Copyright © 2021 by Joanne Gibbs -All rights reserved.

No part of this publication may be reproduced, distributed, or transmitted in any form or by any means, including photocopying, recording, or other electronic or mechanical methods, without the prior written permission of the publisher, except in the case of brief quotations embodied in reviews and certain other non-commercial uses permitted by copyright law.

This Book is provided with the sole purpose of providing relevant information on a specific topic for which every reasonable effort has been made to ensure that it is both accurate and reasonable. Nevertheless, by purchasing this Book you consent to the fact that the author, as well as the publisher, are in no way experts on the topics contained herein, regardless of any claims as such that may be made within. It is recommended that you always consult a professional prior to undertaking any of the advice or techniques discussed within.This is a legally binding declaration that is considered both valid and fair by both the Committee of Publishers Association and the American Bar Association and should be considered as legally binding within the United States.

CONTENTS

INTRODUCTION 7
    What is a Ninja Foodi pressure cooker? 7
    Comparison between Ninja Foodi and instant pot 7
    Advantages of using the Ninja Foodi 14
    Disadvantages of using the Ninja Foodi 14

TIPS FOR GREAT COOKING USING NINJA FOODI 17
    Air fried chicken wings 17
    Air-fried seasoned asparagus............................ 17
    Air fried plate nachos....................................... 17
    Air fryer tacos 17
    Air fried sausage casserole 18
    Pressure-cooked lasagna soup 18
    Pressure-cooked pork chops with cabbage.... 18
    Pressure-cooked-chicken Masala 18
    Ninja Foodi yoghurt... 19

BEGINNER MEALS USING THE NINJA FOODI 20
BENEFITS OF USING FOODI MULTICOOKER..... 21
BREAKFAST AND BRUNCH................................. 22
    Egg and Cheese Scramble................................ 22
    Hash Brown Casserole..................................... 22
    Blueberries Breakfast Mix 22
    Cherries Oat... 22
    Kale - Egg Frittata 22
    Sunrise Millet Pudding..................................... 23
    Breakfast Quinoa.. 23
    Onion Tofu Scramble 23
    Walnut Bowls... 23
    Scrambled Eggs 24
    Butter and Ham Sandwich 24
    Breakfast Casserole.. 24
    Bacon Veggies Combo..................................... 24
    Crunchy Cut Oats... 24
    Polenta Breakfast 24
    Feta and Bacon Omelet 25
    Crust-less Quiche... 25
    Coconut Scramble.. 25
    French Fries and Cheese.................................. 25
    Almond and Berries Cut Oats 26
    Spinach Quiche.. 26
    Sourdough Bread... 26
    Mushroom Omelet 26
    Cheesy Meat Oatmeal...................................... 27
    Baked Omelet 27
    Breakfast Burritos.. 27
    Bacon and Corn Bake 27
    Maple Giant Pancake....................................... 28
    Air Fried Breakfast Sausage............................. 28
    Corned Beef Hash 28
    Gold Potatoes and Bacon................................ 28
    Almond Eggs.. 29
    Simple Corned Beef Hash 29
    Tuna Bowls... 29
    Banana Breakfast Mix 29
    Oatmeal with Carrot... 29
    Cream Cheese and Bread 30
    Spicy Tomato Eggs 30
    Egg, Sausage, and Cheese Cake 30
    Tofu with Mixed Veggies 30
    Brown Rice Breakfast Risotto 31
    Deli Salmon Veggies Cakes 31
    Breakfast Roll Casserole 31
    Turkey Burrito 32

SIDE DISH RECIPES 33
    Turmeric Cauliflower....................................... 33
    Cauliflower Mix.. 33
    Potato Salad 33
    Zucchini Spaghetti... 33
    Garlicky Broccoli 34
    Brussels sprouts.. 34
    Easy Gnocchi... 34
    Warm Potato Salad 34
    Baby Carrots 34
    Zucchini Fries.. 34
    Herbed Sweet Potatoes 35
    Veggie Side Salad 35
    Buttery Broccoli 35
    Sumac Eggplant 35
    Thyme Red Potatoes.. 35
    Buttery Mushrooms... 36
    Cauliflower and Pineapple Salad..................... 36
    Squash Mash.. 36
    Hazelnut Cauliflower Rice 36
    Maple Carrots 36
    Red Cabbage.. 37
    Green Beans Salad... 37
    Roasted Tomato Salad 37
    Mexican Beans 37
    Potato Mash... 37
    Spiced Squash.. 38
    Beans and Tomatoes Mix................................. 38
    Potatoes and Tomatoes.................................... 38
    Creamy Cauliflower 38
    Garlic Mushrooms... 38
    Sweet Potato and Mayo................................... 39
    Yummy Eggplant 39
    Buttery Brussels sprouts.................................. 39
    Asian Style Chickpeas 39
    Brussels sprouts.. 39
    Sweet Potato Mash 40
    Oregano Potatoes 40
    Carrot Puree... 40
    Baked Mushrooms 40
    Roasted Potatoes 40
    Cauliflower Risotto 41
    Paprika Beets.. 41
    Creamy Artichokes... 41

- Broccoli Mash ... 41
- Cumin Green Beans ... 42
- Lemony Carrots ... 42
- Creamy Mushrooms ... 42
- Carrot Fries ... 42

POULTRY RECIPES ... 43
- Black Bean Soup ... 43
- Vegetable Stock Recipe ... 43
- Chicken Stock Recipe ... 43
- Herbed Whole Roasted Chicken ... 43
- Chicken and Chimichurri ... 44
- Cumin Chicken Wings ... 44
- Great Chicken Wings ... 44
- Creamy Asparagus Soup ... 45
- Chicken and Tomatoes ... 45
- Rosemary Turkey ... 45
- Turkey Breast ... 45
- Stuffed Chicken Recipe ... 46

SOUP RECIPES ... 47
- Chicken Noodle Soup Recipe ... 47
- Beef Stock Recipe ... 47
- Potato, Carrot, and Leek Soup Recipe ... 47
- Tomato Soup Recipe ... 48
- Turkey Meatballs in Tomato Sauce ... 48
- Chicken Strips ... 48
- Olive and Lemon Ligurian Chicken ... 49
- Chicken Drumsticks ... 49
- Spicy Chicken ... 49
- Pesto Chicken Breasts ... 50
- Crispy Chicken Thighs with Carrots and Rice Pilaf ... 50
- Chicken and Mushrooms Mix ... 50
- Turmeric Chicken ... 50
- Sweet Chipotle Chicken Wings ... 51
- Spicy Turkey Chili ... 51
- Delicious Frozen Chicken Dinner ... 51
- Asian Chicken Delight ... 52
- Turkey Gluten Free Gravy ... 52
- Cheddar Chicken Breast ... 52
- Chicken Pot Pie Recipe ... 53
- Chicken Casserole ... 53
- Cream of Sweet Potato Soup Recipe ... 53
- Butternut Squash Soup with Chicken ... 54
- Tasty Chicken Soup ... 54
- Colombian Style Chicken Soup Recipe ... 54
- French Onion Soup Recipe ... 54
- Spicy Chili Verde ... 55
- Italian Chicken Masala ... 55
- Indian Butter Chicken ... 55
- Chicken and Rice with Yogurt Sauce ... 56
- Chimichurri Chili Chicken ... 56
- Herb-Roasted Chicken ... 56
- Lemon Dill Chicken and Potatoes ... 57
- Garlicky Chicken Adobo ... 57
- Chicken Curry ... 57
- Portuguese Style Chicken ... 58
- Spicy Thai Chicken Wings ... 58
- Keto Coq Au Vin ... 58
- Piripiri Chicken ... 59
- Shredded Chicken Breast ... 59
- Teriyaki Chicken with Rice and Broccoli ... 59
- Indian Chicken Vindaloo ... 60
- Buffalo Chicken Meatballs ... 60
- Chicken Lemon Sauce Pasta ... 60
- Hungarian Chicken Paprikash ... 61
- Cereal-Crusted Tenders ... 61
- Keto Chicken Pot Pie ... 61
- Chicken Enchilada Dish ... 62
- Salsa Chicken ... 62
- Chicken Puttanesca ... 62
- Spaghetti Squash Chicken Alfredo ... 62
- Chicken Pie Casserole ... 63
- Turkey Meatballs with Pasta ... 63
- Orange Chicken ... 64
- Crack Chicken ... 64
- Chicken and Dumplings ... 64
- Bruschetta Chicken ... 65
- Hungarian Paprika Turkey ... 65
- Lemon Rotisserie Chicken ... 65
- Chicken and Rice Casserole ... 65
- 30-Minutes Moroccan Chicken ... 66
- Moroccan Frozen Chicken ... 66
- Chicken Thighs ... 66
- Crispy Breaded Air Fried Chicken ... 67
- Tasty Chicken Ramen ... 67
- Turmeric Nutty Chicken ... 67
- Roasted Red Pepper Chicken ... 67
- Barbeque Pulled Chicken ... 68
- Air Fried Turkey Breast ... 68
- Chicken with Cashew Cream and Naan ... 68
- Chicken and Brown Rice ... 69
- Peppered Chicken and Potatoes ... 69

BEEF/LAMB ... 70
- Fall-Apart Pot Roast ... 70
- Beef Stroganoff with Egg Noodles ... 70
- Beef Bourguignon ... 70
- Ragù Bolognese ... 71
- Air Fried Beef Satay ... 71
- Keto Indian Kheema ... 71
- Un-Stuffed Beef and Cabbage ... 72
- Mississippi Pot Roast ... 72
- Balsamic Roast Beef ... 72
- Beef Brisket ... 72
- Air fryer Lamb Chops ... 73
- Steak, Potatoes and Asparagus ... 73
- Ropa Vieja ... 73
- Keto Chunky Chili ... 74
- Pot Roast ... 74
- Beef and Egg Noodles ... 75
- Corned Beef and Cabbage ... 75
- Carbonnade ... 75
- Cheese steak Casserole ... 75
- Keto Curried Beef ... 76
- Keto Steak Rolls and Asparagus ... 76

- Tex-Mex Meatloaf ... 76
- Beef Gyros ... 77
- Peppercinis Pot Roast ... 77
- Dinner of Beef Short Ribs ... 77
- Balsamic Beef Pot Roast ... 77
- Shredded Beef Sloppy Joes ... 78
- Beef and Old-School Calico Beans ... 78
- Sticky St. Louis Ribs ... 78
- Beef Short Ribs and Vegetables ... 78

PORK ... 80
- Keto Pulled Pork ... 80
- Country Style Ribs ... 80
- Jamaican Jerk Pork Roast ... 80
- Pork and Pinto Bean Nachos ... 81
- Crispy Pork Carnitas ... 81
- Simple Pulled Pork ... 81
- Pork Chops with Potato Purée and Gravy ... 81
- Chipotle Pulled Pork ... 82
- Smothered Pork Chops ... 82
- Smoky White Beans and Ham ... 82
- Carnitas ... 83
- Apples Pork Chops ... 83
- Pulled Pork with Crispy Biscuits ... 83
- Kalua Pork with Green Cabbage ... 83
- Juicy Kalua Pork ... 84
- Pork Loin, Stuffing, and Gravy ... 84
- Ham and Greens ... 84
- Pork Roast Bacon with Potato Bourbon Mash ... 84
- Slow- Cooked Pulled Pork Apple Sliders ... 85
- Low-Carb Mexican Pulled Pork ... 85
- Pepper Jack Pork Chops ... 85
- Puerto Rican Pork Roast ... 86
- BBQ Pork Chops ... 86
- Braised Pork Belly with Potato and Eggs ... 86
- Bacon Pulled Pork ... 86
- Pork Loin with Vegetables ... 87
- Chinese Pork with Ginger Coconut Potatoes ... 87
- Directions ... 87
- Pork and Fennel Sausage Risotto ... 87
- Sweet and Sour Pork ... 88
- Mexican- styled Pork Pozole ... 88
- Hot and Spicy Pork Shoulder ... 88
- Stir-Fried Pork and Noodles ... 89
- Mushroom Pork ... 89
- Pork Tenderloin with Gravy ... 89
- Hawaiian Pork Roast ... 89
- Very Tender Pork Roast ... 90
- Chinese BBQ Pork with Ginger Almond Sweet Potatoes ... 90
- Air Fryer Pork Taquitos ... 90

FISH AND SEAFOOD ... 91
- Indian Fish Curry ... 91
- Shrimp Chicken Jambalaya ... 91
- Mussels and Chorizo ... 91
- Garlicky Shrimp Scampi ... 92
- Creamy Crab ... 92
- Paella ... 92
- Creamy Shrimp Scampi ... 93
- Brazilian Fish Stew (Moqueca) ... 93
- Seared Shrimp and Rice with Fruity Salsa ... 93
- Keto Clam Chowder ... 94
- Hot Prawns with Cocktail Sauce ... 94
- Garlic Shrimp with Risotto Primavera ... 94
- Catfish with French Sauce ... 95
- Orange Roughy with Black Olive Sauce ... 95
- Salmon with Orange Ginger Sauce ... 95
- Country Grouper ... 95
- Thai Shrimp Soup ... 96
- Shrimp with Tomatoes and Feta ... 96
- Shrimp and Cheesy Butter Grits ... 96
- Low Town Shrimp Boil ... 97
- Red Snapper with miso ... 97
- Wild Salmon Tagine ... 97
- Calamari with Tomato Stew ... 98
- Fish Steaks with Olive Sauce and Tomato ... 98

SOUPS/ STEWS/ SAUCES/ BROTHS ... 99
- Double Bean and Ham Soup ... 99
- Chicken Thigh Soup ... 99
- Kale Chicken Soup ... 99
- North African Lentil and Spinach Soup ... 99
- Barley and Mushroom Soup ... 100
- White Chicken Chili ... 100
- Leek, Potato, and Pea Soup ... 100
- Ground Beef Cabbage Soup ... 100
- Kimchi Beef Stew ... 101
- Oxtails Stew ... 101
- Chicken Taco Soup ... 101
- Beef and Wheat Berry Soup ... 102
- Minestrone Soup ... 102
- Butternut Squash and Apple Soup ... 102
- Potato Leek Soup ... 102
- Chicken and Kale Stew ... 103
- Chinese Hot and Sour Soup ... 103
- Belize Chicken Stew ... 103
- Tomato Basil Soup ... 104
- African Lamb Stew ... 104
- Keto No- Beans Chili ... 104
- French Onion Soup ... 104
- Chinese Pork Soup ... 105
- Vegetable Soup ... 105
- Zuppa Toscana Soup ... 105
- Italian Chicken, Lentil, and Bacon Stew ... 106
- Carrot Ginger and Turmeric Soup ... 106
- Beef Taco Soup ... 106
- Mexican Pork Soup ... 107
- Zucchini Pasta Sauce ... 107
- Vegetable Stock ... 107
- Chicken and Vegetable Noodle Soup ... 107
- Bacon Cheeseburger Soup ... 108
- Chicken Zoodle Soup ... 108
- Homemade Hot Sauce ... 108
- Wild Rice Soup ... 108
- Chili Queso Chicken Soup ... 109
- Tortellini Soup ... 109

- Cauliflower Soup 109
- Creamy Tomato Feta Soup 109
- Spicy Cranberry Sauce 110
- Silky Creamy Chicken Mulligatawny Soup 110
- Spicy Pasta Sauce 110
- Ethiopian Spinach Lentil Soup 110
- Beans Chicken Chili 111
- Bacon Potato Soup 111
- Matzo Ball Soup 111
- Homemade Marinara Sauce 111
- Cabbage Roll Soup 112
- Pot Roast Soup 112
- Sweet Tomato Chutney 112

VEGETARIAN AND VEGAN 113
- Mushroom Rice Pilaf 113
- Spaghetti Squash with Tomatoes 113
- Sweet Potato and Black-Eyed Peas 113
- Vegetable Biryani 114
- Chicory and Carrots Salad 114
- Sweet Potatoes with Thai Peanut Butter Sauce 114
- Curried Peppers Stuffed With Lentil 115
- Spinach Chana Dal 115
- Smoky Lentils and Rice 115
- Zucchini Tomato Medley 115
- Millet, Beans, and Quinoa 116
- Millet and Pinto Bean Chili 116
- Buffalo Wing Potatoes 116
- Vegan Bread 117
- Chickpea Tagine 117
- Pressure-Cooked Summer Squash 117
- Bean Pasta 118
- Sicilian Steamed Leeks 118
- Lemony Broccoli 118
- Risotto with Lima Beans 118
- Vegetable Mélange 119
- Black Beans and Potato 119
- Hearty Ratatouille 119
- Stuffed Acorn Squash with Pecans 119

RICE/PASTA 121
- Mac 'N' Cheese 121
- Cabbage Risotto 121
- Vegetarian Chili Mac 121
- Steamed White Rice 121
- Saffron Rice 122
- Rice Pilaf with Veggies 122
- Cheesy White Wine Risotto 122
- Asparagus and Mushroom Risotto 122
- Lentil Vegetable Risotto 123
- Mexican Rice 123
- Pasta with Arugula Pesto 123
- Rich Spaghetti Dish 123
- Pineapple and Cauliflower Rice 124
- Mushroom Stroganoff 124
- Spicy Farfalle Pasta 124
- Vegan Pasta Puttanesca 124
- Kimchi Fried Rice 125
- Creamy Spaghetti in Pesto Sauce 125
- Marinara with Pasta 125
- Meatless Spaghetti 125
- Coconut Mango Arborio Rice Pudding 126
- Jumbo Shrimp Pasta 126
- Pasta with Meat Sauce 126
- Pasta with Mediterranean Veggies 126
- Cheese- Rich Pasta 127
- Med Tuna Noodle 127
- Vegan Miso Risotto 127

APPETIZERS, SNACKS, AND SIDES 128
- Air Fried Rosemary Chips 128
- Crispy Hot Wings 128
- Slow-Cooked Korean Chicken Wings 128
- Pot Stickers Traditional 128
- Rustic Bell Pepper 128
- Pineapple Cilantro Lime Rice 129
- Caponata 129
- Crab Cheese Wontons 129
- Mediterranean White Bean Dip 130
- Quinoa Salad 130
- Potato with Herbs 130
- Crispy Kale Chips 130
- Jalapeno Hot Popper Dip 130
- Buffalo Chicken Dip 131
- Asian Barbecue Satay 131
- Bacon Cheeseburger Dip 131
- Crispy Popcorn Chicken 131
- Peperonata Sauce 132
- Nacho Covered Prawns 132
- Cajun Shrimp 132
- Pizza Dip 132
- Sweet Potato Tots 132
- Easy Steamed Artichokes 133
- Southwest Asian Falafel 133
- Rosemary Beets 133
- Easy pickled Green Chilies 134
- Beet, Endives and Spinach Salad 134
- Hoisin Meatballs 134
- Cheddar Bacon Ale Dip 135
- Bok Choy and Mushrooms Salad 135
- Black Bean Dip 135
- Chickpeas Meal 135
- Broiled Grapefruit 136
- Texas Cheese Fries in Melted Cheese 136
- Broccoli, Cherries, and Raisins 136
- Mashed Potatoes 136
- Creamy Parmesan Mashed Cauliflower 136
- Spanish Tortilla 137
- Air Fried Bacon Wrapped Asparagus 137
- Hummus 137
- Puff Pastry Banana Rolls 137
- Crispy Chicken Wings 138
- Air Fried Blooming Onion 138
- Bow Tie Pasta Chips 138
- Asian Sticky Wings 138
- Brussels sprouts and Walnuts 139

Fried Ravioli 139
DESSERTS **140**
    Vanilla Tapioca Pudding 140
    Strawberry Jam 140
    Cinnamon Maple Apples 140
    Citrus Canola Cake 140
    Dump Cake 140
    Vanilla Cake 141
    Dried Fruits in Wine Sauce 141
    Banana/ Rum Mix 141
    Peach Cobbler 141
    Upside-Down Cheesecake 141
    Blueberry Pancake Muffins 142
    Pear Cranberry Honey Sauce 142
    Mango Cheesecake 142
    Mexican Pot du Crème 142
    Pressure Cooked Apples 143
    Baked Apples 143
    Dulce de Leche Cake 143
    Peach Dump Cake 143
    Easy Applesauce 143
    Baked Spice Cookies 144
    Chocolaty Rice Pudding 144
    Cranberry Oat Bars 144
    Candied Lemon Peels 144
    Pumpkin Pie Pudding 145
    Hot Peach and Blackberry Cobbler 145
    Apple Dumplings 145
    Egg Leche Flan 146
    Easy Pumpkin Puree 146
APPENDIX : RECIPES INDEX **147**

INTRODUCTION

Becoming a successful cook is a combination of passion and resources (such as cutlery, utensils, and appliances.) Pressure cookers are the best innovation that has happened to cooks both in commercial and domestic setups. These appliances have made cooking enjoyable by reducing electricity use and cook time.

Ninja Foodi pressure cooker is the latest design that may cook almost everything in a modern kitchen. This is because; it comprises of a pressure cooker, air fryer, and dehydrator. You can also prepare main and side meals in one pot. However, using it appropriately requires excellent mastery of its components, and that's why I have compiled this guide. It comprises of model types, description of components and their functionalities, cleaning guide, maintenance, safety precautions, and examples of ninja recipes. By reading through it, answers to disturbing questions will be provided.

What is a Ninja Foodi pressure cooker?

The advancing technology has introduced great innovations that have simplified our daily activities. The food industry is among the growing sectors with new designs of kitchenware, enabling exploration of recipes. Ninja Foodi pressure cooker is among the appliances that cooks are talking about. The multi-purpose pot can air fry, grill, slow cook, pressure cook, steam, sauté, and roast.

It was difficult to switch from my adorable instant pot to a Ninja Foodi. In this, I researched a lot from the internet, inquired from other cooks, and even contacted the company for further details. The truth is; before finding out about the Ninja Foodi, I had never thought of replacing my 3 year-old instant pot. However, I purchased the Ninja Foodi and explored my instant pot recipes using it. The table below compares its specifications, cooking capabilities, and accessories to that of my instant pot.

Comparison between Ninja Foodi and instant pot

Element	Ninja Foodi	Instant pot
Cooking capabilities	Air fry, grill, slow cook, pressure cook, steam, sauté, bake, dehydrate, sear, and roast. It keeps food warm up to 12 hours after cooking.	Low temperature cooking (sous vide,) pressure cook, simmer, sear, boil, ferment, and sauté. It's also a yogurt maker, food warmer, and rice cooker.
Controls	You can customize cooking temperature, pressure levels, and time.	You can set cooking duration, pressure level, temperature, delay start, and warm your food.
Cleaning	Easy since the accessories are ceramic coated.	Easy since its parts can be cleaned by a dishwasher.
sizes	6.5 quart available.	3 quarts, 6, and 8 available.

	8.5 quart for special orders.	
accessories	Pressure cooker lid, air frying/ crisping lid, reversible rack, and an air fryer basket.	Pressure cooker lid and a trivet.
Power consumption	1400W Plus	1100W and below
Start procedure	Switch it on, push start, and set the cooking temperature followed by time.	Set the cooking temperature and time.

Note: Once you become a Ninja Foodi pro, you can prepare all your instant pot recipes using it.

Models of Ninja Foodi pressure cooker

You may be wondering why your appliance lacks some of the specifications explained in this guide. Similar to other devices, Some Ninja Foodi cookers have different features that distinguish them from others. Acquiring it depends on your preferences and cost. Below is a list of the Ninja series alongside their specifications.

1. **Model OP300**

The 1400-watt unit lacks dehydration functions. Its other features include;
- A reversible rack
- Pressure and crisping lids
- 4-quart cook and crisp basket
- 6.5-quart ceramic pot
- 15 recipe guides

2. **Model OP301**
- A reversible rack
- 1400W unit
- Pressure and crisping lids
- 4-quart cook and crisp basket
- 6.5-quart ceramic pot
- 45 recipe guides

3. **Model OP301C**

The 1400-Watt unit appliance conducts the dehydration functions appropriately. Its other specifications include;
- A reversible broil/steam rack
- Pressure and crisping lids
- 4-quart cook and crisp basket
- Cook and crisp layered insert
- 6.5-quart ceramic pot
- 20 recipe guides

4. **Model OP302**
- A reversible broil/steam rack
- Pressure and crisping lids

- 4-quart cook and crisp basket
- 6.5-quart ceramic pot
- 45-plus recipe guides

5. Model OP305
- A reversible broil/steam rack
- Pressure and crisping lids
- 4-quart cook and crisp basket
- Cook and crisp layered insert
- 6.5-quart ceramic pot
- 45-plus recipe guides

6. Model OP401

Besides the 1700-watt unit containing a larger quart, it also executes the dehydration functions. Its other features include;
- A reversible broil/steam rack
- Pressure and crisping lids
- XL 5-quart cook and crisp basket
- Cook and crisp layered insert
- XL 8-quart ceramic pot
- 45-plus recipe guides

Descriptions of the Ninja Foodi accessories

Here, I will name the cooker's accessories and their functions. This will not only guide the potential users but also simplify their purpose to continuing users. It's unfortunate that even after some individuals acquiring the appliance; they continue preparing repetitive recipes due to the complexity of parts functions.

1. The pressure lid

It is a removable part of the ninja Foodi utilized when the device is used as a pressure cooker. It consists of a valve cap found on the lid's underside and a black valve on the Foodi top. These parts should be detached, cleaned, and inspected after using the lid following the manufacturer's directions. When using the lid, the valve should be loose and floating to allow the release of accumulated steam. However, it tightens after pressurizing. When setting the valve to "vent" position, it should be raised. The red button at the lid's top stays depressed when the Foodi is pressurizing before popping up. You should not open the pot when the button has popped up to prevent burns.

2. Air-crisp lid

The lid is screwed on the pot and remains intact even when pressure cooking. However, it remains open except when preparing crisped diets. It contains a fan for hot-air circulation and a heater. It can be flipped up anytime you need to check the cooking progress contrary to the pressure lid, which requires you first to release the built-in pressure.

3.   User's guide

Although I will analyze critical details of the cooker, it's essential to study the comprehensive guide packaged alongside the appliance before using it. It consists of a; maintenance guide, troubleshooting guide, and the Foodi functions.

4.   Ninja cookbook

This is a guide containing more than 45 ninja Foodi recipes. It also comprises of cooking charts that illustrate food timing and settings. However, when following the guidelines, you should consider your seasoning preferences since reviews indicate that the dishes are salty. Also, consider adding your favorite spices and eliminating/replacing the ones you dislike. Similarly, you can follow the quick start guide to understand the package contents and the pressure test. A cooking cheat sheet is also availed containing a roasted chicken recipe.

How to perform the Ninja Foodi functions

As seen from the cooker series, different models consist of varying features. These enable the cooker to execute its design functionalities. For instance; some recipes are cooked with a sealed crisping lid, others tightened pressure lids, and the rest opened pots.Additionally, while cooking different dishes opening the cooker lid is necessary on initial stages. Below is a description of the ninja Foodi functions.

1.   Pressure cooker functions

This is attained with the pressure lid sealed. Its settings are either "High" or "Low." The user can also customize the cooking time up to four hours depending on your recipe. To achieve this, seal the black valve found at the top of the Foodi by turning it. Examples of pressure-cooked meals include; steak, desserts, and one-pot chili among others.

•   When selecting the cooking time, you should consider the ingredient's temperature. For example; a frozen chicken takes longer cooking duration than thawed ones.

•   Also, your cooking version matters a lot. For example; PIP style preferred when preparing meals by putting a pot inside your Ninja Foodi consumes more time than placing food in the cooker directly.

•   When pressure cooking, the cooking time may depend on your food type. This includes food size and density. For instance; larger and denser foods consume more cooking time than smaller and lighter ones. This can be proven by cooking whole potatoes and sliced ones.

What amount of liquid is recommendable when using the pressure cooker? This is a controversial question that has stopped Ninja Foodi owners from using the appliance. The truth is; different recipes demands special treatment. For instance; when preparing a beef stew, I expect to serve it with gravy while plain rice should be dry. Also, depending on what you are cooking, some water will be absorbed while cooking and the rest released as steam. For instance; boiling meat requires more water than boiling pumpkins inconsiderate on what you will be preparing with the boiled ingredient. Similarly, large quantity of meals requires more fluid than smaller portions. In short, the amount of liquid to be added in the pressure cooker depends on what you are cooking and the expected results.

Hint: Thinner may be added to milky-recipes since milk does not generate steam. In doing this, remember some of the fluids will be absorbed by your meal and some released. For a tasty meal, you should also consider using broth in place of water.

2. Steam functions

This is attained by setting the black valve to "vent' instead of "seal." In this, no requirement for temperature adjustment, although the cooking duration can be customized up to half-hour depending on the dish prepared. Examples of steamed dishes include; vegetables, grains, and delicate fish, among others.

3. Slow cook function

The function is a replica of the slow cooker. This is attained with the lid on and black valve set to vent. Also, you can set temperatures high or low, depending on the meal. The feature also allows customization of the cooking duration to 12 hours maximally. Examples of slow-cooked recipes include; risotto and slow-pulled pork, among others.

4. Sear/sauté

When sautéing the meal, you can either seal the pressure lid or open it depending on your familiarity with the cooker. However, if you are new to the appliance, it's advisable to sauté with an open lid to enable regular checking of your meal. The feature allows temperature adjustments from high, medium-high, medium, medium-low, and low. In this, the user is supposed to switch off the cooker manually when the dish is ready since there are no settings for the cooking duration. Examples of sautéed dishes include; caramelized onion and steak, among others.

5. Air crisp

This functionality is attained with a crisping lid "on." The cooker has a setting to adjust the temperature from 300 to 400° F. The cooking duration can also be customized up to an hour. Examples of air frying recipes include; golden chips, crispy chicken, and crispy vegetables, among others.

6. Roast/Bake

It is also attained with a sealed crisping lid. When executing the function, the temperature can be adjusted from 250 to 400° F. The baking or roasting duration can be adjusted to four hours maximally. Examples of baked recipes include; Mediterranean vegetables and roasted potatoes.

7. Broil

The broiling feature also accomplishes its functions when a crisping lid is on. Although it does not have temperature adjustment settings, the cooking duration can be customized to half-hour. Examples of broiling recipes are; Broiled fish, garlic broiled chicken, and broiled beef among others.

8. Dehydration

The dehydration feature is found on some models, and it's executed using a crisping lid. It allows temperature adjustment from 105 to 195° F and cooking time customization from quarter-hour to 12hours. Examples of dehydrated recipes include; beef jerky, vegetable crisps, apples, and fruit leather, among others.

9. One-pot meal

The reversible rack allows the Ninja Cooker to prepare mains and side meals simultaneously. These include; layered grains, vegetables with meat, and fish, among others.

How to release the Ninja Foodi Pressure

The rotating lights demonstrate the pressure-building activity. Its accumulation duration varies depending on the size of the dish and the liquid contents on the pot. When the cooker is pressurizing, its lid locks until the pressure gets released. Here, full pressure is illustrated by the glow of the lid icon light. After that, the pressure cooking begins, and the timer countdown starts. Below are ways to release built-in pressure from your Ninja Foodi;

- **NPR**

After elapsing the cooking duration, the accumulated steam will start releasing naturally to allow lid opening. The process may take up to 30 minutes, depending on the amount of food cooked and the fluid remaining. During NPR, the cooker turns to "keep warm" mode which can be changed by pressing the keep warm button. After all pressure exits the pot, the red valve drops down, allowing lid opening.

- **QPR**

This option is distinguished for recipes that do not require steam softening. Immediately the cooking time elapses, the "keep warm" light switches on. Here, the cook is needed to turn the pressure valve to vent. This activity may consume at least 30 seconds, depending on your dish size and fluid.

Note: After releasing the built-in pressure either in NPR or QPR, the lid should be opened to allow the escape of the remaining pressure. Here, care should be taken to prevent dripping of the pot's vapor on its base. Also, when the pressure is releasing naturally, you can shift to quick-release by turning the pressure valve to vent.

How to use the Ninja Foodi pressure cooker

Before getting into cooking details, I would like to explain the Ninja Foodi abbreviations. This is because; when following a recipe, translating the required function may be confusing due to its shortened language. Besides that, you may find it hard to engage in related discussions. The following list contains the translation of such functions.

1. PIP:pot in pot
2. AC:air crisp
3. NPR:natural pressure release
4. SC:slow cook
5. IR:immediate release
6. TC:tender-crisp
7. AF:air fry
8. PC:pressure cook
9. NR:natural release
10. QR:quick release
11. QPR:quick pressure release

Now that you have understood the Ninja Foodi language, I will explain the recommendable stages you should follow after acquiring the new appliance.

This involves cleaning the washable components after unpacking it. For instance; the inner pot, silicone ring, rack, and basket can be cleaned on a dishwasher. The cooker's lid can be washed by hand while its anti-clog cap can be scrapped using a fine toothbrush. However, the cap should be detached and inspected regularly to prevent spattering of food debris when releasing the accumulated pressure.

A condensation tray should be fitted on the Ninja cooker to collect moisture that may arise when steaming. The tray should also be removed and cleaned after cooking to prevent building-up of moulds due to accumulated vapor.

How to perform a pressure test

If you are not familiar with the Ninja Cooker, it's advisable to conduct a pressure test to understand how it works. This test may also verify the functionality of your cooker. The procedural steps involve;

1. Switch on your Ninja Foodi device, plug it power cable in the wall socket, and turn on the power button.
2. Pour around 3 cups of water in your Ninja pot.
3. Seal the pressure lid tightly by turning the black valve.
4. Press the "pressure" button. In this, use the arrows on the left to select "high."
5. Select the boiling duration (around 8 minutes) using the arrows on the right.
6. Press start. Rotation of lights implies that your cooker is heating.
7. Let the water boil until you see steam escaping from all-round the lid. Stop it.
8. Twist the black vent to a vent position for the steam to exit.
9. When all the in-built pressure has exited, remove the cooker's lid and allow your boiled water to cool.

Note: it's normal for steam to escape through the black valve, red button, or both. However, if you see it exiting all-round the lid surface, you should open the cooker's lid. The above procedure is a template of the Ninja Foodi cooking instructions.

How to use the Ninja Air-fryer

Lovers of crisped recipes, it's now your time to enjoy because Ninjashark has considered you in their innovation. You do not need an extra oven or other air fryers to prepare your favorite snack. Below is the procedure to follow when cooking air-fried meals using your Ninja Foodi;

1. As said earlier, the cooker has two lids. In this, only the crisping lid (already attached to the pot) is utilized.
2. Place the air-frying basket in the cooking pot.
3. You can either place your food on the basket or the grilling pan.
4. Flip down the lid and "switch on" the appliance.
5. Use the air-fryer chart to predict the cooking duration.
6. Press in the "air fry" button.
7. Customize the cooking temperature using +/- buttons.

8. Customize the cooking time using +/- buttons.
9. Hit start.

How to transform the Ninja cooker to an air fryer, pressure cooker, or slow cooker

Having said a lot about the cooker's accessories and functionality, I thought explaining its transformation concept was essential.

- A Ninja Foodi package consists of an attached air fryer lid to be flipped down when baking, broiling, or roasting. Also, a basket is inserted when preparing related recipes.
- In case you want to use your cooker as pressure or slow cooker, you will have to close the pressure lid. The lid resembles that of the instant pot. It comes along with a rack which is fitted inside the Ninja Foodi. It's also used when sautéing your meal using the "sauté" setting.

However, the new kitchenware has received mixed reactions from users and potential users. This depends on your love of exploration. Below are some of the benefits and limitations of the device according to its users.

Advantages of using the Ninja Foodi

- It reduces the cooking time.
- The multi-purpose cooker plays the role of four kitchen appliances.
- It's affordable compared to the total cost of individual devices.
- The gadget comes with a detailed user manual which it's easier to follow.
- Cleaning the Ninja cooker is easy since most parts are ceramic-coated.
- It has a digital screen that displays the pressure-building progress.
- It has a timer and temperature setting that mitigates cooking guesswork.

Disadvantages of using the Ninja Foodi

- Being a compact unit, its large size does not save the kitchen space.
- After air-frying, double cleaning is required (for the layered insert and the basket.)Who finds fun in cleaning?
- Sometimes the lid may leak when the pot is releasing pressure. This may happen when you start cooking without confirming its "seal" position.
- It's hard to predict cooking time for new recipes. This requires regular opening of the cooker which entails releasing the in-built pressure.
- The Ninja cooker sizes are limited (6-quarts and 8-quarts); therefore, buyers do not enjoy their freedom of choice.
- Their baskets are also small for larger meals. That means the user is forced to cook in batches.
- The attached air fryer lid inconveniences the user.This is because; it's usually open unless you are air crisping.

How to clean and maintain the Ninja Foodi

The appliance should be well cleaned after cooking to prevent the accumulation of food debris. Its cleaning instructions involve;

1. Unplugging the unit from the wall socket.
2. The cooker's base should not be immersed in water or put in the dishwasher. Its control panel and base should be wiped with a damp towel.
3. You can wash the basket, pot, diffuser, and silicone ring in a dishwasher.
4. The pressure valve and anti-clog cap can be cleaned using soapy water.
5. Do not disassemble the pressure valve when cleaning.
6. The crisping lid should be wiped using wet clothing.
7. Avoid using scouring pads to scrub food residue stuck on the rack, basket, or pot. If scrubbing is essential, a non-abrasive cleanser or a brush soaked in a liquid soap can be used. Also, soaking the pot in water for some time helps when removing stuck foods.
8. After cleaning the components, you can air-dry them for the next use.
9. The silicone ring should be taken off by pulling it outward part by part. Fixing it back involves placing it on the rack and pressing it down systematically.
10. Food debris should be removed from the anti-clog cap and ring immediately after use.
11. A damaged silicone ring should be replaced to allow pressure cooking and prevent its explosion.

Several elements may limit efficient use of your ninja Foodi cooker, and that's why I have compiled the below troubleshooting guide. They include;

1. The cooker taking long to pressurize
- Pressure-building up depends on the temperature of the cooking pot, ingredients, and the cooking temperature. Before making any judgments, you should confirm the status of the named elements.
- Check whether your silicone ring is in good condition and well-positioned.
- Confirm that your pressure lid is locked. The release valve should be in seal position when cooking.

2. Slow cont-down timer
Confirm whether you set the cooking duration in minutes or hours. This is because; when cooking, time should decrease in minutes.

3. Lights displaying on the screen when steaming or pressure cooking
This implies that your cooker is pressurizing. When the rotating lights stop, you can set your cook time to begin the countdown.

4. The pressure lid is not getting off
This is a safety feature. The lid opens after all pressure exits from your Ninja cooker. You can either use quick release or natural release depending on your recipe. Open the lid by turning it anticlockwise, lifting it, and placing it away. In this, the pressure valve should be loose to enable its transitioning from seal to vent.

5. Cooker producing a hissing sound
First, verify that you have positioned the pressure valve to a seal position. If it continues, check whether its silicone ring is well-installed by removing and inserting it.

6. The timer counting upwards instead of downwards

If you are experiencing this, do not worry. It implies that the cooking time has elapsed; therefore, your Ninja Foodi has reached the "keep warm" mode.

If you encounter more challenges, you can refer to the cooker's manual or inquire from its dealers.

Ninja Foodi safety precautions

After using the Ninja cooker, I identified a number of things that should be avoided by every user. This is to protect the gadget, its user, and the environment. They include;

- Spraying the inner pot with aerosol. This causes baking up of its base, making it hard to clean.
- Predicting the water portion well, especially when using the pressure cooking function. This may affect the final product. For instance; cooking a stew with low levels of water may dry it up. Similarly, cooking rice with large portions of water may leave it gravy.
- Similar to other home appliances, the Ninja cooker should be unplugged when not in use to prevent unexpected switching. This may cause burning off your home, damaging of the appliance, and even human accidents.
- The device should not be used on a stove. Turning on the stove's burner may melt the appliance ruining it.
- Avoid covering the pressure valve.
- Confirm that all parts are well-assembled before using your Ninja cooker.
- Avoid long power cords to reduce risks of getting entangled or being grabbed by children. Also, use pots recommended by the manufacturer to prevent electric shocks.
- Power cords, cooker base, plugs, and the crisping lid should not be immersed in liquids to prevent electric shock.
- Do not force opening the cooker's lid. The accumulated steam locks it. In this, you should either consider quick release or natural release to avoid scald issues.
- Avoid touching the appliance's hot surfaces when cooking to prevent burning accidents. If need be, use hot pads, knobs, handles, or oven mitts.
- Do not use a damaged silicone ring to prevent the pot from exploding, causing body burns.
- Care should be taken when preparing "expanding" meals using the cooker. In this, place the ingredients halfway or as instructed by the recipe.
- The unit should not be used when preparing instant rice.
- Allow the Ninja Foodi to cool before cleaning or tampering with it.

TIPS FOR GREAT COOKING USING NINJA FOODI

Now that you have learned all essential details about the Ninja cooker usage, I have compiled some mouth-watering recipes for your trial.

Air fried chicken wings

Prep time: 4 MINUTES | Cooking time: 20 minutes | Servings: 4 people

Ingredients
- A pound of chicken wings
- A tablespoon of olive oil
- ½ teaspoon of salt
- A pinch of pepper
- 4 teaspoons of barbeque sauce

Cooking procedure
1. Spread the air fryer basket with half of the olive oil.
2. Align the chicken wings on the oiled basket.
3. Spray the wings with the remaining oil followed by salt and pepper depending on your seasoning preferences.
4. Flip-down the lid and cook the wings at 390° for around 10 minutes. Ensure the wings temperature is around 165°.
5. Flip their other side and cook with the same settings for time and temperature.
6. Transfer the golden-brown wings on a large bowl and spread them with the barbeque sauce.
7. Serve warm alongside rice, chips, or any other preferred meal.

NUTRITION: CALORIES 168KCAL, FAT 13G, SODIUM 52G, PROTEIN 11G

Air-fried seasoned asparagus

Prep time: 8 MINUTES | Cooking time: 10 minutes | Servings: 4 people

Ingredients
- 200g of trimmed asparagus
- A teaspoon of olive oil
- ½ teaspoon of garlic salt
- 50g of sliced mushrooms

Cooking procedure
1. Put the trimmed asparagus on the air fryer basket.
2. Spread it with olive oil.
3. Add your sliced mushrooms and season with garlic salt to attain your preferred taste.
4. Close the crisping lid and cook your asparagus at 390° for around 5 minutes.
5. Flip-up the cooker's lid and check whether your meal is ready. Turn it.
6. Cook its other side using the same cooker settings.
7. Transfer your seasoned asparagus to serving plates and enjoy.

NUTRITION: CALORIES 63KCAL, FAT 6G, CARBOHYDRATES 1G, PROTEIN 1G

Air fried plate nachos

Prep time: 10 MINUTES | Cooking time: 5 minutes | Servings: 4 people

Ingredients
- An ouch of tortilla chips
- An ouch of grilled chicken
- Drained and rinsed black beans
- A cup of white queso
- Halved grape tomatoes
- 2 Diced green onions

Cooking procedure
1. Line the air fryer basket with an aluminum foil and spread it with non-stick spray.
2. Mix the grilled chicken with beans and chips to form nachos.
3. Pour the queso over the nacho.
4. Cover the mixture with tomatoes and onions.
5. Close the air frying lid having set the fryer to 355°-Cook for around 5 minutes.
6. Open the lid and check whether your nacho attained your desired texture.
7. Serve your crispy nacho while warm.

NUTRITION: CALORIES 271KCAL, FAT 13G, CARBOHYDRATES 18G, PROTEIN 13G

Air fryer tacos

Prep time: 15 MINUTES | Cooking time: 8 minutes | Servings: 12 people

Ingredients
- 10 taco shells
- Rinsed and drained black beans
- A package of gluten-free taco seasoning
- Shredded lettuce
- A pound of ground turkey
- Mexican cheese (shredded)
- 2 sliced tomatoes
- A teaspoon of olive oil.
- A diced onion
- Salsa and other toppings

Cooking procedure
1. Put your turkey on a medium-sized skillet and fry until it turns brown.
2. Drain excess oil from your turkey and add the taco seasoning until it attains your desired taste.
3. Combine taco shells with lettuce, beans, cheese, and browned turkey to form tacos.
4. Line the air fryer basket with foil and spread it with olive oil.
5. Add your tacos to the fryer and close its lid.

6. Cook your turkey tacos for 4 minutes having set it to around 355° depending on your cooker settings.
7. Add salsa alongside other toppings and continue cooking at 355° for 4 minutes.
8. Serve your tacos warm.
NUTRITION: CALORIES 237KCAL, FAT 9G, CARBOHYDRATES 28G, PROTEIN 15G

Air fried sausage casserole

Prep time: 10 MINUTES | Cooking time: 20 minutes | Servings: 4 people
Ingredients
- A pound of hash browns
- A pound of ground sausage
- A diced bell pepper (green)
- A diced bell pepper (red)
- A diced bell pepper (yellow)
- ¼ cup of diced sweet onions
- 4 eggs
- A pound of shredded cheese

Cooking procedure
1. Line your air fryer basket with foil and place hash browns on it.
2. Add the ground sausage.
3. Top the mixture with the diced onions, shredded cheese, and peppers.
4. Close the crisping lid and cook the ingredients at 355° for around 10 minutes.
5. Open the lid and stir your casserole.
6. Crack the eggs and whisk them in separate bowls.
7. Pour them over your cooked casserole and continue cooking at 355° for 10 minutes.
8. Season your casserole with salt and pepper to attain your desired taste. Serve hot.
NUTRITION: CALORIES 573KCAL, FAT 45.3G, CARBOHYDRATES 23.4G, PROTEIN 31.3G

Pressure-cooked lasagna soup

Prep time: 10 MINUTES | Cooking time: 10 minutes | Servings: 6 people
Ingredients
- A pound of ground beef
- 20 OZ of meat sauce
- A cup of mozzarella cheese(shredded)
- A crushed garlic clove
- A cup of spinach leaves(fresh)
- 1 teaspoon of dried basil
- 12 oz of lasagna noodles
- 6 cups of water

Cooking procedure
1. Set your cooker to sauté mode and put the ground beef in it.
2. Cook the beef until it tenderizes and its fluid drains.
3. Turn the cooker off and add meat sauce followed by spinach, garlic, water, and basil. Stir the mixture.
4. Break your noodles into reasonable pieces and add it to the meat mixture.
5. Close the pressure lid and cook the mixture for 4 minutes.
6. Quick-release the accumulated steam and open the lid.
7. Transfer your cooked lasagna soup into a dish and serve with cheese toppings. Enjoy.
NUTRITION: CALORIES 339KCAL, FAT 25G, CARBOHYDRATES 13G, PROTEIN 34G

Pressure-cooked pork chops with cabbage

Prep time: 15 MINUTES | Cooking time: 10 minutes | Servings: 6 people
Ingredients
- 2 pounds of boneless pork chops
- A small-sized cabbage (roughly chopped)
- 2 cups of chicken broth
- ½ cup of butter
- ½ cup of steak seasoning
- A chopped pepper
- A teaspoon of salt

Cooking procedure
1. Pour the steak seasonings over the pork chops in a bowl.
2. Transfer the seasoned chops to the pressure pot.
3. Add cabbage chunks and chicken broth to the pork mixture. Add pepper and salt to your preferred taste.
4. Spread butter over the mixture and cook it on high-pressure mode for around 10 minutes.
5. Let the built-in steam release naturally for quarter-hour. Hit the quick-release button for any remaining pressure to exit.
6. Transfer your pork chops with cabbage to serving plates and enjoy.
NUTRITION: CALORIES 424KCAL, FAT 23G, CARBOHYDRATES 13G, PROTEIN 40G

Pressure-cooked-chicken Masala

Prep time: 10 MINUTES | Cooking time: 13 minutes | Servings: 4 people
Ingredients
- A cup of chicken broth
- A cup of Marsala wine
- 2 pounds of chicken breast
- A cup of flour
- 3 garlic cloves
- 2 teaspoons of butter
- 16 oz of mushrooms
- 2 teaspoons of olive oil

Cooking procedure

1. Subdivide your chicken breast into halves and season each with pepper and salt.
2. Dip the halves into a bowl containing flour for coating.
3. Set your Ninja Foodi to sauté mode and add butter followed by crushed garlic.
4. Add the coated chicken to the sautéed contents and cook each side for around 3 minutes or until it turns golden brown.
5. Add mushrooms, chicken broth, and Marsala wine into the chicken mixture.
6. Set the cooker to high-pressure mode and cook the added contents for around 10 minutes.
7. Select quick-release pressure.
8. Transfer your chicken Masala to a large bowl and serve hot alongside white rice.

NUTRITION: CALORIES 364KCAL, FAT 22G, CARBOHYDRATES 14G, PROTEIN 27G

Ninja Foodi yoghurt

Prep time: 5 MINUTES | Cooking time: 14 hours | Servings: 8people

Ingredients
- 8 cups of milk
- ¼ cup of plain yoghurt

Cooking directions

1. Pour the milk into the Ninja inner pot.
2. Set the cooker to sauté mode and boil the milk until it reaches 181° while stirring it frequently to prevent scorching.
3. Stop the cooker and remove the pot. Place it on a cool surface and leave it until the milk reaches around 110°.
4. Add plain yoghurt to the milk and stir.
5. Seal the pot with an aluminum foil and return it to the Ninja cooker.
6. Flip down the crisping lid and cook the contents on dehydration mode for around 8 hours. Here, the cooking temperature should be set to around 180°.
7. Incubate your yoghurt by continuing cooking it with the same settings for around 6 hours.
8. Switch off your cooker and remove the inner pot.
9. Place it in the refrigerator and allow it to cool for around 12 hours.
10. Strain it until you attain your preferred texture.
11. You can add your favorite sweeteners and other mix-ins to obtain your desired flavor.

NUTRITION: CALORIES 153KCAL, FAT 8G, CARBOHYDRATES 12G, PROTEIN 7G

BEGINNER MEALS USING THE NINJA FOODI

Although there are hundreds of recipes experts can prepare using the cooker, I have compiled easy dishes to familiarize beginner users with the appliance. Everyone starts from somewhere!

- Crispy bacon
- Tasty popcorns
- Roasted chicken
- Fluffy rice
- Creamy yogurt
- Roasted yam

You can also try other Ninja Foodi recipes following its packaged manual. As time goes, you will get used to preparing a variety of meals using the appliance. In this, you should consider water portions to attain your preferred output. Also, study the listed safety precautions to avoid scald injuries.

The innovation of Foodi multi-cooker is something we cannot ignore. The outstanding feature of the appliance is its ability to air crisp, pressure cook, and slow cook. If you love one-pot cooking, then Ninja Foodi might impress you. The pot allows multiple cooking. For instance; you can pressure cook, roast, and steam your veggies; melt and brown your cheese, pressure cook your chicken and air fry it in one pot.

The pre-programmed multi-cooker is safe and easy to use- you only need to use the correct button depending on the recipe. Besides that, it's strong and durable. The Foodi package has a reversible rack and a crisping basket that allows the user to cook multiple recipes simultaneously. Its versatility and efficiency offers relief and comfort to your kitchen.

Moreover, the Ninja Foodi has both pressure cooking and air frying lids whereby the air frying lid is permanently attached while the pressure cooking is separate. Different buttons are displayed for performing functions such as ;pressure cooking, slow cooking, steaming, searing/ sautéing, air crisping, keeping warm, baking/ roasting, and broiling. Also, the Foodi has buttons for time control, temperature adjustment, and start/stop cooking. A 6.5 quart-wide inner pot is available for large servings.

Air crisping/air frying function: The mode is attained when the crisping lid is 'on'. In this, the temperature settings ranges between 300 and 400°F, and the cooking time can be set in two-minute increments, but cannot exceed one hour. Interestingly, the cook can open the crisping lid to check or toss the meal. Opening the lid to check the food's progress suspends the cooking which resumes after closing it.

However, it's advisable to preheat the unit for some minutes before air frying. The action prepares the device for the cooking ahead. Pre-heating involves pressing the start button when beginning and stop button when finishing. Air crisping enables you to cook crispy French fries, onion rings, zucchini wedges, and chicken tenders without using a lot of oil. Pressure-cooked food can also be air-fried when making tender-crisp.

Pressure cook: Pressure cooking locks in moisture and reveals the taste of foods. It cooks fast and produces flavorful meals. It also allows you to cook frozen foods without thawing. The Pressure function occurs after closing the pressure lid. Foods can be cooked for 4 hours continuously on low or high pressure. In this, cook time is set in one-minute increments for 1 hour. After the hour-mark, time can be added in five-minute increments and foods pressure cooked for 4 hours.

To pressure cook, place the pressure lid on, and seal the lid. Select the Pressure button on the control panel and the unit will switch to high pressure automatically. If your recipe requires low pressure-cooking, set it to low mode. Otherwise, continue resetting the cooking duration. In this, press the start/ stop button and the device will enable a dull countdown on the display.As the pressure builds the digital display becomes visible, eliminating guesswork. Once the Foodi is fully pressurized, the countdown begins and when it ends, it switches to keep warm mode automatically (which starts counting up.) The mode keeps the food warm at safe temperatures for up to 12 hours.

After pressure cooking, it's safe to release the accumulated steam/pressure before opening the lid. This can be done using two ways;

a) Quick release: Turn the release valve on the vent position. All the build-up pressure will exit the pot within two minutes allowing you to open the lid. The user should perform this cautiously since the hot steam can cause body burns. The quick -pressure release strategy is perfect for vegetables, eggs, or any food that does not require steam to tenderize.

b) Natural release: In this, do not turn the valve; the pressure exit by its own. When the pot depressurizes, the red float valve drops allowing you to open the lid. This method is helpful when making stocks, soups, and stews because as the pressure drops, the food keeps on cooking.

Note: Pressure cooking happens when the valve is turned to seal position. However, the seal and vent positions of the valve are clearly labeled to avoid human error.

Foodi delivers all the cooking functions you want from your kitchen appliance. Its control panel contains various functions that are easy to execute. Besides pressure cooking and air frying, the multi-cooker can bake, grill, steam, sauté, slow cook, and even dehydrate.

Slow cook: The function uses the pressure lid with the release valve set to vent position. Slow cooking might be done on high or low pressure and time set for up to 12 hours in 15-minute increments. It works perfectly for soups, stews, bone beef ribs, and pot roasts.

Steam: The function uses the pressure lid with the valve set to vent position. However, no temperature control is required to activate the Foodi to this mode. The steam function is ideal for fish and vegetables.

Sear/Sauté: This is the only setting that needs no lid. It has 5 temperature settings: low, medium-low, medium, medium-high, or high setting.

Bake/Roast: The function uses the air-frying lid. It operates between the temperature of 250 and 400 degrees Fahrenheit. The maximum cook time is one hour which can be adjusted in single-minute increments. After one hour, the duration can be extended to four hours in five-minute increments. This is ideal for roasted meats and baked foods.

Broil: The function is attained by putting your ingredients into the multi-cooker, pressing the broil function, setting the cooking duration, and pressing the start/stop button.

The Ninja Foodi is simple to master since its basic steps are the same;
- Put your ingredients into the pot
- Insert the crisping basket or the reversible rack depending on what you are making,
- Select your cooking function,
- Adjust the timer/temperature settings using the arrow buttons,
- Press start. The visible window displays the cooking progress including food timing and the status of the lid among others.

If you hate cleaning utensils, the Ninja pot should not bother you. This is due to its ceramic coating that simplifies washing no matter what it had cooked. It cleans in seconds, wiping-off all residue and oils at a snap of the fingers.

It's convenient to use the Ninja multi-cooker instead of four kitchen appliances. The Foodi is reliable, user-friendly, and saves your kitchen space. Besides that, the cook can prepare multiple recipes simultaneously whether pressure cooking, slow cooking, air frying, or roasting.

BENEFITS OF USING FOODI MULTICOOKER

After hearing about the new appliance in the market, we decided to test its functionality, convenience, and efficiency. In this, we prepared different recipes and found some of the benefits below.

- Allows multiple cooking. The Foodi can air-fry, sauté, bake, pressure cook, slow cook, grill, steam, and roast. It comes with a pressure lid and an air-frying basket.
- The Foodi can replace four small appliances. These includes; an air-fryer, a pressure cooker, a dehydrator, and a pressure cooker.
- The removable basket that allows fats to drain makes the Ninja Foodi a perfect air fryer. Besides that, it cooks faster than I thought-all meals cooked in half the time set.
- It allows the pressure to release naturally saving those nervous for quick release.
- It's safer than the instant pot since the user controls the cooking. In this, the cook inputs the cooking duration and temperature contrary to the instant pot which has time delays and other preset programs.
- It has more functions than the instant pot.

BREAKFAST AND BRUNCH

Egg and Cheese Scramble

This is a flavor-rich and nutritious meal perfect for energizing your day. It is rich in 255 calories, 16.69 fats, 15.13 protein, and 2.52 net carbs.
Preparation time: 5 minutes |Cook time: 3 minutes | Servings: 2

Ingredients
- 4 large eggs, beaten
- ½ tablespoon of cream cheese
- ½ teaspoon of olive oil
- 2 tablespoons of grated cheddar cheese
- Salt and pepper

Directions
1. Combine the cream cheese with the beaten eggs in a bowl. Add some salt and pepper and whisk well.
2. Grease the Foodi's base with organic olive oil.
3. Select the sauté function, set heat to medium-high, and cook time to 3 minutes. Allow the pot to preheat for around 45 seconds.
4. Add the egg mixture using a spatula. When the eggs are almost cooked, add the cheddar cheese and cook for a minute.
5. Transfer your scramble to plates and serve with sausage or bacon.

Hash Brown Casserole

Preparation time: 10 minutes | Cook time: 25minutes | Servings: 1

Ingredients
- 3 tablespoons of organic olive oil
- 48 oz. of frozen hash browns
- 1 onion, chopped
- 6 eggs
- 1/4 cup of milk
- 1/2 cup of cheddar cheese, shredded
- 1b of ham, cubed

Directions
1. Press the sauté function and let the Ninja Foodi preheat for some minutes.
2. Add the olive oil followed by onions and sauté them until they tenderizes.
3. Add the hash browns and close the crisping lid.
4. Set the Foodi to Air Crisp mode and cook for quarter-hour. Remember to open your hash brown half way.
5. Combine the eggs with milk together in a bowl and whisk.
6. Pour the mixture over the hash browns and cook for ten minutes.
7. Add the cubed ham and cheese on top and allow it to rest for a minute. Serve your casserole warm.

Blueberries Breakfast Mix

A healthy mix!
Preparation time: 5minutes | Cook Time: 20 minutes |Servings: 6

Ingredients
- 2 glasses of oats
- 1/3 cup of brown sugar
- 1 teaspoon of baking powder
- A teaspoon of cinnamon powder
- 2 cups of almond milk
- 2 cups of blueberries
- 2 tablespoons of butter
- Cooking spray

Directions
1. Pour all the ingredients into a bowl and stir.
2. Insert the reversible rack in the Foodi and place the baking pan on it. Grease it lightly with the cooking spray and add oats and blueberries.
3. Select the bake function, set the temperature to 325°F, and cook time to 20 minutes.
4. Transfer your blueberries mix to a bowl and ladle into serving plates. Enjoy.

Cherries Oat

You will love this!
Preparation time: 5minutes | Cook time: 15 minutes |Servings: 4

Ingredients
- 3 cups of almond milk
- 4 whole eggs, whisked
- 1 tablespoon of brown sugar
- 1/4 teaspoon of cinnamon powder
- 4 tablespoons of cream cheese
- 1/4 glasses of cherries, pitted and chopped
- 1 and 1/2 cups of rolled oats, divided

Directions
1. Combine the ingredients in a bowl and well.
2. Pour them into the Foodi pot and close the pressure lid. Cook on high mode for 15 minutes.
3. Release the pressure naturally for ten minutes and quick release the rest.
4. Subdivide your cherries oat between plates and enjoy.

Kale - Egg Frittata

Preparation time: 10minutes |Cook Time: 10 minutes |Servings: 6

Ingredients
- 11/2 cups of kale, chopped

- 1/4 cup of cheese, grated
- 6 large eggs
- Cooking spray
- 1 cup of water
- 2 tablespoons of heavy cream
- 1/2 teaspoon of nutmeg, freshly grated
- Salt and pepper

Directions
1. Mix the eggs with cream, nutmeg, salt, and pepper in a bowl.
2. Add the kale and cheese and stir to combine.
3. Grease the cake pan lightly with cooking spray and cover the pan using an aluminum foil.
4. Put the egg mixture in the pan. Pour some water into the pot and fix the reversible rack. Place the pan on the rack and close the lid.
5. Press the pressure button, set the temperature to high mode, and cook time to 10 minutes. Press the start button and quick release the pressure once the set duration elapses.
6. Subdivide your egg-frittata among six plates and enjoy.

Sunrise Millet Pudding

A fantastic breakfast option!
Preparation time: 5 minutes | Cooking time: 12 minutes | Servings: 4

Ingredients
- 1/2 cup of water
- 2/3 cup of millet
- 1 1/2 cups of coconut milk or almond, unsweetened
- 4 pitted dates, chopped
- 1/2 teaspoon of cinnamon
- 1 teaspoon of pure vanilla flavoring

Directions
1. Put all the ingredients in the pot except cinnamon and the vanilla flavoring. Stir.
2. Close the pressure lid and select pressure cook, warm, and 12 minutes cook time. Let the pressure release naturally.
3. Open the pressure lid and add vanilla extract followed by cinnamon. Stir.
4. Serve your pudding with chopped fruits and preferred sweetener.

Breakfast Quinoa

Preparation time: 5 minutes |Cook time: 1 minute |Servings: 4-6

Ingredients:
- 1 1/2 cups of quinoa, well-rinsed and drained
- 2 1/4 cups of broth
- 1 tablespoon of canola oil
- 2 tablespoons of maple syrup
- 2 teaspoons of cumin
- 2 teaspoons of turmeric
- 1/2 teaspoon of vanilla
- 1/4 teaspoon of ground cinnamon

Optional garnishing: chopped pecans, sliced almonds, or fresh berries

Directions:
1. Add water and quinoa into the Ninja multi-cooker. Stir and add the remaining ingredients.
2. Close the pressure lid and set the release valve to "seal".
3. Set the cooking time to one minute at high mode. Do a 10 minute natural-pressure release and then quick release the remaining steam.
4. Open the lid carefully and fluff the quinoa. Serve drizzled with maple and garnish with any of the toppings.

Onion Tofu Scramble

Preparation time: 5minutes |Cook Time: 8 minutes |Servings: 2

Ingredients
- 2 blocks of tofu, cubed
- 4 tablespoons of butter
- Black pepper and salt
- 1 cup of cheddar cheese, grated
- 2 medium-sized onions, sliced

Directions
1. Combine the black pepper, salt, and tofu in a bowl.
2. Sauté butter and onions for 3 minutes and then add the seasoned tofu.
3. Let it cook for two minutes and add the grated cheddar cheese.
4. Close the crisping lid and set the Foodi to air crisp mode.
5. Set the cooking duration to 3 minutes and temperature to 340F. Serve your scramble while hot.

Walnut Bowls

Preparation time: 10 minutes | Cook Time: 12minutes |Servings: 4

Ingredients
- 1 cup of rolled oats
- A cup of walnut, chopped
- 1 cup of cashew milk
- 1/4 cup of sugar
- 1 tablespoon of soppy butter

Directions
1. Put all the ingredients into the Ninja Foodi.
2. Seal the pressure lid and cook on high mode for 12 minutes.
3. Release the pressure naturally for ten minutes and quick release the rest.
4. Subdivide your walnut delicacy amongst bowls and enjoy.

Scrambled Eggs

Preparation time: 5 minutes |Cook time: 3 minutes |Servings: 2
Ingredients
- ¼ cup of milk
- 4 whole eggs, beaten
- 1 tablespoon of butter
- Pepper and salt

Directions:
1. Whisk the eggs in the bowl and add milk. Stir the mixture until it froths. Add salt and pepper and stir again.
2. Preheat the Foodi on Sauté and melt the butter.
3. Add the frothed eggs and stir. Cook for 3 minutes.

Butter and Ham Sandwich

Preparation time: 5 minutes | Cook Time: 8 minutes | Servings: 2
Ingredients
- 4 slices of bread
- 4 teaspoons of butter
- 4 ham slices
- 4 slices of cheddar cheese

Directions
1. Spread the butter on the bread slices and subdivide ham and cheese between two slices.
2. Cover each of the topped slices with one slice of bread. Cut into two equal parts and place them in the Foodi basket.
3. Close the crisping lid and select the air crisp function. Set the cooking time to 8 minutes.
4. When the time elapses, remove the sandwiches from the basket and subdivide it between two plates. Serve for breakfast.

Breakfast Casserole

Preparation time: 10 minutes | Cook Time: 20 minutes | Servings: 6
Ingredients
- 3 cups of hash browns
- 1/2 lb of ground turkey-breakfast sausage
- 6 eggs
- 1/2 cup of milk
- 1/4 teaspoon of black pepper
- 1/2 teaspoon of kosher salt
- 1 cup of shredded Colby cheese

Directions
1. Brown the sausages on sauté mode and transfer them to a bowl.
2. Add a cup of water to the Ninja pot and insert the reversible rack.
3. Combine the eggs with milk, salt and pepper in the bowl.
4. Grease the baking dish lightly and add the hash browns. Put the browned sausages into the dish and pour the egg mix over it.
5. Sprinkle the shredded cheese over the mixture and cover it with the aluminum foil.
6. Place the baking dish on the rack and close the crisping lid.
7. Choose the bake/roast function and set the temperature to 375°F.
8. Set the cooking time to 15 minutes and remember to check its progress frequently.

Bacon Veggies Combo

Preparation time: 10 minutes |Cook Time: 25 minutes | Servings: 4
Ingredients
- 4 bacon slices
- 1 green bell pepper, seeded and chopped
- 1/2 cup of Monterey jack cheese
- 1 tablespoon of mayonnaise, preferably avocado
- Sautéed corn
- 2 scallions, chopped

Directions
1. Place the bacon slices into the basket and put it in the pot.
2. Add the mayonnaise on top and add corn, sweet peppers, scallions, and cheese.
3. Close the crisping lid and select the bake/roast function.
4. Cook with a temperature of 365F for 25 minutes. Serve your combo hot.

Crunchy Cut Oats

Preparation time: 2 minutes | Cook time: 5 minutes | Servings: 3
Ingredients
- 1/2 cup of cut oats
- 1 tablespoon of canola oil
- 2 glasses of water
- Salt

Directions:
1. Combine all the ingredients in the Foodi and close the pressure lid. Select the pressure cook function and cook on high mode for 5 minutes.
2. Do a 10 minutes natural release and quick release the remaining steam.
3. Open the lid and stir for some seconds. Allow the oat breakfast sit for 5 minutes and serve with your favorite toppings and sweeteners.

Polenta Breakfast

Preparation time: 5 minutes | Cook time: 10 minutes | Servings: 6
Ingredients
- 1 1/2 glasses of polenta flour

- 1 teaspoon of salt
- 5 glasses of vegetable broth

Directions:
1. Boil broth and salt on sear/ sauté mode.
2. Add the polenta flour and stir.
3. Close the pressure lid and cook o high mode for 8 minutes.
4. Quick release the accumulated steam and open the Foodi's lid.
5. Whisk the polenta mixture to smoothen and transfer the meal into serving plates.

Feta and Bacon Omelet

Preparation time: 5 minutes |Cook Time: 15 minutes | Servings: 4

Ingredients
- 4 eggs, beaten
- 1/2 lb of bacon, chopped
- 1 tablespoon of organic olive oil
- 1/2 cup of corn
- 1 tablespoon of parsley, chopped
- 1 tablespoon of feta cheese, crumbled
- Salt and black pepper

Directions
1. Press the sauté function and add the oil. When it heats, add the chopped bacon and stir. Let it cook 5 minutes.
2. Add the remaining ingredients except cheese and stir well.
3. Now, sprinkle the cheese over the mixture and close the air-frying lid. Cook the ingredients on air crisp mode for ten minutes. Serve hot.

Crust-less Quiche

Preparation time: 10 minutes | Cook Time: 30 minutes |Servings: 2

Ingredients
- 1/2 cup of Kalamata olives, chopped
- 4 eggs
- 1/4 cup of onions, chopped
- 1/2 cup of milk
- 1/2 cup of tomatoes, chopped
- 1 cup of crumbled feta cheese
- 1 tablespoon of basil, chopped
- 1 tablespoon of oregano, chopped
- 2 tablespoons of extra-virgin olive oil
- Salt and pepper

Directions
1. Smear the multi-cooker pot with organic olive oil.
2. Beat the eggs into a bowl and add milk. Stir well and season with pepper and salt.
3. Add the remaining ingredients and mix thoroughly.
4. Pour the mixture into the oiled pot and close the crisping lid.
5. Select the Air Crisp button and cook for 30 minutes at 325°F. Cool and serve.

Coconut Scramble

Preparation time: 10 minutes | Cook Time: 15 minutes |Servings: 4

Ingredients
- 4 eggs
- 4 tablespoons of coconut milk
- 1 red onion, chopped finely
- 1 tablespoon of canola or coconut oil
- 4 tablespoons of chives
- 4 tablespoons of grated cheddar cheese

Directions
1. Press the sauté button on the Foodi multi-cooker. Add the oil and heat it.
2. Add the chopped onions and stir. Sauté the contents for 3 minutes.
3. Combine the remaining ingredients in a bowl and stir.
4. Pour the mixture into the browned onion and toss.
5. Press the air crisp button and cook for 10 minutes (stir after 5 minutes of cooking.) Serve the scramble while hot.

French Fries and Cheese

Preparation time: 15 minutes | Cook Time: 45 minutes | Servings: 6

Ingredients
- 1 ½ lb of Idaho potatoes, sliced thickly
- 6 cups of cold water
- 2 tablespoons of essential olive oil
- 4 tablespoons of butter
- ¼ cup of all-purpose flour
- 1 ¼ cups of chicken stock
- 2 ½ cups of beef stock
- 1 tablespoon of apple cider vinegar
- 2 tablespoon of ketchup
- 2 teaspoons of Worcestershire sauce
- 1 teaspoon of salt
- ½ teaspoon of ground black pepper
- 1 tablespoon of cornstarch
- 2 cups of fresh mozzarella cheese, diced

Directions
1. Soak the sliced potatoes in water for 30- 45 minutes.
2. Insert the basket in the Foodi and close the crisping lid.
3. Select the air crisp function and set the temperature to 390°F. Preheat the multi-cooker pot for 5 minutes.
4. Drain the potatoes and toss with oil. Add them into the basket and air fry for 30 minutes at the same temperature.

5. Open the crisping lid after every ten minutes and shake the basket to toss. Remove them and set aside.
6. Preheat the pot on sauté mode for 5 minutes to melt the butter.
7. Add the flour and stir until golden brown.
8. Add the beef and chicken stock. Whisk until they smoothen.
9. Add ketchup followed by Worcestershire sauce, vinegar, salt, and pepper.
10. Let it boil for 10 minutes over low temperature.
11. Combine cornstarch with a tablespoon of water and add it to the sauce. Stir until it thickens. Serve your French fries with cheese and gravy.

Almond and Berries Cut Oats

Preparation time: 5 minutes | Cook time: 5 minutes | Servings: 4
Ingredients
- 1 cup of cut oats
- 1 ½ cups of almond milk
- ½ cup of water
- 3 tablespoons of maple syrup
- 1 cup of mixed berries
- ¼ cup almonds, sliced
- 1 teaspoon of vanilla flavoring

Directions:
1. Combine all the ingredients and close the pressure lid. Cook them for 5 minutes.
2. Release pressure naturally for ten minutes and quick release the remaining steam. Serve the oat breakfast while hot.

Spinach Quiche

Preparation time: 10 minutes | Cook Time: 35 minutes| Servings: 6
Ingredients
- 10 ounce of spinach (frozen and thawed)
- 1 tablespoon of butter, melted
- 5 whole eggs, whisk
- Kosher salt
- Freshly ground black pepper
- 3 cups of cheddar cheese, shredded

Directions
1. Sauté the butter and spinach for 3 minutes and transfer them to a bowl.
2. Put the melted butter into a separate bowl. Add the shredded cheese, salt, and pepper.
3. Subdivide the mixture amongst greased molds (previously greased) and put them in the Ninja multi-cooker.
4. Select the bake/ roast function and cook for 30 minutes at a temperature of 360°F.
5. Remove your spinach quiche from the pot and cut them into wedges. Serve warm.

Sourdough Bread

Preparation time: 15 minutes |Cook Time: 40 minutes |Servings: 1
Ingredients
- 1 ½ cups of water, divided
- 1 ½ teaspoons of dry yeast
- 1 teaspoon of sugar
- 1 cup of plain Greek yogurt
- 3 cups of all-purpose flour
- 2 teaspoons of kosher salt
- Cooking spray

Directions
1. Add yeast and sugar to a half cup of hot water and stir. Stir the sugary water for 5 minutes or until it becomes foamy.
2. Add flour, yoghurt, and salt to the foamy mixture and mix for 2 minutes using a high-speed mixer.
3. Preheat the multi-cooker for a minute and set it to bake/ roast mode at 250F.
4. Shape the dough into a ball and leave it covered (in the pot) for two hours or until it rises.
5. Place a parchment paper on the reversible rack and grease it with the cooking spray.
6. Transfer the risen dough to the greased paper and shape it into a ball. Cover it with a towel and set aside for 15 minutes.
7. Subdivide the dough into 4" pieces of ½" depth approximately.
8. Pour the remaining water into the pot and insert the rack (containing the risen dough) in the Foodi.
9. Close the crisping lid and set the multi-cooker to roast mode.
10. Set the temperatures to 325° F and cook time to 40 minutes.
11. After the bread is cooked, remove it from the rack and let it rest for two hours before serving.

Mushroom Omelet

Preparation time: 5 minutes| Cook Time: 20 minutes| Servings: 4
Ingredients
- 6 white mushrooms, sliced
- 1 tablespoon of organic olive oil
- 4 eggs, beaten
- 2 tablespoons of bacon, chopped
- 1/2 cup of coconut milk
- 1 tablespoon of cilantro, chopped
- Salt and black pepper
- Shredded mozzarella cheese

Directions
1. Press the sauté function of the Foodie multi-cooker. Add the oil and heat it.
2. Add the onion and bacon while stirring and sauté for 5 minutes.

3. Add the sliced mushrooms and sauté for 5 minutes.
4. Add the remaining ingredients and stir.
5. Close the crisping lid and set the Foodi to air crisp mode. Cook 10 minutes and serve hot.

Cheesy Meat Oatmeal

Preparation time: ten minutes| Cook Time: 12 minutes |Servings: 2
Ingredients
- 1 beef sausage, chopped
- 3 oz. of salami, chopped
- 4 slices of chopped prosciutto
- 1 tablespoon of ketchup
- 1 cup of mozzarella cheese, grated
- 4 eggs
- 1 tablespoon of chopped onion

Directions
1. Preheat your Ninja Foodi on 300°F. Set it to Air Crisp mode.
2. Whisk the egg in a bowl. Add the ketchup and whisk.
3. Add the onion and stir again.
4. Grease the Foodi basket with the cooking spray. Add the sausage and cook them for two minutes or until they turn brown.
5. Meanwhile, mix the egg mixture with the chopped salami, mozzarella cheese, and prosciutto. Pour the mixture over the sausage and stir.
6. Close the crisping lid and let it cook for 10 minutes. Serve your meat oatmeal hot.

Baked Omelet

Preparation time: ten minutes| Cook Time: 35 minutes| Servings: 6
Ingredients
- ½ cup of milk
- 8 eggs
- Kosher salt and pepper
- 1 cup of cheddar cheese, shredded
- 1 cup of cooked ham, diced
- 1/3 cup of green bell pepper, diced
- 1/3 cup of red bell pepper, diced
- ½ cup of fresh chives, diced

Directions
1. Close the crisping lid and preheat the unit on bake/ roast mode for 5 minutes having set the temperature to 315°F.
2. Combine the milk with eggs, salt, and pepper in a bowl and add the remaining ingredients. Stir.
3. Pour the mixture into a greased baking pan (8 inches) and place it on a rack.
4. Place the rack in the preheated pot and close the crisping lid.
5. Bake/roast the omelet on the same temperature settings for 35 minutes. Enjoy.

Breakfast Burritos

Cook Time: 20 minutes| Preparation time: 20 minutes |Servings: 4
Ingredients
- ½ cup of milk
- 8 large eggs
- ¼ teaspoon of black pepper
- ½ teaspoon of kosher salt
- 1 tablespoon of extra virgin olive oil
- 5 oz. of fresh Mexican chorizo
- 1 cup of yellow onion, chopped
- 1 cup of poblano Chile, chopped
- ½ cup of water
- 4 ounces (about 1 cup) of Mexican cheese, blend
- 4 large flour tortillas
- ½ cup of Pico de Gallo
- ½ cup of fresh cilantro leaves, loosely packed

Directions
1. Mix the eggs with milk in a bowl. Add salt and pepper. Stir.
2. Preheat the Foodi on sauté mode and cook the chorizo in oil for 5 minutes or until they brown.
3. Add onions and poblano. Cook while stirring frequently for 5 minutes or until they tenders. Stop the sauté mode.
4. Place the chorizo mixture on a foil-lined pan.
5. Pour water into the Ninja Foodi and put the pan in the reversible rack.
6. Spread the egg mixture over the chorizo mixture. Sprinkle the contents with cheese evenly.
7. Insert the rack in the Foodi and close the pressure lid.
8. Cook the mixture on high mode for 20 minutes. Quick release the pressure and open the pressure lid.
9. Place tortillas on a flat surface and subdivide the egg/sausage mixture among them.
10. Top up with two teaspoons of Pico de Gallo and two teaspoons of cilantro.
11. Fold the tortillas' sides and roll up. Enjoy.

Bacon and Corn Bake

Preparation time: 10 minutes| Cook Time: 35 minutes| Servings: 6
Ingredients
- 4 bacon slices, chopped
- 1 cup of cheddar cheese, grated
- ½ cup of heavy cream
- 2 cups of corn
- 4 eggs, whisked
- 1 yellow onion, chopped

- 1 tablespoon of essential olive oil
- 1 teaspoon of thyme, chopped
- 2 teaspoons of garlic, grated
- Salt and pepper

Directions
1. Set your Foodi to sauté mode, add oil, and allow it heat.
2. Add the onions and cook for two minutes.
3. Add the chopped bacon, corn, garlic, and thyme. Stir and cook for 5 minutes.
4. Mix the remaining ingredients in the pot and close the crisping lid.
5. Select the bake mode and set the cooking temperature to 320°F.
6. Cook for twenty minutes and serve.

Maple Giant Pancake

Preparation time: 25 minutes| Cook Time: 10 minutes| Servings: 6
Ingredients
- 3 cups of flour
- 1/2 cup of essential olive oil
- 1/3 cup of water
- 5 eggs
- 3/4 cup of sugar
- 2 tablespoon of maple syrup
- 1 and ½ teaspoon of baking soda
- ½ teaspoon of salt
- A dollop of whipped cream

Directions
1. Mix the flour, eggs, sugar, water, baking soda, and salt in a bowl. Use the mixer to blend it.
2. Pour the mixture into the Ninja Foodi and let it rest for 15 minutes.
3. Close the lid and seal the pressure release valve.
4. Press the pressure cook button and cook on low mode for 10 minutes.
5. Quick release the pressure and open the lid carefully.
6. Remove the pancake using a spatula and place it on a platter.
7. Spread your giant pancake with maple syrup. Serve it with whipped cream toppings.

Air Fried Breakfast Sausage

Preparation time: 5 minutes| Cook Time: 10 minutes| Servings: 4
Ingredients
- 4 medium sausages
- 1 teaspoon of celery salt
- 1 teaspoon of garlic powder
- 1 egg

Directions
1. Chop the sausages into mince.
2. Add egg, celery salt, and garlic powder to the minced sausages.
3. Form 4 patties and put them in the air crisp basket.
4. Close the crisping lid and press the press crisp function.
5. Set the temperature to 350°F and timer for ten minutes.
6. Select the start/ stop button.
7. Remove the breakfast sausage and serve.

Corned Beef Hash

Preparation time: 15 minutes| Cook Time: 35 minutes| Servings: 6
Ingredients
- 1/2 lb of cooked corned beef, diced
- 2 tablespoons of canola oil
- 1 red bell pepper, chopped
- 1 onion (peeled and chopped)
- 2 medium white potatoes (peeled and diced)
- 3 teaspoons of salt, divided
- 1/2 teaspoon of ground black pepper
- 6 eggs

Directions
1. Sauté the corned beef. Add oil, onion, and potatoes to it.
2. Add 2 teaspoons of salt and pepper. Sauté the seasonings until the onions brown.
3. Cook for 5 minutes or until a crust forms at the bottom while stirring frequently.
4. Cook for five more minutes and stir.
5. Crack the eggs over the potatoes and close the crisping lid.
6. Broil for 10 minutes. Serve the beef hash with hot sauce. You can also garnish with parsley.

Gold Potatoes and Bacon

Preparation time: 10minutes| Cook Time: 40 minutes| Servings: 8
Ingredients
- 2 gold potatoes, cubed
- 8 oz. of bacon, chopped
- 4 eggs, beaten
- 1 red bell pepper, chopped
- 1 yellow onion, chopped
- Salt and black pepper
- 1 teaspoon of sweet paprika

Directions
1. Set the Foodi to sauté mode. Add the bacon and cook for 5 minutes.
2. Add the bell pepper, onions, and gold potatoes. Sauté the mixture for 5 more minutes.
3. Add eggs, paprika, salt, and black pepper.
4. Set the Foodi to air fry mode and close the crisping lid.

5. Cook the contents for thirty minutes at a temperature of 300°F. Remember to flip at around 15 minutes. Serve hot.

Almond Eggs

Preparation time: 5 minutes| Cook Time: 15 minutes| Servings: 4

Ingredients
- 4 eggs, whisked
- 1 tablespoons of essential olive oil
- 1 red onion, chopped
- 3 oz. of almond milk
- 2 oz. of grated cheese
- Splash of Worcestershire sauce

Directions
1. Select the sauté function on your Ninja Foodi.
2. Add the oil and heat it. Add the chopped onions and stir. Cook for 5 minutes.
3. Combine the remaining ingredients in a bowl and pour them over the sautéed onions.
4. Stir the contents and close the crisping lid.
5. Select the bake function, set temperatures to 375°F, and cook time to 10 minutes. Subdivide your almond eggs between plates and enjoy.

Simple Corned Beef Hash

Preparation time: 5 minutes |Cook Time: 8 minutes |Servings: 6

Ingredients
- 2 medium cans of corned beef, diced
- 12 white potatoes, medium-sized
- 4 large carrots
- 1 large white onion
- 1 and ½ cups of beef stock
- 1 teaspoon of parsley
- Salt and pepper

Directions
1. Dice the corn beef and set aside.
2. Prepare the vegetables by dicing the carrots, potatoes, and onions.
3. Put the diced veggies in the Foodi and add the beef stock.
4. Close the pressure lid on and seal the pressure valve.
5. Cook at high mode for ten minutes.
6. Quick release the pressure when the cooking time elapses.
7. Open the lid and add salt and pepper.
8. Add the diced beef and set the multi-cooker to Sauté mode. Let it cook for two minutes and serve hot.

Tuna Bowls

Preparation time: 5 minutes |Cook Time: 8 minutes |Servings: 4

Ingredients
- 16 oz. of canned tuna (drained and flaked)
- 1 red onion, chopped
- ½ cup of baby spinach
- 2 spring onions, chopped
- 1 tablespoons of lime juice
- 3 tablespoons of melted butter

Directions
1. Set your Ninja Foodi to sauté mode and preheat it for a minute.
2. Add butter and melt. Add onions to the butter and cook for 2 minutes while stirring.
3. Add the remaining ingredients and stir.
4. Close the pressure lid and set the release valve to seal position.
5. Cook the ingredients for 5 minutes and quick release the accumulated pressure after the cooking time elapses.
6. Subdivide the tuna bowls amongst four plates and enjoy.

Banana Breakfast Mix

Preparation time: 5 minutes| Cook Time: 15 minutes| Servings: 6

Ingredients
- 3 bananas (peeled and sliced)
- 1 egg, beaten
- 1 and ½ cups of coconut milk
- 2 glasses of rolled oats
- ½ cup of brown sugar
- 1 tablespoon of baking powder
- 1 teaspoon of vanilla extract
- 1 teaspoon of cinnamon powder
- Cooking spray

Directions
1. Grease the Foodi pot lightly using the cooking spray.
2. Add all the ingredients and close the pressure lid.
3. Cook on high mode for 15 minutes.
4. Allow the pressure to release naturally for 10 minutes.
5. Quick release the remaining pressure and stir. Serve hot.

Oatmeal with Carrot

Preparation time: 10 minutes| Cook time: 13 minutes |Servings: 6

Ingredients:
- 1 tablespoon of butter
- 1 cup of cut oats
- 1 cup of carrots, grated
- 4 cups of water
- 1 teaspoon of pumpkin pie spice
- 3 tablespoons of maple syrup
- ¼ teaspoon of salt

- ¼ cup of dried apricots, chopped
- ½ cup of slivered almonds
- ½ cup of raisins

Directions
1. Put butter into the Foodi and melt it on sauté mode.
2. Add the oats and sauté for 3 minutes while stirring consistently.
3. Add the water, carrots, maple syrup, spices, and salt.
4. Close the pressure lid and set the release valve to "seal."
5. Cook the ingredients on high mode for ten minutes.
6. Let the steam exit naturally for 10 minutes and quick release the rest.
7. Open the pressure lid and add cinnamon, almonds, apricots, and raisins. Stir. Let your oatmeal rest for 5 minutes before serving.

Cream Cheese and Bread

Preparation time: 10 minutes| Cook Time: 15 minutes| Servings: 6

Ingredients
- 8 ounces of cream cheese
- 12 ounces of bread loaf, cubed
- 2 glasses of heavy cream
- 4 eggs
- ½ cup of brown sugar
- 1 teaspoon of cinnamon powder
- 1 teaspoon of vanilla flavoring
- Cooking spray

Directions
1. Grease the baking pan with the cooking spray.
2. Add all the ingredients and mix well.
3. Place the reversible rack in the pot and put the rack on it. Close the crisping lid.
4. Set the Foodi to air crisp mode and cook the ingredients over 325°F for 15 minutes.
5. Subdivide your cheese delicacy amongst six plates.

Spicy Tomato Eggs

Preparation time: 10 minutes| Cook Time: 20minutes| Servings: 4

Ingredients
- 1 red bell pepper, chopped
- 2 tomatoes, cubed
- 4 eggs, whisked
- 1 yellow onion
- 2 tablespoons of organic olive oil
- 1 teaspoon of sweet paprika
- 1 teaspoon of garlic powder
- 1 teaspoon of onion powder
- Salt and pepper

Directions
1. Set your Foodi to sauté mode and heat some olive oil.
2. Add the bell pepper to the heated oil let it cook for five minutes while stirring occasionally.
3. Add the cubed tomatoes, onion powder, garlic powder, paprika, salt, and pepper. Stir. Cook the ingredients for five more minutes.
4. Add the eggs and toss well.
5. Close the pressure lid and cook on high mode for 12 minutes.
6. Natural-release the accumulated pressure for ten minutes. Subdivide your spiced tomato eggs amongst four plates.

Egg, Sausage, and Cheese Cake

Preparation time: 20 minutes| Cook Time: 10minutes|Servings: 4

Ingredients
- 8 eggs, beaten
- 8 oz. of breakfast sausage, chopped
- 3 slices of bacon, chopped
- 1 red bell pepper, chopped
- 1 green bell pepper, chopped
- 1 cup of green onion, chopped
- 1 cup of cheddar cheese, grated
- 1teaspoon of red chili flakes
- ½ cup of milk
- 4 bread slices, ½ inches cubed
- 2 cups of water
- Salt and black pepper

Directions
1. Combine all the ingredients except the bread cubes and water in a bowl.
2. Pour the egg mixture into a greased Bundt pan.
3. Squeeze the bread cubes in the egg mixture using a spoon
4. Pour water into the Ninja Foodi and insert the reversible rack.
5. Place the pan on the rack and close the pressure lid. Ensure the release valve is set to seal position.
6. Cook on high mode for 6 minutes and quick release the accumulated pressure.
7. Slit the egg mixture using a knife and close the crisping lid.
8. Cook on bake/roast mode for four minutes over the temperature of 380°F.
9. Remove the egg mixture from the pan by inverting the pan over a platter.
10. Slice the mixture and serve it alongside your preferred sauce.

Tofu with Mixed Veggies

Preparation time: 20 minutes| Cook time: 12 minutes| Servings: 4
Ingredients:
- 2 tablespoons of essential olive oil
- 1 package (16-oz) of extra-firm tofu (drained and pressed)
- ½ onion, sliced
- ½ zucchini, chopped
- ½ green bell pepper, chopped
- 1 cup of broccoli, chopped
- 1 can (14.5-oz) of diced tomatoes
- ½ teaspoon of dried rosemary
- ¼ cup of vegetable broth
- 1 teaspoon of dried thyme
- 1 pinch of dried basil
- ½ teaspoon of oregano
- Ground black pepper
- ¼ cup of nutritional yeast

Directions
1. Wrap tofu in paper towels and press it for 5 minutes. Cut it into bite-size pieces.
2. Sauté the tofu pieces until they turn light brown.
3. Add garlic, onions and bell pepper. Let it cook for 3 minutes.
4. Add the zucchini, tomatoes, broccoli, and herbs.
5. Close the pressure lid and cook 4 minutes.
6. Quick release the accumulated pressure and serve. Sprinkle each plate with black pepper and yeast.

Brown Rice Breakfast Risotto

Preparation time: 5 minutes| Cook time: 25 minutes| Servings: 4
Ingredients
- 2 tablespoons of butter
- 1 ½ cups of short grain brown rice
- 2 medium bananas, mashed lightly
- 1/3 cup of brown sugar
- 1 ½ teaspoons of cinnamon
- ½ teaspoon of salt
- 3 cups of light coconut milk
- 1 cup of dry white wine
- Chopped walnuts

Directions:
1. Smear some butter on your Foodi's base and melt it on sauté mode.
2. Add the rice and cook for two minutes while stirring constantly.
3. Add the bananas, cinnamon, salt, sugar, milk, and wine.
4. Close the pressure lid and cook on high mode for 22 minutes.
5. Natural-release the in-built pressure and serve with chopped walnuts garnishing.

Deli Salmon Veggies Cakes

Preparation time: 20 minutes| Cook time: 15 minutes| Servings: 4
Ingredients
- 25-oz of packed salmon flakes (steamed)
- 1cup of breadcrumbs
- 1 red onion, finely diced
- 1 red pepper (seeded and diced)
- 4 tablespoons of butter, divided
- 4 tablespoons of mayonnaise
- 2 teaspoons of Worcestershire sauce
- ¼ cup of parsley, chopped
- 1 teaspoon of garlic powder
- 2 teaspoons of olive oil
- Salt and black pepper
- 3 eggs, beaten
- 3 large potatoes cut into chips

Directions
1. Preheat the Foodi by setting it to sauté mode.
2. Add the oil and butter. Sauté the contents until the butter melt.
3. Add the onions and red pepper. Let it cook for 6 minutes and turn off the sauté mode.
4. Combine the salmon flakes with breadcrumbs, garlic powder, Worcestershire sauce, mayonnaise, parsley, salt, black pepper, sautéed red bell pepper, and onions in a bowl. Mix well using a spoon to breakdown the salmon.
5. Form 4 patties from the mixture and add the remaining butter.
6. Fry for 5 minutes to melt the butter while flipping.
7. Close the crisping lid and bake/roast for 4 minutes at 320°F.
8. Serve your cake with salad. You can also spray it with herb vinaigrette for additional flavor.

Breakfast Roll Casserole

Preparation time: 5 minutes| Cook time: 20 minutes| Servings: 4
Ingredients:
- 12 eggs
- 1 cup of milk
- A crescent roll, halved
- ½ pound of pork sausage, cooked
- Salt and Pepper

Directions:
1. Mole the halved crescent rolls into balls and set aside.
2. Cook the sausage and drain it using towels.
3. Put all the ingredients into the Ninja Foodi except the reserved rolls.
4. Now, add the crescent roll balls and close the pressure lid.

5. Set the release valve to seal position and cook on high mode for 15 minutes.
6. Release the in-built pressure naturally and open the pressure lid. Serve hot.

Turkey Burrito

Preparation time: 5minutes| Cook Time: 6 minutes |Servings: 2

Ingredients
- 1 turkey breast (cooked and shredded)
- 3 eggs, whisked
- 1 red pepper, sliced
- 1 avocado (peeled, pitted, and sliced)
- Salt and pepper
- 2 tablespoons of shredded mozzarella cheese
- 2 corn tortillas
- Cooking spray

Directions
1. Smear the pan with the cooking spray.
2. Add salt, pepper, and the whisked eggs into a pan and mix.
3. Add the remaining ingredients except cheese and tortilla. Whisk well.
4. Fix the reversible rack in the pot and place a pan on it. Cover the pan's content with a foil and closes the pressure lid.
5. Cook on high mode for10 minutes and then quick release the accumulated steam.
6. Place the tortillas on a clean surface and subdivide the egg mixture equally amongst them. Top each of them with mozzarella cheese and enjoy.

SIDE DISH RECIPES

Turmeric Cauliflower

Preparation and cooking time: 30 minutes |Servings: 4

Ingredients:
- 2 cups of cauliflower florets
- 1 cup of veggie stock
- A handful of cilantro, chopped.
- 2 garlic cloves, minced.
- 2 tablespoons of essential olive oil
- 2 tablespoons of turmeric powder
- Salt and black pepper

Directions:
1. Set the Foodi to Sauté mode and add oil.
2. Heat it and add the garlic. Cook for a minute.
3. Add all the ingredients to the pot (except the cilantro) and toss.
4. Set your multi-cooker to baking mode and cook at 380 °F for 20 minutes.
5. Add the cilantro and toss. Subdivide your turmeric cauliflower amongst plates as a side dish.

Cauliflower Mix

Preparation and cooking time: 20 minutes |Servings: 4

Ingredients
- 1 ½ cups of white cauliflower, florets separated
- 1 ½ cups of purple cauliflower, florets separated
- 2 garlic cloves, minced.
- ½ cup of peas
- 1 carrot, cubed.
- 2 spring onions, chopped
- 2 and ½ teaspoons of soy sauce
- 2 teaspoons of organic olive oil
- A pinch of salt and black pepper

Directions:
1. Set the Foodi to Sauté mode and add oil. Heat it up.
2. Add the onions and garlic and stir. Cook for three minutes.
3. Add the carrots, cauliflower, soy sauce, salt, pepper, and peas.
4. Toss and close the pressure lid. Cook on high mode for 8 minutes.
5. Release the pressure naturally for ten minutes. Subdivide your cauliflower mix between plates as a side dish.

Potato Salad

Preparation and cooking time: 25 minutes |Servings: 6

Ingredients
- 2 lb of red potatoes, scrubbed
- 1 yellow onion, chopped
- 5 bacon strips, chopped
- 2 celery stalks, chopped
- ¼ cup of apple cider vinegar
- 1 cup of sauerkraut
- ½ cup of scallions, chopped
- ½ cup of water
- 1 tablespoon of mustard
- ¼ teaspoon of sweet paprika
- 1 teaspoon of sugar
- A pinch of salt and black pepper

Directions:
1. Put the potatoes and water into the Ninja Foodi and close the pressure lid.
2. Cook on high mode for 5 minutes and release the pressure naturally for 10 minutes
3. Cool the potatoes, peel, and cube them.
4. Clean the Foodi and set it to sauté mode. Add the bacon and stir. Cook for 5 minutes
5. Add the onions and stir. Cook for another 5 minutes.
6. Add vinegar and toss. Cook for one minute.
7. Add the scrubbed potatoes and the remaining ingredients. Toss and cook until the potatoes soften.
8. Subdivide your potato salad between plates as a side dish.

Zucchini Spaghetti

Preparation and cooking time: 10 minutes |Servings: 4

Ingredients
- 3 zucchinis cut with a spiralizer
- 1 cup of sweet peas
- 1 cup of cherry tomatoes, halved
- 6 basil leaves, torn
- 1 tablespoon of extra virgin olive oil
- A pinch of salt and black pepper
- spaghetti

For the pesto:
- 1/3 cup of pine nuts
- ¼ cup of parmesan, grated
- ½ cup of extra virgin olive oil
- 3 cups of basil leaves
- 2 garlic cloves
- A pinch of salt and black pepper

Directions
1. Mix ½ tablespoon of oil with 3 cups basil, garlic, pine nuts, parmesan, salt, and pepper in a blender. Pulse well.
2. Set the Foodi to sauté mode and add the remaining oil. Heat it up.

3. Add the zucchini, spaghetti, peas, tomatoes, and the pesto. Toss and close the pressure lid. Cook on high mode for 5 minutes.
4. Release the in-built pressure naturally for four minutes and quick release the rest.
5. Open the lid and add the torn basil leaves.
6. Toss and subdivide your zucchini spaghetti between plates as a side dish.

Garlicky Broccoli

Preparation and cooking time: 30 minutes |Servings: 4

Ingredients
- 1 broccoli head, florets separated
- 3 garlic cloves, minced
- 2 tablespoons of lemon juice
- 2 tablespoons of parsley, chopped
- 1 tablespoon of essential olive oil

Directions:
1. Set the Foodi on sauté mode and add oil. Heat it up.
2. Add the garlic, broccoli, and lemon juice. Toss and cook for two minutes
3. Close the pressure lid and cook on high mode for 15 minutes.
4. Let the accumulated pressure release for 10 minutes naturally. Subdivide your garlicky broccoli between serving plates as a side dish.

Brussels sprouts

Preparation and cooking time: 22 minutes |Servings: 4

Ingredients
- 1 lb of Brussels sprouts (trimmed and halved)
- 2 tablespoons of garlic, minced
- 6 teaspoons of extra virgin olive oil
- Salt and black pepper

Directions
1. Put all the ingredients into your Foodi's air crisp basket. Stir.
2. Insert the basket into the multi-cooker and set it to air crisp mode.
3. Cook the sprouts at 400 °F for 12 minutes.
4. Subdivide your Brussels sprouts between plates as a side dish.

Easy Gnocchi

Preparation and cooking time: 32 minutes | Servings: 6

Ingredients
- 50 oz. of potato gnocchi
- 10 oz. of baby spinach
- ½ cup of goat cheese, crumbled
- ¼ cup of parmesan, grated
- 1/3 cup of white flour
- 3 and ½ cups of heavy cream
- 1 ½ cups of chicken stock
- A pinch of salt and black pepper

Directions:
1. Set the Foodi to Sauté mode and heat it up.
2. Add the stock, cream, flour, salt, pepper, and nutmeg. Whisk well and cook for 8 minutes.
3. Add the spinach and gnocchi.
4. Sprinkle the mixture with parmesan and goat cheese.
5. Set the Foodi to bake mode and cook at 325 °F for 15 minutes.
6. Subdivide your gnocchi side dish amongst plates.

Warm Potato Salad

Preparation and cooking time: 30 minutes |Servings: 4

Ingredients
- 2 gold potatoes cut into wedges
- 3 tablespoons of heavy cream
- 1 tablespoon of canola oil
- Salt and black pepper

Directions
1. Put the potatoes in the air crisp basket and insert it in the Foodi.
2. Set the multi-cooker to air crisp mode and cook at 400 °F for 10 minutes
3. Transfer the potatoes to a bowl and clean the Foodi.
4. Set it to sauté mode and add oil. Heat it up.
5. Put the potato wedges, salt, pepper, and cream into the pot.
6. Toss and cook for 10 minutes.
7. Subdivide your salad between plates as a side dish

Baby Carrots

Preparation and cooking time: 25 minutes |Servings: 4

Ingredients:
- 1 lb of baby carrots, trimmed
- 2 tablespoons of lime juice
- 2 teaspoons of essential olive oil
- 1 teaspoons of herbs de Provence

Directions:
1. Put all the ingredients into a bowl and toss.
2. Transfer them into a crisping basket and fix it in the Foodi. Add the trimmed carrots and close the crisping lid.
3. Air-fry the mixture at 350 °F for 15 minutes. Subdivide your carrot side dish between plates.

Zucchini Fries

Preparation and cooking time: 22 minutes |Servings: 4

Ingredients
- 2 small zucchinis cut into fries
- 2 eggs, whisked
- 1 cup of bread crumbs
- ½ cup of white flour
- Cooking spray
- Salt and black pepper

Directions:
1. Mix flour, salt, and pepper in a bowl. Stir.
2. Put the breadcrumbs in another bowl and add the whisked eggs.
3. Dredge the zucchini fries in the bread crumb mixture and transfer them to the Foodi's air crisp basket.
4. Fix the basket in the Foodi and grease the fries with the cooking spray.
5. Set the multi-cooker to air crisp mode and cook at 400 °F for 12 minutes.
6. Subdivide your zucchini side dish between plates.

Herbed Sweet Potatoes

Preparation and cooking time: 25 minutes |Servings: 6

Ingredients
- 3 lb of sweet potatoes, wedged
- ½ cup of parmesan, grated
- 2 garlic cloves
- 2 tablespoons of butter, melted
- ½ teaspoon of parsley, dried
- ¼ teaspoon of sage, dried
- ½ tablespoon of rosemary, dried
- Salt and black pepper

Directions
1. Combine all the ingredients in the Foodi's baking dish. Toss.
2. Insert the reversible rack in the pot and place the baking dish on it.
3. Set the multi-cooker to baking mode and cook at 360 °F for 20 minute.
4. Divide the sweet potatoes side dish between plates and enjoy.

Veggie Side Salad

Preparation and cooking time: 22 minutes |Servings: 4

Ingredients
- 1 eggplant, cubed
- 1 green bell pepper, chopped
- 1 bunch of cilantro, chopped
- 2 garlic cloves, minced
- 1 yellow onion, chopped
- 1 tablespoon of tomato sauce
- 1 tablespoon of extra virgin olive oil
- Salt and black pepper

Directions:
1. Set the Foodi to Sauté mode and add the oil. Heat it up.
2. Add all the ingredients (except the cilantro) and toss.
3. Close the pressure lid and cook on high mode for 12 minutes.
4. Release pressure naturally for 10 minutes.
5. Subdivide your veggie side dish between plates and enjoy.

Buttery Broccoli

Preparation and cooking time: 35 minutes |Servings: 4

Ingredients
- 1 broccoli head, florets separated
- ½ cup of chicken stock
- ½ cup of parmesan, grated
- 2 garlic cloves, minced
- 1 yellow onion, chopped
- 2 tablespoons of parsley, chopped
- 3 tablespoons of butter
- Salt and black pepper

Directions:
1. Set the Foodi to Sauté mode and add the butter. Melt it.
2. Add onions and the garlic. Stir and cook for 5 minutes
3. Add the remaining ingredients (except the parsley and the parmesan) and toss. Set your Foodi to baking mode and cook at 360 °F for 20 minutes.
4. Sprinkle it with cheese and parmesan. Toss and subdivide the buttery side dish between plates.

Sumac Eggplant

Preparation and cooking time: 25 minutes |Servings: 6

Ingredients
2 lb of eggplants, cubed
1 tablespoon of organic olive oil
1 teaspoon of sumac
1 teaspoon of garlic powder
Juice extracted from a lime.

Directions
1. Set the Foodi to sauté mode and add oil. Heat it up.
2. Add the eggplant, garlic powder, sumac, and lime juice. Toss and close the pressure lid.
3. Cook on high mode for 15 minutes.
4. Release the pressure for 10 minutes naturally.
5. Subdivide the eggplant mixture between plates as a side dish.

Thyme Red Potatoes

Preparation and cooking time: 40 minutes | Servings: 4

Ingredients:

- 4 red potatoes, thinly sliced
- 1 tablespoon of organic olive oil
- 2 teaspoons of thyme, chopped
- Salt and black pepper

Directions:
1. Mix all the ingredients in a bowl and toss.
2. Transfer the mixture to an air crisp basket and insert it in the Foodi.
3. Set the multi-cooker to air crisp mode and cook at 370 °F for 30 minutes.
4. Subdivide your thyme-potatoes between serving plates as a side dish

Buttery Mushrooms

Preparation and cooking time: 20 minutes |Servings: 4

Ingredients
- 1 lb of button mushrooms, halved
- 3 tablespoons of butter, melted
- 2 tablespoons of parmesan, grated
- 1 teaspoon of Italian seasoning
- A pinch of salt and black pepper

Directions
1. Set the Foodi to Sauté mode and add butter. Heat it up to melt.
2. Add the mushrooms followed by the remaining ingredients and toss.
3. Close the pressure cooking lid and cook on high mode for 10 minutes.
4. Release the pressure naturally for 10 minutes. Subdivide the buttery mushroom between serving plates as a side dish.

Cauliflower and Pineapple Salad

Preparation and cooking time: 30 minutes |Servings: 6

Ingredients
- 2 cauliflower florets
- 1 pineapple (peeled and cubed)
- 1 mango (peeled and cubed)
- 1 cup of chicken stock, heated up
- 2 teaspoons of essential olive oil
- Salt and black pepper

Directions
1. Set the Foodi to sauté mode and add the oil. Heat it up and add the cauliflower. Cook for 5 minutes.
2. Add the remaining ingredients to the pot and close the pressure lid.
3. Cook on high mode for 15 minutes and release the steam naturally for 10 minutes.
4. Subdivide your pineapple salad between serving plates as a side dish.

Squash Mash

Preparation and cooking time: 30 minutes |Servings: 4

Ingredients
- 1 cup of veggie stock
- 2 tablespoons of butter, melted
- 2 tablespoons of sour cream
- 1 butternut squash (peeled and cubed)
- Salt and black pepper

Directions:
1. Mix the squash with the stock, salt, and pepper in your Foodi. Toss and close the pressure lid.
2. Cook on high mode for twenty minutes.
3. Release the stress naturally for 10 minutes.
4. Mash the squash well and add butter followed by the sour cream.
5. Whisk well and subdivide the mash between four serving plates a side dish.

Hazelnut Cauliflower Rice

Preparation and cooking time: 32 minutes |Servings: 4

Ingredients
- 1 spring onion, chopped
- 2 garlic cloves, minced
- 2 cups of cauliflower rice
- 2 cups of chicken stock
- ½ cup of hazelnuts (toasted and chopped)
- 1 tablespoon of cilantro (chopped)
- 1 teaspoon of essential olive oil
- Salt and black pepper

Directions:
1. Set the Foodi to Sauté mode and add the oil. Warm it and add onions. Add the minced garlic and stir. Cook for 3 minutes.
2. Add the cauliflower rice, stock, hazelnuts, salt, and pepper. Toss and close the pressure lid. Cook on high mode for 20 minutes.
3. Release the accumulated steam naturally for 10 minutes.
4. Add the chopped cilantro and toss.
5. Subdivide your cauliflower rice between serving plates as a side dish.

Maple Carrots

Preparation and cooking time: 25 minutes |Servings: 6

Ingredients
- 2 lbs of carrots, roughly cubed
- 1 tablespoon of canola oil
- 2 tablespoon of maple syrup
- 1 tablespoon of parsley, chopped

Directions
1. Mix all the ingredients in a bowl and transfer the mixture into an air crisp basket.
2. Fit the basket in the Foodi and set it to crisping mode.

3. Cook at 350 °F for 20 minutes.
4. Subdivide the maple carrots between serving plates as a side dish.

Red Cabbage

Preparation and cooking time: 30 minutes |Servings: 2

Ingredients
- 1 red cabbage head, shredded
- 1 cup of sour cream
- 1 red onion, chopped
- 4 bacons (sliced and chopped)
- Salt and black pepper

Directions
1. Set the Foodi to sauté mode and add the bacon.
2. Stir and brown it for four minutes.
3. Add onions, cabbages, salt, and pepper to the bacon.
4. Stir and cook for four minutes.
5. Add the sour cream and toss well. Close the pressure lid and cook on high mode for 12 minutes.
6. Release the pressure naturally for ten minutes.
7. Subdivide your red cabbage between the serving plates as a side dish.

Green Beans Salad

Preparation and cooking time: 30 minutes |Servings: 4

Ingredients
- 1 ½ lb of green beans, trimmed
- ½ lb of shallots, chopped
- ¼ cup of walnuts, chopped
- 2 tablespoons of olive oil
- Salt and black pepper

Directions:
1. Combine all the ingredients in the crisping basket and fix it in the Foodi
2. Set the multi-cooker to air crisp mode and cook at 360 °F for 20 minutes.
3. Subdivide your beans' salad between serving plates as a side dish.

Roasted Tomato Salad

Preparation and cooking time: 16 minutes |Servings: 2

Ingredients
- 20 oz. of cherry tomatoes, cut into quarters
- ½ cup of cilantro
- 1 white onion, roughly chopped
- 1 jalapeno pepper, chopped
- Juice extracted from one lime
- 1 tablespoon of extra virgin olive oil
- Salt and black pepper

Directions:
1. Set the Foodi to sauté mode and add the oil. Heat it and add the onions.
2. Stir and sauté the onions for three minutes.
3. Add the remaining ingredients and toss.
4. Set the Ninja Foodi to roast mode and cook at 380 °F for 4 minutes.
5. Subdivide your tomato salad between serving plates as a side dish.

Mexican Beans

Preparation and cooking time: 30 minutes |Servings: 4

Ingredients:
- A cup of canned garbanzo beans, drained
- 1 cup of canned cranberry beans, drained
- A cup of chicken stock
- 1 bunch of parsley, chopped
- 1 small red onion, chopped
- 1 garlic herb, minced
- 2 celery stalks, chopped
- 5 tablespoons of apple cider vinegar
- 4 tablespoons of organic olive oil
- Salt and black pepper

Directions:
1. Set the Foodi to sauté mode and add the oil. Heat it up and add onions and the minced garlic. Stir and sauté the seasonings for 5 minutes.
2. Add the remaining ingredients and toss. Close the pressure lid and cook on high mode for 15 minutes.
3. Natural-release the accumulated moisture and open the lid.
4. Subdivide your Mexican beans between serving plates as a side dish.

Potato Mash

Preparation and cooking time: 20 minutes |Servings: 4

Ingredients
- 3 gold potatoes (peeled and cubed)
- ½ cup of cheddar cheese, shredded
- 1 cup of heavy cream
- 1 cup of water
- ¼ cup of butter, melted
- A pinch of salt and black pepper

Directions:
1. Put the potatoes and water in the Foodi and close the pressure lid.
2. Cook on high mode for ten minutes and release the pressure naturally for another ten minutes.
3. Drain the potatoes and transfer them to a bowl.
4. Mash them and add butter, cheese, cream, salt, and pepper. Stir.

5.   Subdivide your potato mash between serving plates as a side dish.

Spiced Squash

Preparation and cooking time: 25 minutes |Servings: 4
Ingredients
- 6 oz of squash, cubed
- 2 oz of heavy cream
- 1 small yellow onion, chopped
- 2 garlic cloves, minced
- 2 tablespoons of extra virgin olive oil
- ½ teaspoon of cinnamon powder
- ½ teaspoon of allspice
- ½ teaspoon of nutmeg, ground
- ½ teaspoon of ginger, grated

Directions:
1.   Set the Foodi to sauté mode and add the oil. Heat it up.
2.   Add onions and garlic. Stir and cook for 5 minutes.
3.   Add the remaining ingredients and toss.
4.   Set the Foodi to baking mode and cook everything at 360 °F for fifteen minutes.
5.   Subdivide your squash between serving plates as a side dish.

Beans and Tomatoes Mix

Preparation and cooking time: 30 minutes |Servings: 6
Ingredients
- 1 lb of canned red kidney beans, drained
- ½ lb of cherry tomatoes, cut into quarters
- 1 yellow onion, chopped
- 4 garlic cloves, chopped
- 2 spring onions, minced
- 1 teaspoon of essential olive oil
- 2 tablespoons of cilantro, minced
- 2 tablespoons of tomato sauce
- Salt and black pepper

Directions
1.   Mix all the ingredients (except cilantro) in your Foodi's baking pan and toss.
2.   Insert the reversible rack in the equipment and place the baking pan on it.
3.   Set the Foodi to baking mode and cook everything for 20 minutes.
4.   Add the minced cilantro and stir. Subdivide your tomatoes side dish between plates and enjoy.

Potatoes and Tomatoes

Preparation and cooking time: 25 minutes |Servings: 6
Ingredients
- 15 oz of potatoes, cubed
- 6 oz of canned tomatoes, chopped
- 2 spring onions, chopped
- 2 tablespoons of extra virgin olive oil
- ½ teaspoon of nutmeg, ground
- Salt and black pepper

Directions:
1.   Set the Foodi to sauté mode and add the oil. Heat it up and add the onions.
2.   Stir and cook for 3 minutes.
3.   Add the potatoes, nutmeg, tomatoes, salt, and pepper to the onions.
4.   Toss and close the pressure lid. Cook on high mode for fifteen minutes.
5.   Release the accumulated vapor naturally for ten minutes.
6.   Subdivide the side dish between plates and enjoy.

Creamy Cauliflower

Preparation and cooking time: 25 minutes |Servings: 4
Ingredients
- 1 cauliflower head, florets separated
- ½ cup of Italian bread crumbs
- ¼ cup of raisins
- ½ cup of heavy cream
- ½ cup of parmesan, grated
- 1 cup of beer
- 1 tablespoon of white flour
- A teaspoon of nutmeg, ground
- A pinch of salt and black pepper

Directions:
1.   Combine beer with the raisins, cauliflower, salt, pepper, and nutmeg in your Foodi.
2.   Toss and close the pressure lid. Cook the ingredients on high mode for 3 minutes.
3.   Release the pressure naturally for four minutes and quick release the rest.
4.   Add the cream mixed with the flour and toss. Set the Foodi to sauté mode and continue cooking for 5 more minutes.
5.   Mix the bread crumbs with cheese in a bowl. Stir and pour it over the cauliflower mixture.
6.   Close the crisping lid and set the Foodi to air crisp mode. Cook at 390 °F for ten minutes.
7.   Subdivide your creamy cauliflower between serving plates as a side dish.

Garlic Mushrooms

Preparation and cooking time: 30 minutes |Servings: 4
Ingredients
- 1 lb of brown mushrooms, halved
- 1 tablespoon of garlic, minced
- A tablespoon of lime juice
- 1 tablespoon of chives, chopped

- 2 tablespoons of extra virgin olive oil
- Salt and black pepper

Directions:
1. Set the Foodi to sauté mode and add the oil. Warm it and add garlic and mushrooms.
2. Toss and sauté for 5 minutes
3. Add the lime juice and set the multi-cooker to baking mode. Cook at 380 °F for 15 minutes. Add the chives and toss.
4. Subdivide the mushroom side dish between serving plates and enjoy.

Sweet Potato and Mayo

Preparation and cooking time: 30 minutes |Servings: 2

Ingredients
- 2 sweet potatoes (peeled and cut into wedges)
- 4 tablespoons of mayonnaise
- 2 tablespoons of organic olive oil
- ½ teaspoon of curry powder
- ¼ teaspoon of coriander, ground
- ½ teaspoon of cumin, ground
- A pinch of ginger powder
- Salt and black pepper

Directions:
1. Mix the sweet potato wedges with salt, pepper, coriander, curry powder, and oil in the crisping basket. Toss well.
2. Insert the basket in the Foodi and set it to air crisp mode.
3. Cook the potatoes at 380 °F for 20 minutes. Remember to shake the pot at the 10th minute.
4. Transfer the potatoes to a bowl and add the remaining ingredients. Toss and serve as a side dish.

Yummy Eggplant

Preparation and cooking time: 25 minutes |Servings: 4

Ingredients
- 4 eggplants (cut into cubes)
- 1 red onion, chopped
- 1 tablespoon of smoked paprika
- 1 tablespoon of organic olive oil
- Salt and black pepper

Directions:
1. Set the Foodi to Sauté mode and add the oil. Heat it up and add the eggplants followed by the remaining ingredients. Stir.
2. Close the pressure lid and cook on high mode for fifteen minutes.
3. Release the pressure naturally for 10 minutes.
4. Subdivide your yummy eggplants between serving plates as a side dish.

Buttery Brussels sprouts

Preparation and cooking time: 30 minutes |Servings: 8

Ingredients:
- 3 lbs of Brussels sprouts, trimmed
- 1 lb of bacon, chopped
- 1 yellow onion, chopped
- 2 cups of heavy cream
- 4 tablespoons of butter, melted
- 1 teaspoon of extra virgin olive oil
- Salt and black pepper

Directions:
1. Put the Brussels sprouts in the crisping basket and insert it in your Ninja Foodi.
2. Set it to air crisp mode and cook at 370 °F for 10 minutes.
3. Transfer the cooked sprouts to a bowl and clean the Foodi.
4. Set the multi-cooker to sauté mode and add oil and butter. Heat it to melt the butter.
5. Return the sprouts to the Foodi and add the chopped bacon.
6. Add onions and stir. Continue cooking the ingredients for five more minutes.
7. Subdivide the sprouts between plates as a side dish.

Asian Style Chickpeas

Preparation and cooking time: 30 minutes |Servings: 4

Ingredients
- 30 oz of canned chickpeas, drained
- 2 tablespoons of olive oil
- 2 teaspoons of garam Masala
- ¼ teaspoon of mustard powder
- ½ teaspoon of garlic powder
- 1 teaspoon of sweet paprika
- A pinch of salt and black pepper

Directions:
1. Mix all the ingredients in a bowl and toss well.
2. Set the Ninja Foodi to sauté mode and heat it up for 3 minutes.
3. Add the chickpeas mixture and sauté them for 6 minutes
4. Transfer them to the Foodi's basket and set it to air crisp mode.
5. Cook the mixture at 400 °F for fifteen minutes.
6. Subdivide your chickpeas side dish between plates as a side dish.

Brussels sprouts

Preparation and cooking time: 25 minutes |Servings: 4

Ingredients

- 1 lb of Brussels sprouts, halved
- 4 bacon strips (cooked and chopped)
- 1 tablespoon of extra virgin olive oil
- 2 teaspoons of garlic powder
- A pinch of salt and black pepper

Directions:
1. Mix all the ingredients in a bowl (except bacon) and toss.
2. Put the Brussels sprouts in the crisping basket and set it to air crisp mode.
3. Cook at 390 °F for twenty minutes.
4. Subdivide the Brussels sprouts between plates and top them with bacon.

Sweet Potato Mash

Preparation and cooking time: 20 minutes |Servings: 4

Ingredients:
- 1 ½ lbs of sweet potatoes (peeled and cubed)
- 1 cup of chicken stock
- 1 tablespoon of honey
- A tablespoon of butter, softened
- Salt and black pepper

Directions:
1. Mix the sweet potatoes with stock, salt, and pepper in your Foodi. Close the pressure lid and cook for 15 minutes. Release the pressure naturally for ten minutes
2. Mash the potatoes and add the softened butter followed by honey.
3. Whisk well and subdivide the mash between serving plates as a side dish.

Oregano Potatoes

Preparation and cooking time: 35 minutes |Servings: 2

Ingredients:
- 4 gold potatoes (cut into wedges)
- 4 garlic cloves, minced
- ½ cup of water
- 2 tablespoons of essential olive oil
- 1 tablespoon of oregano, chopped
- Juice extracted from a lemon
- A pinch of salt and black pepper

Directions:
1. Pour water into the Foodi and insert a basket into it.
2. Put potatoes in the basket and close the pressure lid. Cook it on low mode for four minutes.
3. Release the pressure naturally for 10 minutes and drain the potatoes. Transfer them to a large bowl and set aside.
4. Clean the Ninja pot and set it to sauté mode. Add oil and heat.
5. Add the potatoes followed by the remaining ingredients and toss.
6. Set the Foodi to roast mode and cook at 400 °F for twenty minutes.
7. Subdivide your oregano potatoes between serving plates and enjoy.

Carrot Puree

Preparation and cooking time: 25 minutes |Servings: 4

Ingredients
- 1 lb of carrots (peeled and halved)
- A yellow onion, chopped
- ½ cup of chicken stock
- ¼ cup of heavy cream
- Salt and black pepper

Directions:
1. Mix all the ingredients (except cream) in your Ninja Foodi.
2. Close the pressure lid and cook on high mode for 15 minutes.
3. Release the accumulated vapor naturally for ten minutes
4. Mash everything and add cream. Whisk.
5. Subdivide your carrot puree between plates as a side dish.

Baked Mushrooms

Preparation and cooking time: 25 minutes |Servings: 4

Ingredients
- 1 lb of white mushrooms, halved
- 1 tablespoon of oregano, chopped
- 2 tablespoons of mozzarella cheese, grated
- 2 tablespoons of organic olive oil
- 1 tablespoon of parsley, chopped
- 1 tablespoon of rosemary, chopped
- Salt and black pepper

Directions:
1. Set the Foodi to sauté mode and add the oil. Heat it up and mix all the ingredients (except cheese.)
2. Spread the grated cheese over the mixture and set the Foodi to baking mode.
3. Cook the mushrooms mixture over 380 °F for 15 minutes.
4. Subdivide your mushroom side dish between plates as a side dish

Roasted Potatoes

Preparation and cooking time: 35 minutes |Servings: 4

Ingredients:
- 1 lb of baby potatoes, halved
- ½ cup of parsley, chopped
- ½ cup of mayonnaise
- 2 tablespoons of tomato paste

- 2 tablespoons of extra virgin olive oil
- 1 tablespoons of smoked paprika
- A tablespoon of garlic powder
- 2 tablespoons of white wine vinegar
- 3 teaspoons of hot paprika
- A pinch of salt and black pepper

Directions:
1. Combine the potatoes with hot paprika, oil, smoked paprika, garlic powder, salt, and pepper in a bowl. Toss well.
2. Put the potatoes in the crisping basket and insert it in the Foodi.
3. Set the multi-cooker to air crisp mode and cook the potatoes at 360 °F for 25 minutes.
4. Transfer the mixture to a bowl and add tomato paste, mayo, vinegar, and parsley.
5. Toss your roasted potatoes and serve as a side dish.

Cauliflower Risotto

Preparation and cooking time: 32 minutes |Servings: 4

Ingredients
- 1 cauliflower head, diced
- 15 oz of water chestnuts, drained
- 1 egg, whisked
- A tablespoon of ginger, grated
- 1 tablespoon of freshly squeezed lemon juice
- 2 tablespoons of olive oil
- 4 tablespoons of soy sauce
- 3 garlic cloves, minced

Directions:
1. Set the Foodi to sauté mode and add the oil. Heat it up.
2. Add the minced garlic and cauliflower rice. Toss and cook for three minutes.
3. Add soy sauce, chestnuts, and ginger.
4. Toss and close the pressure lid. Cook on high mode for 15 minutes.
5. Release the accumulated pressure naturally for four minutes and quick release the rest for a minute.
6. Set the Ninja Foodi to sauté mode and add the egg.
7. Stir well and cook for 2 more minutes.
8. Subdivide your risotto between plates and serve as a side dish.

Paprika Beets

Preparation and cooking time: 45 minutes |Servings: 4

Ingredients:
- 2 lbs of small beets (trimmed and halved)
- 1 tablespoon of olive oil
- 4 tablespoons of sweet paprika

Directions:
1. Mix all the ingredients in a bowl. Put the beets in the crisping basket and insert it into the Foodi.
2. Set the multi-cooker to air crisp mode and cook the beets over 380 °F for 35 minutes.
3. Subdivide your beets between serving plates as a side dish.

Creamy Artichokes

Preparation and cooking time: 30 minutes |Servings: 4

Ingredients
- 15 oz of canned artichoke hearts
- 1 ½ tablespoons of thyme, chopped
- 2 garlic cloves, minced
- 1 yellow onion, chopped
- A cup of heavy cream
- 1 tablespoon of olive oil
- 1 tablespoon of parmesan, grated
- Salt and black pepper

Directions:
1. Set the Foodi to sauté mode and add the oil. Heat it.
2. Add onions and garlic. Stir the seasonings and sauté for 5 minutes.
3. Add the remaining ingredients (except the thyme and parmesan) and toss.
4. Set the Foodi to baking mode and cook at 370 °F for 15 minutes.
5. Spread parmesan and thyme and continue baking for five more minutes.
6. Subdivide your creamy artichoke between plates and serve.

Broccoli Mash

Preparation and cooking time: 21 minutes |Servings: 4

Ingredients
- 1 broccoli head (florets separated and steamed)
- ½ cup of veggie stock
- ½ teaspoon of turmeric powder
- 1 tablespoon of olive oil
- A tablespoon of chives, chopped
- 1 tablespoon of butter, melted
- Salt and black pepper

Directions:
1. Set the Foodi to sauté mode and add the oil. Heat it up and add the broccoli florets. Cook them for 4 minutes.
2. Add the remaining ingredients (except butter and chives) and close the pressure lid.
3. Cook everything on high mode for 12 minutes.

4. Release the pressure naturally for ten minutes. Mash the cooked broccoli and add butter and chives.
5. Stir your broccoli mash and subdivide it between plates.

Cumin Green Beans

Preparation and cooking time: 20 minutes |Servings: 6

Ingredients:
- 1 lb of green beans, trimmed
- 2 garlic cloves, minced
- 1 tablespoon of olive oil
- ½ teaspoon of cumin seeds
- Salt and black pepper

Directions:
1. Combine all the ingredients in a bowl and toss well.
2. Transfer the green beans mixture to a crisping basket and insert it in the Foodi.
3. Set the appliance to air crisp mode and cook the mixture over 370 °F for 15 minutes,
4. Subdivide the side dish between plates and enjoy.

Lemony Carrots

Preparation and cooking time: 25 minutes |Servings: 2

Ingredients:
- 1 lb of baby carrots, trimmed
- 2 teaspoons of organic olive oil
- 2 teaspoons of sweet paprika
- Juice extracted from two lemons.
- Salt and black pepper

Directions:
1. Combine all the ingredients in a bowl and toss them well.
2. Transfer the mixture into the crisping basket and insert it into the Foodi.
3. Set the appliance to air crisp mode and cook at 400 °F for fifteen minutes.
4. Subdivide the lemony carrots between plates and serve as a side dish.

Creamy Mushrooms

Preparation and cooking time: 32 minutes |Servings: 4

Ingredients
- 8 oz of mushrooms, sliced
- 4 oz of heavy cream
- 2 garlic cloves, minced
- 1 yellow onion, chopped
- 1 tablespoon of essential olive oil
- 2 tablespoons of parmesan, grated
- 1 tablespoon of parsley, chopped

Directions:
1. Set the Foodi to sauté mode and add the oil.
2. Heat it up and add onions and garlic. Stir and cook for three minutes.
3. Add the mushrooms, salt, pepper, and cream. Toss and close the pressure lid. Cook on high mode for 20 minutes.
4. Release the stress naturally for ten minutes. Add parmesan and parsley. Toss and subdivide your creamy mushroom between four plates.

Carrot Fries

Preparation and cooking time: 25 minutes |Servings: 4

Ingredients
- 4 mixed carrots cut into sticks
- 2 garlic cloves, minced
- 2 tablespoons of rosemary, chopped
- 2 tablespoons of olive oil
- Salt and black pepper

Directions:
1. Mix all the ingredients in a bowl.
2. Transfer the carrot mixture into an air crisp basket and fix it in the Foodi.
3. Set the multi-cooker to air crisp mode and cook the fries over 380 °F for fifteen minutes.
4. Subdivide your carrot fries between plates and serve as a side dish.

POULTRY RECIPES

Black Bean Soup

Preparation and cooking time: 70 minutes |Servings: 6

Ingredients
- 2 yellow onions, chopped
- 2 cups of black beans
- 5 cups of water
- 1 cup of brewed coffee
- 1 cup of sour cream
- Zest and juice extracted from one lemon
- 1 red bell pepper, chopped
- 1 jalapeno pepper, chopped
- 4 garlic cloves, minced
- 2 bay leaves
- 2 celery stalks, chopped
- 1 tablespoon of tomato paste
- 3 tablespoons of canola oil
- 1 tablespoon of cumin, ground
- A pinch of salt and black pepper

Directions:
1. Set the Foodi to sauté mode and add the oil.
2. Heat it up and add onions, bay leaves, red bell pepper, garlic, celery, jalapeno, salt, and pepper.
3. Stir and cook the mixture for 10 minutes.
4. Add cumin, tomato paste, water, and beans. Stir and close the pressure lid.
5. Cook on high mode for 50 minutes
6. Release the pressure naturally for 10 minutes.
7. Add lime zest and lime juice. Stir and subdivide the soup between bowls.
8. Top each serving with sour cream and enjoy.

Vegetable Stock Recipe

Preparation and cooking time: 11 minutes |Servings: 6

Ingredients
- 2 large unpeeled yellow onions (with roots removed and sliced lengthwise)
- 1 bunch of fresh flat leaf parsley
- 2 medium tomatoes (fresh or canned)
- 2 unpeeled garlic cloves
- 2 medium carrots, halved
- 2 celery stalks, halved
- 1 tablespoon of black peppercorns
- 2 bay leaves
- Cold water

Directions:
1. Put vegetables, spices, and herbs into the multi-cooker.
2. Cover them with cold water and close the pressure lid.
3. Cook the ingredients on high mode for 10 minutes.
4. Pressure release the accumulated pressure naturally for 30 minutes and quick release the rest.
5. Carefully, strain the cooker contents over a stainless bowl and let it cool at room temperature.
6. Reserve the solids or discard them. Freeze your veggie stock for some days before using it.

Chicken Stock Recipe

Preparation and cooking time: 70 minutes |Servings: 10 cups

Ingredients:
- 2 ½ lbs of chicken carcasses
- 2 carrots, diced
- 2 bay leaves
- 4 garlic cloves, crushed
- 1 teaspoon of peppercorn
- 2 celery stalks, diced
- 2 onions with the outer layers, diced
- 1 tablespoon of apple cider vinegar (*optional*)
- 10 cups of water
- Your favorite fresh herbs

Directions:
1. *Optional step*: Brown the chicken carcasses in your Ninja multi-cooker with one tablespoon of oil. This flavors the stock, turning it brown. Add a half cup of water/100ml to deglaze the pot.
2. Put all the ingredients into the Ninja Foodi multi-cooker.
3. Close the pressure lid and cook on high mode for sixty minutes. This can be attained by pressing the pressure button and the time management button to regulate your cooking. Release the in-built pressure naturally and open the lid.
4. Strain the stock using a colander and discard the solids.
5. Store your chicken stock in the refrigerator until it forms a layer of gel.
6. Skim off the fat on the top layer. You can use your chicken stock immediately and even freeze some of it for future use.

Herbed Whole Roasted Chicken

Preparation and cooking time: 50 minutes |Servings: 4

Ingredients:
- A raw chicken (4 ½ - 5 lb)
- 1 tablespoon of black peppercorns
- 4 tablespoons of kosher salt (divided into two)
- ¼ cup of hot water
- ¼ cup of honey

- ¼ cup of freshly squeezed lemon juice
- 5 sprigs of fresh thyme
- 5 cloves garlic (peeled and smashed)
- 1 tablespoon of canola oil/ cooking spray
- 2 teaspoons of ground black pepper

Directions
1. Rinse the chicken and tie its legs using a cooking twine.
2. Mix the freshly squeezed lemon juice with warm water, honey, and two tablespoons of kosher salt in a bowl.
3. Pour mixture to the Foodi and add peppercorns, thyme, and garlic.
4. Place the tied chicken in the crisping basket and fix it in the Foodi.
5. Close the pressure lid and ensure the release valve is in the seal position.
6. Select the pressure button and cook over high temperature mode for 22 minutes. Press the start/stop button to start cooking.
7. When the cooking duration elapses, allow the pressure to release naturally for five minutes.
8. Quick release the remaining pressure by moving the release valve to the vent position. Open the pressure lid and brush the chicken with the canola oil. Season it with the remaining salt and pepper.
9. Close crisping lid and Select the air crisp button. Set the temperature to 400°F and air-fry the chicken for 8 minute or until it attains your desired crispness.
10. Cooking ends when the internal temperature reaches 165°F.
11. Remove your crisped chicken from the basket using 2 large serving forks.
12. Let it rest for around 5 minutes before serving.

Chicken and Chimichurri

Preparation and cooking time: 45 minutes |Servings: 2

Ingredients
- 2 chicken breasts (Skinny and bony)
- 1 tablespoon of organic olive oil
- 1 tablespoon of fennel, ground
- A tablespoon of chili powder
- 1 tablespoon of sweet paprika
- 1 teaspoon of garlic powder
- A teaspoon of onion powder
- 1 teaspoon of cumin, ground
- A pinch of salt and black pepper

For the Chimichurri:
- ¼ cup of extra virgin olive oil
- ½ bunch of parsley
- 4 garlic cloves, minced
- 1 shallot, chopped
- ½ bunch of cilantro
- Zest and juice from one lemon

Directions:
1. Mix paprika with salt, pepper, fennel, chili powder, garlic powder, onion powder, a tablespoon of oil, and cumin in a bowl.
2. Add the chicken breasts and toss them well.
3. Insert the crisping basket in the Foodi and transfer the tossed chicken into it.
4. Set the multi-cooker to air crisp mode and cook the meat over 375 °F for 35 minutes.
5. Mix cilantro with the remaining oil, parsley, garlic, shallot, lemon zest and the freshly squeezed lemon juice into the blender. Pulse well.
6. Subdivide your chicken breasts between plates. Serve alongside the Chimichurri sauce.

Cumin Chicken Wings

Preparation and cooking time: 30 minutes |Servings: 4

Ingredients
- 8 chicken wings, halved
- ¼ cup of chicken stock
- 2 garlic cloves, minced
- 1 tablespoon of essential olive oil
- 2 teaspoons of cumin, ground
- Salt and black pepper

Directions:
1. Put the chicken wings in the Foodi's basket.
2. Set the multi-cooking appliance to air crisp mode and cook them at 360 °F for ten minutes.
3. Transfer the wings to a bowl and clean the Foodi cooker. Preheat it on sauté mode for a minute and add oil.
4. Heat it up and add the crisped chicken followed by the remaining ingredients.
5. Stir and sauté everything for around 10 minutes. Serve your cumin chicken wings while hot.

Great Chicken Wings

Preparation and cooking time: 30 minutes |Servings: 4

Ingredients
- 2 lbs of chicken wings
- 2 tablespoons of buffalo sauce
- ½ cup of water
- 2 tablespoons of canola oil

Directions:
1. Pour the water into the Foodi and fix the air crisp basket. Put the chicken wings in the basket and close the pressure lid.
2. Cook the wings over high mode for 5 minutes. Allow the pressure to release naturally for 10 minutes.
3. Set the appliance to air crisp mode and cook the wings at 390 °F for 15 minutes.

4. Transfer your chicken wings into a bowl and serve with a buffalo sauce.

Creamy Asparagus Soup

Preparation and cooking time: 11 minutes |Servings: 4

Ingredients
- 1 lb of asparagus (tough ends removed and cut into 1-inch pieces)
- 3 green onions (sliced crosswise into 1/4-inch pieces)
- 1 tablespoon of extra-virgin olive oil
- 4 cups of salt-free Chicken Stock
- 1 teaspoon of ground white pepper (plus more as needed)
- 1/2 cup of heavy cream
- 1 tablespoon of unsalted butter
- 1 tablespoon of all-purpose flour
- 2 teaspoons of salt

Directions:
1. Preheat the Ninja Foodi multi-cooker on sauté mode add the oil.
2. Heat it and add the green onions and salt.
3. Sauté the green onions for some minutes and add asparagus and stock.
4. Close the pressure lid and cook on high mode for 5 minutes.
5. Meanwhile, *make a blond roux*: mix butter and flour in a small saucepan cook and cook over low heat while constantly stirring.
6. Remove from heat when all butter has melted, it begins foaming, and turning golden beige.
7. Release the accumulated pressure naturally from the asparagus mixture.
8. Add salt and pepper to the blond roux and puree using an immersion blender.
9. You can also add more seasonings to get your desired taste.
10. Swirl cream into the asparagus soup before serving. Enjoy!

Chicken and Tomatoes

Preparation and cooking time: 25 minutes |Servings: 4

Ingredients
- 2 chicken breasts (skinless, boneless, and cubed)
- ¼ cup of cheddar, grated
- ½ cup of tomatoes, chopped
- ½ cup of heavy cream
- ¾ cup of chicken stock
- 2 garlic cloves, minced
- 2 tablespoons of basil, chopped
- 1 tablespoon of organic olive oil
- A tablespoon of rosemary, chopped
- 1 teaspoon of chili powder
- Salt and black pepper

Directions
1. Set the Foodi on sauté mode and add the oil. Heat it.
2. Add the garlic, tomatoes, rosemary, chili, salt, and pepper. Stir and cook for 5 minutes.
3. Add the remaining ingredients and toss.
4. Close the pressure lid and cook on high mode for 15 minutes.
5. Release the pressure naturally for 10 minutes. Subdivide your appetizing chicken between bowls and enjoy.

Rosemary Turkey

Preparation and cooking time: 60 minutes |Servings: 4

Ingredients
- 2 turkey breasts (skinless, boneless, and halved)
- 1 tablespoon of lime juice
- 2 tablespoons of olive oil
- 2 teaspoon of garlic powder
- 1 teaspoon of rosemary, dried
- Salt and black pepper

Directions:
1. Mix all the ingredients in a bowl and toss.
2. Insert the basket in the Foodi and add the turkey breasts.
3. Set the appliance to air crisp mode and cook at 370 °F for 35 minutes having flipped the turkey halfway.
4. Serve hot with a side salad.

Turkey Breast

Preparation and cooking time: 70 minutes |Servings: 4

Ingredients
- 1 frozen turkey breast with a frozen gravy packet
- 1 whole onion

Directions:
1. Put all ingredients in the Ninja Foodi multi-cooker.
2. Lock the pressure lid and cook on high mode for 30 minutes.
3. Release the in-built pressure naturally and open the lid.
4. Turn your turkey breast for overall cooking and close the pressure lid again.
5. Cook on high mode for 30 minutes and release the accumulated steam naturally.
6. Close the crisping and air-fry the chicken 360°F for 10 minutes. Remember to check its progress after 5 minutes.
7. Crisp your turkey breast for another 5 minutes if it needs browning.

8. Remove it from the Foodi and slice it for serving alongside its gravy.

Stuffed Chicken Recipe

Preparation and cooking time: 30 minutes |Servings: 4

Ingredients
- 4 chicken breasts, skinless
- 1 cup of baby spinach, frozen
- 1/2 cup of crumbled feta cheese
- 2 tablespoons of Olive oil
- 2 teaspoons of dried parsley
- 1/2 teaspoon of dried oregano
- 1/2 teaspoon of garlic powder
- Salt and black pepper
- 1 cup of water

Directions:
1. Wrap the chicken in plastic and place it on a cutting board.
2. Pound it flat to a quarter inch thickness using a rolling pin. Remove the plastic wrap.
3. Mix spinach, salt, and feta cheese in a bowl and add the mixture on the chicken breasts. Wrap the chicken using toothpicks to secure the spinach filling.
4. Season the chicken pieces with oregano, parsley, garlic powder, and pepper.
5. Select sear/sauté mode on the Foodi Ninja and heat some oil.
6. Add the stuffed chicken and sear each of its sides to golden brown. You can work on batches if necessary.
7. Remove the chicken from the Foodi and pour some water into it.
8. Scrap the pot's base using a spoon to remove any stuck food pieces.
9. Insert the reversible rack in the Foodi and place the chicken on it.
10. Lock the pressure lid and cook it on high mode for 10 minutes.
11. Release the accumulated pressure quickly and close the crisping lid.
12. Cook the chicken on bake/roast made at 370 F for five minutes.
13. Transfer the chicken to a bowl and serve it alongside sautéed asparagus and tomato slices.

SOUP RECIPES

Chicken Noodle Soup Recipe

Preparation and cooking time: 25 minutes | Servings: 6

Ingredients
- 2 large chicken breasts (1lb), bony and skinless
- 1 medium red onion, halved
- 6 cups of chicken broth
- 2 medium carrots
- 2 fresh thyme sprigs
- 2 fresh sage sprigs
- 2 medium garlic cloves, peeled
- 4-ounces of wide egg noodles
- 1 tablespoon of minced fresh dill fronds
- 2 tablespoons of extra virgin olive oil
- 1/2 teaspoon of salt

Directions:
1. Heat some oil on sauté mode in the Ninja Foodi multi-cooker.
2. Add the chicken and brown both of its sides well on both sides for around 4 minutes.
3. Add chicken broth, onions, carrots, salt, thyme, sage, and garlic. Lock the pressure lid.
4. Cook the spiced chicken on high mode for 18 minutes. Quick release the accumulated vapor and open the lid.
5. Transfer the chicken to a cutting board and leave it for some minutes to cool. Debone and chop it into bite-size pieces.
6. Pour the onion, carrots, thyme, sage, and garlic from the pot to a bowl.
7. Put noodles and dill into the Foodi and lock the pressure lid.
8. Cook the dill mixture on high mode for four minutes and quick release the accumulated steam.
9. Open the lid and add the chopped chicken pieces. Stir.
10. Cover it loosely and set it aside for a few minutes to warm. Serve and enjoy.

Beef Stock Recipe

Preparation and cooking time: 110 minutes | Servings: 6

Ingredients
- 2 lb of beef soup bones
- 1 large onion (quartered with skin)
- 2 teaspoons of ground pepper
- 1 teaspoon of ground Himalayan salt
- 2 tablespoons of garlic, minced
- 3 tablespoons of apple cider vinegar
- 3 large carrots
- 1 bay leaf
- 3 celery sticks
- A handful of fresh parsley
- Water

Directions:
1. *Optional*: Ideally, baking the bones on 375°F for thirty minutes before pressure cooking them helps to draw out the marrow.
2. Put the bones, veggies, and seasonings into the Ninja Foodi multi-cooker.
3. Add apple cider vinegar and cover with water. The quantity of water depends on your amount of vegetables. You can also add other greens.
4. Lock the pressure lid and cook the mixture on high mode for 90 minutes.
5. Quick release the accumulated vapor after the cooking time elapses.

Potato, Carrot, and Leek Soup Recipe

Preparation and cooking time: 11 minutes | Servings: 4

Ingredients
- 1 lb of carrots (coarsely chopped)
- 1 bouquet of garnishing (parsley sprigs, bay leaf, and a sprig of thyme)
- 1 large potato (peeled and coarsely chopped)
- 1 medium leek (white and pale green parts only, coarsely chopped)
- 1 tablespoon of organic olive oil
- 2 tablespoons of unsalted butter
- 2 teaspoons of salt
- 4 cups of salt-free chicken stock
- Freshly ground black pepper
- 1/4 cup of heavy cream
- 1/8 teaspoon of freshly grated nutmeg
- Fresh thyme sprigs or chopped fresh chives (for serving)

Directions:
1. Preheat the Ninja Foodi multi-cooker on sauté mode.
2. Add oil and butter and cook until the butter has melted.
3. Add the chopped leeks and salt and sauté for five minutes or until the leeks softens while stirring frequently.
4. Add the carrots and continue cooking for five minutes or until they turn golden on one side. Add the potatoes, stock, pepper, and the garnishing ingredients.
5. Lock the pressure lid and cook on high mode for ten minutes.
6. When the set time expires, release the in-built vapor naturally.
7. Transfer the garnished mixture into an immersion blender and puree.
8. Add the heavy cream and nutmeg. Stir.

9. Ladle the soup into bowls and top each serving with a thyme sprig or a few chopped chives.

Tomato Soup Recipe

Preparation and cooking time: 11 minutes |Servings: 2 to 4

Ingredients
- 1 can (14.5-ounce) of fire- roasted tomatoes
- 1 small roasted red bell pepper (cut into chunks about 1/4 cup)
- 1/2 cup of sliced onion
- 3/4 cup of chicken stock or low-sodium broth
- 1/4 cup of dry or medium-dry sherry
- 3 tablespoons of extra virgin olive oil
- 1 tablespoon of heavy whipping cream (optional)
- 1 medium garlic cloves, sliced or minced
- 1/8 teaspoon of ground cumin
- 1/8 teaspoon of freshly ground black pepper
- Kosher salt

Directions:
1. Set the Ninja Foodi multi-cooker to sauté and heat the olive oil until it shimmers and flows like water.
2. Add the onions and sprinkle with kosher salt. Cook for five minutes or until the onions browns while stirring constantly.
3. Add the garlic and cook for two minutes or until it browns.
4. Add sherry and simmer for 2 minutes or until it reduces to half, scraping up any browned bits from the bottom of the pot.
5. Add tomatoes, the roasted red bell pepper, and chicken stock into the Foodi.
6. Lock the pressure lid and cook on high mode for ten minutes. Quick release the accumulated steam.
7. Transfer the mixture into an immersion blender and add cumin and pepper. Add more salt if necessary.
8. Add the heavy cream and blend.
9. Be careful if at all you are using a standard blender. Steam can blow off its lid if the soup it hot. In this, you can blend in batches to avoid filling the jar.
10. Ladle your tomato soup into bowls and enjoy.

Turkey Meatballs in Tomato Sauce

Preparation and cooking time: 15 minutes |Servings: 4

Ingredients
- 1 lb of ground turkey
- 1 large egg (beaten in a small bowl)
- A can (28-ounce) of tomatoes (drained and roughly chopped- 3 ½ cups)
- 1 medium yellow onion, chopped
- 2 medium celery stalks, thinly sliced
- 1/2 cup of plain dried breadcrumbs
- 1/4 cup of finely grated parmesan cheese (1/2-ounce)
- 2 tablespoons of unsalted butter
- 1/2 cup of chicken broth
- 1 tablespoon of packed fresh oregano leaves, minced
- 1/4 teaspoon of grated nutmeg
- 1/4 cup of heavy cream
- 1/2 teaspoon of dried oregano
- 1/2 teaspoon of dried rosemary
- 1/2 teaspoon of ground black pepper
- 1/2 teaspoon of salt

Directions
1. Mix the ground turkey with egg, breadcrumbs, cheese, oregano, rosemary, pepper and a quarter teaspoon of salt in a large bowl.
2. Mold 12 balls from the mixture.
3. Melt the butter in the Ninja Foodi multi-cooker on sauté mode.
4. Add the onion and celery and cook for three minutes or until the onions turn translucent while stirring frequently.
5. Add tomatoes, broth, oregano, and the remaining salt.
6. Drop the meatballs to the sauce and close the pressure lid.
7. Cook the mixture on high mode for ten minutes and quick release the pressure.
8. Open the pressure lid and turn the Foodi to sauté mode.
9. Add cream and nutmeg and simmer for a minute while stirring constantly.
10. Allow it to cool before using. You can also refrigerate for future usage.

Chicken Strips

Preparation and cooking time: 25 minutes |Servings: 4

Ingredients:
- 2 chicken breasts (skinless, boneless, and cut into strips)
- 2 eggs, whisked
- 1 cup of rice flour
- 3 cups of any cereal, crushed
- A pinch of salt and black pepper

Directions:
1. Mix the flour with salt and pepper in a bowl.
2. Put the eggs in another bowl. Combine cereal, salt, and pepper in a third bowl and stir.

Dredge each chicken strip in the flour mixture, egg, and seasoned cereal.
3. Transfer the coated chicken to a crisping basket and set your Foodi to air crisp mode.
4. Cook the chicken on 390 °F for fifteen minutes.
5. Subdivide your chicken strips between plates and serve.

Olive and Lemon Ligurian Chicken

Preparation and cooking time: 35 minutes |Servings: 6-8
Ingredients
- 3.5-ounce (100g) of black gourmet salt
- Cured olives taggiesche, French or Kalamata
- 3 sprigs of fresh rosemary (two for chopping, one for garnishing)
- 1 whole chicken (cut into parts or package of bony and skinless)
- 1/2 cup (125ml) of dry white wine
- 2 garlic cloves, chopped
- 2 sprigs of fresh sage
- 1/2 couple of parsley leaves and stems
- 3 lemons (3/4 cup or 180ml juice extracted)
- 4 tablespoons of extra virgin organic olive oil
- 1 teaspoon of sea salt
- 1/4 teaspoon of pepper
- 1 fresh lemon (for garnishing, optional)

Directions:
1. Prepare the marinade by mixing chopped garlic, rosemary, sage, and parsley.
2. Place them in a container and add the fresh lemon juice, olive oil, salt, and pepper.
3. Mix well and set aside.
4. Remove skin from your chicken and reserve it for the chicken stock.
5. Preheat the Ninja Foodi and spread it with olive oil. Add the skinless chicken pieces and brown them for around 5 minutes on sauté mode.
6. De-glaze the Foodi white wine for three minutes or until it drains.
7. Return the chicken pieces beginning in the following order; dark meat wings, legs, thighs, and breasts on top.
8. Pour the remaining marinade to cook the chicken. Do not worry about its quantity, the chicken will release more fluid.
9. Lock the pressure lid and cook the chicken on high mode for ten minutes. Quick release the accumulated pressure and open the pressure lid.
10. Close the crisping lid and set the Foodi to air crisp mode. Set temperature to 390°F and cooking time to 10 minutes. Remember to check the cooking progress after 5 minutes since the remaining time will brown the chicken.
11. Remove the chicken pieces from the Ninja pot and transfer it to a serving platter. Cover it with a foil tightly.
12. Open the lid and cook the remaining liquid until it becomes thick syrup.
13. Return the chicken pieces to the Ninja Foodi to warm-up.
14. Mix and spoon the thick glaze over the chicken pieces and simmer before serving.
15. Sprinkle with fresh rosemary, olives, and lemon slices. Remember, olives are bitter.

Chicken Drumsticks

Preparation and cooking time: 30 minutes |Servings: 4
Ingredients
- 10 chicken drumsticks
- 1 cup of coconut milk
- ¼ cup of cilantro, chopped
- A few spring onions, chopped
- 4 garlic cloves, minced
- 1 tablespoon of lime juice
- 2 tablespoons of oyster sauce
- 1 tablespoon of ginger, grated
- 1 teaspoon of Chinese five spices
- 1 teaspoon of essential olive oil
- Salt and black pepper

Directions:
1. Mix the spring onions with ginger, garlic, oyster sauce, five spice, salt, pepper, oil and, coconut milk in a blender. Pulse well.
2. Put the chicken drumsticks in the Foodi's baking pan and pour the spring onions mix over it.
3. Insert the reversible rack in the Food and place the baking pan on it.
4. Set the multi-cooker pot to baking mode and cook on 370 °F for 20 minutes.
5. Subdivide the chicken mixture between plates and top it with cilantro.
6. Pour lime juice over it and serve.

Spicy Chicken

Preparation and cooking time: 30minutes |Servings: 6
Ingredients
- 3 and ½ lbs of chicken breasts
- 1 ¼ cups of yellow onion, chopped
- 1 cup of chicken stock
- 1 tablespoon of extra virgin olive oil
- A tablespoon of fresh lemon juice
- 2 tablespoons of green onions, chopped
- 2 teaspoons of hot paprika
- 2 teaspoons of red pepper flakes
- Salt and black pepper

Directions:
1. Set the Foodi to sauté mode and add the oil. Heat it and add the yellow onion. Stir and sauté the onions for two minutes.
2. Add all the ingredients and toss. Lock the pressure lid and cook on high mode for 18 minutes.
3. Release the in-built pressure naturally for ten minutes.
4. Close the crisping lid and cook the chicken with the stock over 370 °F for 12 minutes. Subdivide your spicy chicken between plates and enjoy.

Pesto Chicken Breasts

Preparation and cooking time: 40 minutes |Servings: 4

Ingredients:
- 2 chicken breasts (boneless, skinless, and halved)
- 4 garlic cloves, minced
- 1 cup of parsley, chopped
- ½ cup of extra virgin olive oil
- ¼ cup of burgundy or merlot wine
- A pinch of salt and black pepper

Directions:
1. Mix parsley with garlic, salt, pepper, oil, and wine in a blender. Pulse well.
2. Combine the chicken with parsley pesto in the Foodi's baking pan and toss well
3. Put the reversible rack in the Foodi and place the baking pan on it.
4. Set the multi-cooker pot to baking mode and cook on 370 °F for 30 minutes.
5. Subdivide the pesto chicken breasts between plates and serve.

Crispy Chicken Thighs with Carrots and Rice Pilaf

Preparation and cooking time: 25 minutes |Servings: 4

Ingredients
- 4 raw chicken thighs (boneless but skinny)
- 1 box (6-ounces) of rice pilaf
- 2 tablespoons of honey, warmed
- 1/2 teaspoon of smoked paprika
- 1 3/4 cups of water
- 1 tablespoon of butter
- 4 carrots (peeled and halved lengthwise))
- 2 teaspoons of kosher salt, divided
- 1 tablespoon of extra-virgin essential olive oil
- 2 teaspoons of poultry spice
- 1/2 teaspoon of ground cumin

Directions:
1. Put rice pilaf, water, and butter into the Ninja Foodi and stir.
2. Fix the reversible rack in the pot and place carrots at the center.
3. Arrange the chicken thighs, skin side up, across the carrots.
4. Lock the pressure lid ensuring that the pressure release valve is in the seal position.
5. Cook the thighs over high mode for four minutes.
6. Meanwhile, mix warm honey, smoked paprika, cumin, and a teaspoon of salt in a bowl.
7. Quick release the accumulated steam when the cooking time elapses.
8. Brush the carrots with seasoned honey.
9. Brush the chicken with olive oil, and then season it with poultry spice and remaining salt.
10. Close the crisping lid. Select the broil function and set the cooking time to 10 minutes.
11. Serve chicken with carrots and rice.

Chicken and Mushrooms Mix

Preparation and cooking time: 30 minutes |Servings: 4

Ingredients:
- 2 lbs of chicken breasts (skinless, boneless, and cubed)
- 12 brown mushrooms, halved
- 1 sweet onion, chopped
- 2 garlic cloves, minced
- 1 red bell pepper, chopped
- 2 tablespoons of cheddar cheese, shredded
- 2 tablespoons of canola oil
- Salt and black pepper

Directions:
1. Set the Foodi to sauté mode and add the oil. Heat it.
2. Add the onions, garlic, salt, and pepper. Toss and sauté for 3-4 minutes
3. Add the chicken pieces and toss. Brown them for 2-3 minutes.
4. Add the remaining ingredients (except the cheese) and toss.
5. Lock the pressure lid and cook on high mode for 10 minutes.
6. Release the accumulated pressure naturally for 10 minutes.
7. Subdivide your chicken and mushrooms mix between plates. Serve with cheese toppings.

Turmeric Chicken

Preparation and cooking time: 25 minutes |Servings: 4

Ingredients
- 2 chicken breasts (skinless, boneless, and cubed)
- 2 tablespoons of canola oil
- 1 tablespoon of turmeric powder

- A tablespoon of fresh lemon juice
- 1 tablespoon of ginger, grated
- A tablespoon of sweet paprika
- Salt and black pepper

Directions:
1. Set the Foodi to sauté mode and add the oil. Heat it up.
2. Add the chicken and toss. Brown it for 4-5 minutes
3. Add the remaining ingredients and toss. Loc the pressure lid and cook on high mode for 10 minutes.
4. Release the accumulated pressure naturally for ten minutes.
5. Subdivide your turmeric chicken between bowls and enjoy.

Sweet Chipotle Chicken Wings

Preparation and cooking time: 25 minutes |Servings: 2

Ingredients
- 3 tablespoons of Mexican hot sauce like Valentina brand
- 1 teaspoon of minced canned chipotle in adobo sauce
- 1 cup of water
- 2 tablespoons of honey

Directions:
1. If you are using whole wings, cut off of the tips and discard. Break the wings on the joint into two pieces.
2. Add the water and insert the steamer basket or trivet on the Foodi.
3. Place the wings on the trivet and lock the pressure lid. Cook the wings on high mode for 10 minutes.
4. Meanwhile, mix the Mexican sauce with honey and chipotle in a bowl.
5. Quick release the in-built steam from the Foodi once the cooking time elapses.
6. Close the crisping lid and set the multi-cooker to air crisp mode.
7. Set the temperature to 390°F and cooking time to ten minutes.

Spicy Turkey Chili

Preparation and cooking time: 55 minutes |Servings: 4

Ingredients:
- 1 lb of ground turkey
- 1/4 cup of your preferred hot sauce
- 1 can (15-ounce) of fire-roasted and diced tomatoes
- 1 can (15-ounce) of kidney beans, including their liquid
- 1 medium yellow onion, diced
- 2 green bell peppers (seeded and diced)
- 2 fresh cayenne peppers (chopped and seeded)
- 4 garlic cloves, chopped
- 1 cup of grated Monterey Jack cheese
- 1 tablespoon of olive oil
- 1 teaspoon of ground cumin
- 1/2 teaspoon of dried oregano leaves
- 1/4 cup of chopped cilantro

Directions:
1. Set the Ninja Foodi multi-cooker to sauté mode and add the oil.
2. Add the onions, peppers, and garlic and sauté for 10 minutes or until the onions browns. Add cumin and oregano, sauté for two more minutes.
3. Add the ground turkey and stir using a spatula to break.
4. Sauté the turkey for 5 minutes or until it turns opaque.
5. Add the sauce, canned tomatoes, and kidney beans. Stir.
6. Close the pressure lid and cook on high mode for 45 minutes.
7. Release the in-built pressure naturally and open the lid.
8. Top it with grated cheese and cilantro and serve with rice or cornbread.

Delicious Frozen Chicken Dinner

Preparation and cooking time: 50 minutes |Servings: 2

Ingredients:
- 2 frozen chicken breasts (8 - 10 ounces each)
- 2 tablespoons of organic olive oil, divided
- 1 small onion (peeled and diced)
- 3/4 cup of chicken stock
- 1 bag (12-ounces) of green beans, trimmed
- 1 teaspoon of black pepper, divided
- 1/4 cup of fresh parsley, chopped
- 1 cup of wild rice blend
- 3 teaspoons of kosher salt, divided
- 1 tablespoon of Moroccan seasoning "Ras el Hanout"
- 1/4 cup of honey mustard sauce

Directions:
1. Allow your Foodi to preheat on sear/sauté mode for five minutes.
2. Add a tablespoon of oil and onion. Cook it for 3 minutes or until the onion browns while stirring constantly.
3. Add wild rice, two teaspoons of salt, and the Moroccan seasoning.
4. Cook while stirring until the rice blends with oil (becomes shiny.) Add chicken stock and stir.

5. Place the frozen chicken breasts on the reversible rack and insert it in the Foodi.
6. Lock the pressure lid and cook on high mode for 22 minutes.
7. Meanwhile, toss the green beans in a bowl containing the remaining oil, salt, and pepper.
8. When pressure cooking is complete, allow the pressure release naturally for ten minutes.
9. Quick release the remaining pressure by turning the release valve to the vent position.
10. Take off the reversible rack from the Foodi and add parsley into the rice.
11. After that, add the green beans to the rice.
12. Brush all sides of the chicken breasts with honey mustard sauce and return the rack into the pot.
13. Close the crisping lid and select the broil option. Cook the dishes for 10 minutes.
14. Cooking ends when the internal temperature reaches 165°F.
15. Serve your chicken with green beans and rice.

Asian Chicken Delight

Preparation and cooking time: 40 minutes |Servings: 4

Ingredient
- 2 chicken breasts (skinless, boneless, and cubed)
- 14 oz of water
- 2 red chilies, chopped
- 1 bunch of spring onions, chopped
- A tablespoon of ginger, grated
- 1 tablespoon of rice wine
- A tablespoon of olive oil
- 1 tablespoon of soy sauce
- 1 teaspoon of sesame oil

Directions:
1. Set the Foodi to sauté mode and add essential olive oil and the sesame seed oil. Heat them up.
2. Add chilies, spring onions, and ginger. Stir and cook for three minutes.
3. Add the remaining ingredients and toss.
4. Close the pressure lid and cook the products on high mode for 25 minutes.
5. Release the accumulated pressure naturally for ten minutes.
6. Subdivide your chicken delight into bowls and enjoy.

Turkey Gluten Free Gravy

Preparation and cooking time: 55 minutes |Servings: 6

Ingredients
- 1 4 - 5 lb bony and skinny turkey breast
- 2 tablespoons of ghee or butter
- Coconut oil for AIP
- 1 medium onion (cut into medium dices)
- 1 large carrot (cut into medium dices)
- 1 celery rib (cut into medium dice)
- 1 garlic clove (peeled and smashed)
- 1 ½ cups of bone broth (preferably from chicken or turkey bones)
- Black pepper (omit for AIP diet)
- 2 teaspoons of dried sage
- 1/4 cup of dry white wine
- 1 bay leaf
- 1 tablespoon of tapioca starch optional
- Salt

Directions:
1. Preheat your Food on sauté mode. Pat the turkey breast dry and season them generously with salt and pepper. Melt the cooking fat in the Ninja Foodi Multi-cooker.
2. Brown the turkey breasts (skin side down) for 5 minutes and transfer them to a plate.
3. Add onion, carrot, and celery to the Foodi and cook for 5 minutes or until they soften.
4. Add garlic and sage. Cook them for around 30 seconds.
5. Add wine and cook for 3 minutes or until it starts drying. Put broth and bay leaf.
6. Stir while scrapping the food pieces stuck at the pot's bottom.
7. Add the turkey (skin side up) and lock the pressure lid. Cook the ingredients on high mode for 35 minutes.Quick release the accumulated vapor and open the lid.
8. Close the crisping lid and set the Ninja pot to air crisp mode. Set the temperature to 375°F and cooking time to ten minutes. Remember to check the progress after 5 minutes since the remaining minutes will brown the dish.
9. Transfer the turkey breast to a carving board or plate and cover it loosely using a foil as you prepare the gravy.
10. Transfer the cooking fluid and vegetables to an immersion blender and puree.
11. Heat the puree until it thickens.
12. Slice your turkey breast and serve alongside hot gravy. Enjoy!

Cheddar Chicken Breast

Preparation and cooking time: 30 minutes |Servings: 4

Ingredients
- 16 oz of salsa
- 1 lb of chicken (boneless and skinless)
- 1 ½ cup of cheddar cheese, grated
- ¼ cup of cilantro, chopped
- A teaspoon of sweet paprika
- 1 tablespoon of essential olive oil

- Salt and black pepper

Directions:
1. Combine all the ingredients (except the cheese) in your Foodi's baking pan. Sprinkle the cheese over the chicken.
2. Insert the reversible rack in the Foodi and place the baking pan on it.
3. Set the multi-cooker to baking mode and cook at 380 °F for 20 minutes.
4. Subdivide your cheddar chicken breast between plates and enjoy.

Chicken Pot Pie Recipe

Preparation and cooking time: 35 minutes |Servings: 6

Ingredients
- 2 lb of uncooked chicken breasts (boneless and skinless, cut into 1" cubes)
- 1/2 stick (1/4 cup) of unsalted butter
- 1/2 large onion (peeled and diced)
- 1 large carrot (peeled and diced)
- 2 garlic cloves (peeled and minced)
- 1 stalk celery, diced
- 1/2 cup of frozen peas
- 1 ½ teaspoons of fresh thyme, minced
- 2 teaspoons of kosher salt
- 1/2 teaspoon of black pepper
- 1/2 cup of heavy cream
- 1 cup of chicken broth
- A tablespoon of fresh Italian parsley, minced
- 1/4 cup of all-purpose flour

Directions:
1. Preheat your Foodi on sear/sauté mode for five minutes.
2. Add butter and let it melt.
3. Add onions, carrots, and garlic, and sauté them for 3 minutes or until the carrot softens.
4. Add the chicken breasts followed by broth to the sautéed contents.
5. Close the pressure lid and ensure that the release valve remains in the vent position.
6. Cook the chicken mixture over high mode for 5 minutes. Quick release the in-built pressure when the cook time elapses and opens the lid.
7. Reset the pot to sear/sauté mode and add the remaining ingredients (except the pie crust).
8. Stir the mixture for three minutes or until the sauce thickens and bubbles.
9. Align the pie crust over the filling mixture, folding the edges whenever necessary.
10. Make a small cut at the center of the pie crust for the steam to exit when baking.
11. Close the crisping lid and set the Foodi to broil mode. Cook for 10 minutes.
12. When the cooking time ends, detach the pot from the unit and place it on a heat-resistant surface.
13. Let your pot pie rest for 10 to 15 minutes before serving.

Chicken Casserole

Preparation and cooking time: 40 minutes |Servings: 4

Ingredients
- 1 lb of chicken meat, ground
- 12 eggs, whisked
- 1 cup of baby spinach
- ½ teaspoon of sweet paprika
- 1 tablespoon of organic olive oil
- Salt and black pepper

Directions:
1. Mix all the ingredients (except oil) in a bowl.
2. Insert the reversible rack in the Foodi and place the baking pan on it. Add oil.
3. Pour the chicken mixture in the pan and cook the casserole on baking mode, having set the temperature to 350 °F and cooking time to 30 minutes.
4. Subdivide your chicken casserole between plates and serve for breakfast.

Cream of Sweet Potato Soup Recipe

Preparation and cooking time: 11 minutes |Servings: 6

Ingredients
- 2 lbs of sweet potatoes-2large-sized (peeled and cut into 2-inch pieces)
- 8 tablespoon of unsalted butter (cut into small pieces)
- 1/2 teaspoon of ground cinnamon
- 1/2 teaspoon of ground ginger
- 1/4 teaspoon of baking soda
- 2 ½ cups of chicken broth
- 1/2 cup of heavy cream
- 1 teaspoon of salt

Directions:
1. Melt the butter in a Ninja Foodi until it browns.
2. Add sweet potatoes, salt, cinnamon, ginger, and baking soda.
3. Pour a half cup of water over the ingredients and lock the pressure lid.
4. Cook them on high mode for 15 minutes and quick release the accumulated pressure.
5. Open the pot and add chicken broth followed by cream.
6. Puree the soup using an immersion blender by ladling it in batches.
7. Subdivide the soup between bowls and enjoy.

Butternut Squash Soup with Chicken

Preparation and cooking time: 11 minutes |Servings: 6

Ingredients
- 1 ½ lbs of fresh baked butternut squash (peeled and cubed)
- 1 cup of chicken (seasoned, cooked, and diced)
- 1 onion, diced
- 1 garlic herb, minced
- 2 cans of chicken broth
- 1 cup of orzo, cooked
- 1/2 cup of celery, diced
- 1/2 cup of carrots, diced
- 2 tablespoons of red pepper flakes
- 2 tablespoons of dried parsley flakes
- 1 tomato, diced
- 3 tablespoons of butter
- 1/4 teaspoon of black pepper(freshly ground)

Directions:
1. Set the Ninja Foodi multi-cooker to sauté mode and melt the butter. Add onions, garlic, celery, and carrots.
2. Add the chicken broth, red pepper flakes, dried parsley flakes, black pepper, baked butternut squash, and the diced tomatoes.
3. Lock the pressure lid and cook on high mode for 15 minutes. Quick release the accumulated steam and blend the mixture.
4. Return the puree to the Foodi and add the diced chicken.
5. Add orzo and cook on high mode for 5 minutes. Quick release the in-built pressure and open the lid.
6. Serve your squash soup with fresh dinner rolls and butter.

Tasty Chicken Soup

Preparation and cooking time: 45 minutes |Servings: 8

Ingredients
- 3 peeled carrots (chopped into potato-sizes)
- 4 cups of water
- 32-ounces of chicken stock
- 2 frozen chicken breasts (boneless and skinless)
- 4 washed diced potatoes (medium-sized)
- ½ large onion, diced
- Salt and pepper

Directions:
1. Mix the chicken broth with chicken, potatoes, onion, carrots, salt, and pepper in the Foodi.
2. Lock the pressure lid and cook on high mode for 35 minutes.
3. Allow the pressure to escape for 15 minutes naturally. Quick release the rest and open the lid.
4. Ladle the chicken soup into bowls and enjoy.

Colombian Style Chicken Soup Recipe

Preparation and cooking time: 11 minutes |Servings: 4

Ingredients:
- 3 bony chicken breasts (2 lb or 907g)
- 5 cups (1.2 L) of water
- 1 ½ teaspoons of kosher salt
- 1 ½ lbs of Yukon gold potatoes (cut into ½", 13 mm pieces)
- 1 ear corn (cut into 4 pieces)
- 1 medium yellow onion, halved
- 2 medium carrots (halved crosswise)
- 2 ribs of celery (halved crosswise)
- 1/4 cup of sour cream
- 1 tablespoon of capers, rinsed
- 1/4 teaspoon of freshly ground black pepper
- An avocado
- 1 teaspoon of dried oregano
- 1 lime, quartered
- 8 sprigs of fresh cilantro

Directions:
1. Mix onions with carrots, celery, chicken, water, and salt in your Foodi.
2. Lock the pressure lid and cook on high mode for fifteen minutes. Quick release the accumulated vapor and close the lid.
3. Transfer the chicken to a large bowl. After cooling, shred it into pieces while peeling its skin and detaching the bones.
4. Reserve the celery mixture and clean the Foodi.
5. Mix potatoes with corn and broth. Lock the pressure lid and cook on high mode for 2 minutes. Quick release the accumulated pressure and open the lid.
6. Add the chicken and pepper.
7. Subdivide the soup among bowls. Peel, pit, and slice the avocado.
8. Top the soup with avocado, sour cream, capers, oregano, and cilantro.
9. You can also squeeze some juice from the lime for more flavor

French Onion Soup Recipe

Preparation and cooking time: 40 minutes |Servings: 4

Ingredients:
- 1-ounce (1/3 cup) of Gruyere or any Swiss-style cheese (coarsely grated)
- 1/4 cup of dry sherry
- 2 cups of low-sodium chicken broth

- 1/2 cup of beef stock, Mushroom Stock, or low sodium broth
- 4 cups of thinly sliced (white or yellow) onions, divided
- 2 thin slices of French or Italian bread
- 1/2 teaspoon of kosher salt
- 1/2 teaspoon of Worcestershire sauce
- 2 tablespoons of unsalted butter, divided
- 1/4 teaspoon of dried thyme
- 1 teaspoon of sherry vinegar or dark wine vinegar

Directions:
1. Set the Ninja Foodi to sauté mode and melt a teaspoon of butter.
2. Add a cup of onions and kosher salt. Stir to coat it with butter.
3. Cook the onions for 4 minutes or until it browns. Stir and continue cooking for 4 minutes.
4. Remove the onions from the pan and reserve.
5. Pour the sherry into the pot and stir while scrapping its base to remove the stuck bits. When the sherry begins evaporating add the remaining butter and allow it to melt.
6. Add the remaining onions and season with a half teaspoon of the kosher salt.
7. Lock the pressure lid and cook the mixture on high mode for 25 minutes. Quick release the accumulated steam and open the lid. The cooked onions should be watery.
8. Add the chicken broth, beef Stock, Worcestershire sauce, and thyme. Cook the mixture on high mode for 10 minutes. Quick release the accumulated steam to open the lid.
9. Add the sherry vinegar and taste. If the soup tastes bland, add some salt or vinegar. Add the remaining cup of onions and warm as you prepare the cheese toasts.
10. Preheat the Foodi and add two tablespoons of cheese and sprinkle the rest over the 2 bread slices.
11. Place the bread slices on a sheet pan and broil for 3 minutes or until the cheese melts. Smear one tablespoon of the reserved cheese on the two bowls.
12. Ladle the soup into bowls and top them with a toast slice.

Spicy Chili Verde

Preparation time: ten minutes| Cook Time: 25 minutes| Servings: 4
Ingredients
- 2 lbs (7-8) of chicken thighs (boneless and skinless)
- 12 oz of tomatillos (husked and quartered)
- 4 oz of jalapeño peppers (stemmed, seeded, and chopped)
- 8 oz of poblano peppers (stemmed, seeded, and chopped)
- 4 oz (1/2) of onions, chopped
- 5 garlic cloves
- 1/4 cup of water
- 2 teaspoons of ground cumin
- 1 1/2 teaspoons of salt
- 1/4 oz of cilantro leaves, chopped
- 1 tablespoon of fresh lime juice

Directions
1. Combine the tomatillos with jalapeños, poblano, onions, and water in the Foodi.
2. Sprinkle it with salt, garlic, and cumin. Add the chicken thighs.
3. Close the pressure lid and cook them on high mode for 15 minutes.
4. Allow the accumulated vapor to escape naturally for 10 minutes and then perform quick release.
5. Open the lid and place the chicken on a cutting board. Cut the chicken pieces.
6. Add the lime juice and cilantro to the Foodi and puree the mixture with an immersion blender.
7. Return the chicken to the pot and set it to sear/sauté mode. Boil it for 10 minutes with stirring frequently until it thickens. Serve while garnished with cilantro.

Italian Chicken Masala

Preparation time: 5 minutes| Cook Time: 15 minutes| serving: 4
Ingredients
- 2 lb of chicken, halved
- 3 garlic cloves
- 16 oz of mushrooms
- 1 cup of Masala wine
- 1 cup of flour
- A cup of chicken broth
- 2 tablespoons of butter
- 2 tablespoons of essential olive oil

Directions
1. Season the chicken breasts with salt and pepper. Coat them with flour.
2. Set Ninja Foodi to sauté mode and then add butter, organic olive oil, and garlic.
3. Place the chicken in and cook per side for 3 minutes until brown.
4. Add the broth, wine and mushrooms and set the cooker on Manual High Pressure and cooking time for ten minutes. Perform an instant release.
5. Serve and get with pasta.

Indian Butter Chicken

Preparation time: 5 minutes |Cook Time: 20minutes|Servings: 4
Ingredients

- 4 oz of butter (cubed and divided)
- 1 pound of chicken thighs or breast
- 1 can (14 oz) of tomatoes, diced
- 5 garlic cloves
- 2 teaspoons of ginger, minced
- 1 teaspoon of turmeric
- A teaspoon of paprika
- 1 teaspoon of salt
- 1/2 teaspoon of cayenne pepper
- 2 teaspoons of garam Masala
- 1 teaspoon of ground cumin
- 4 oz of heavy cream
- 1/2 cup of cilantro, chopped

Directions
1. Preheat the Ninja Foodi on sear/sauté mode for two minutes.
2. Melt half of the butter and add garlic. Cook for some seconds.
3. Add the chicken, turmeric, ginger, diced tomatoes, half of the garam Masala, ground cumin, cayenne, and salt. Stir.
4. Lock the pressure lid and cook the turmeric mixture on high mode for five minutes.
5. Release the accumulated steam naturally for 10 minutes and quick release the rest. Open the lid and press the sauté function.
6. Add the heavy cream and the remaining butter. Simmer for 2 minutes and top with cilantro. Serve alongside your favorite rice, preferably basmati.

Chicken and Rice with Yogurt Sauce

Preparation time: 20 minutes| Cook Time: 23 minutes| Servings: 6-8
Ingredients
- 2 pounds of boneless and skinless chicken thighs (cut in pieces)
- 1 packet (1 oz) of mild taco seasoning
- 2 cans (10 oz. each) of enchilada sauce
- A bag (16 oz) of frozen mixed vegetables
- 1 cup of water
- 2 cups of uncooked jasmine rice

Sauce:
- 1 cup of Greek yogurt
- 1/2 jalapeño pepper (deseeded and chopped finely)
- 1/4 cup of fresh mint, minced
- 1/4 cup of fresh cilantro, minced
- 2 tablespoons of vegetable oil

Directions
1. Brown the chicken with the taco seasoning on sauté mode.
2. Add the frozen vegetables into the Foodi contents.
3. Add water, rice, and the enchilada sauce.
4. Cook on high mode for two minutes and release the accumulated pressure naturally for 10 minutes. Quick release the rest.
5. Combine all the sauce ingredients in a bowl.
6. Serve your chicken-rice topped with the yogurt sauce.

Chimichurri Chili Chicken

Preparation time: 15 minutes| Cook Time: 35 minutes| Servings: 2
Ingredients
- 2 teaspoons of kosher salt
- 1 tablespoon of chili powder
- A teaspoon of fresh cracked black pepper
- 1 tablespoon of ground paprika
- A tablespoon of ground fennel
- 1 teaspoon of garlic powder
- 1 teaspoon of onion powder
- A teaspoon of ground cumin
- 2 raw chicken breasts (3/4- lb. each), bony and skinny
- 1 tablespoon of coconut oil

For the Chimichurri:
- 1/4 cup of extra virgin olive oil
- 1/2 bunch of fresh parsley
- 1/2 bunch of fresh cilantro
- 1 shallot (peeled and quartered)
- Zest and juice from a single lemon
- 4 garlic cloves, peeled
- 1 teaspoon of kosher salt

Directions
1. Combine all the dried spices in a bowl.
2. Pat-dry the chicken by coating it with oil. Season the chicken with the spice mixture.
3. Preheat the Foodi for 5 minutes on air crisp mode over a temperature of 375°F.
4. Transfer the chicken to the basket and close the crisping lid. Air-fry the seasoned chicken for 35 minutes.
5. Meanwhile, mix all the Chimichurri ingredients and puree them using a blender.
6. Leave the air-fried chicken for 5 minutes to cool and serve it with Chimichurri.

Herb-Roasted Chicken

Preparation time: 10minutes|Cook Time: 40 minutes| serving: 4
Ingredients
- A raw chicken (about 5 lb)
- 1/4 cup of freshly squeezed lemon juice (from 2 lemons)
- 1/4 cup of water
- 2 tablespoons + 2 teaspoons of kosher salt, divided
- 1/4 cup of honey
- 1 tablespoon of black peppercorns

- 5 sprigs thyme, fresh
- 5 garlic cloves (peeled and smashed)
- 1 tablespoon of canola oil
- 2 teaspoons of ground black pepper

Directions
1. Wash the chicken and tie its legs using a cooking twine.
2. Combine fresh lemon juice with honey, warm water, and two tablespoons of salt in a small bowl.
3. Transfer the mixture to the Foodi and add garlic, thyme, and peppercorns.
4. Put the chicken in a crisping basket and insert it in the Foodi. Secure the pressure lid and cook it on high mode for two minutes.
5. Let the accumulated pressure escape naturally for five minutes and quick release the rest.
6. Open the lid and brush the chicken with oil. After that, season it generously with salt and pepper.
7. Close the crisping lid and press the air crisp button. Set the temperature to 400°F and the cooking time to 8 minutes. Ensure that your chicken has gotten your desired crispness.
8. Serve it hot alongside rice, mashed potatoes, or chips.

Lemon Dill Chicken and Potatoes

Preparation time: 15 minutes| Cook Time: 15minutes|Servings: 4

Ingredients
- 4 boneless and skinless chicken breasts
- 2 lbs of Yukon gold potatoes, sliced thickly
- 1/4 cup of butter, melted
- 1 cup of chicken broth
- 1/4 cup of fresh lemon juice, freshly squeezed
- 2 tablespoons of cornstarch
- 2 garlic cloves, minced
- 2 tablespoons of chopped fresh dill weed
- 1/4 teaspoon of pepper
- 1 teaspoon of salt

Directions
1. Combine the melted butter with broth, cornstarch, juice, dill, garlic, salt, and pepper in a bowl.
2. Add potatoes into the Ninja Foodi and cover them with the chicken breast.
3. Pour the lemon-dill mixture over the chicken mixture.
4. Secure the pressure lid and cook the mixture on high mode for 15 minutes.
5. Perform a quick release of pressure and open the lid. Serve your chicken breasts with the remaining dill sauce.

Garlicky Chicken Adobo

Preparation time: 10 minutes |Cook Time: 35 minutes| Servings 4

Ingredients
- 2 pounds of chicken thighs (boneless and skinless)
- 1/2 cup of soy sauce, low-sodium
- 1/3 cup of white vinegar
- 1 onion, sliced
- 5 cloves garlic, minced
- 3 bay leaves
- 2 tablespoons of organic olive oil
- 1/4 teaspoon of cayenne
- Salt and black pepper
- 2 sliced scallions (for serving)
- Cooked white rice (for serving)

Directions
1. Set your Foodi to sear/sauté mode.
2. Rub the chicken thighs with salt and pepper.
3. Spray the Foodi with essential olive oil and add half from the chicken thighs.
4. Brown all their sides and transfer them to an empty bowl. Repeat the procedure for the remaining thighs.
5. Add soy sauce, onion, vinegar, cayenne, and garlic in the Foodi pot. Stir thoroughly.
6. Return the chicken thighs to the pot. Add onions and bay leaves.
7. Seal the pressure lid and cook the chicken on high mode for ten minutes.
8. Let the pressure release naturally and uncover the lid. Sauté the sauce for 10-15 minutes or until it thickens.
9. Remove the bay leaves and serve your chicken and sauce alongside cooked rice topped with the sliced scallions.

Chicken Curry

Preparation time: 15 minutes| Cook Time: 12 minutes| Servings: 4

Ingredients
- 1 lb of uncooked chicken cutlets
- 3 tablespoons of flour
- Kosher salt and pepper
- 1 large egg, beaten
- 1 cup of panko bread crumbs
- 3-4 tablespoons of peanut oil
- 1 1/2 cups of water
- 1 cup of raw basmati rice
- 1 small onion (peeled and cubed)
- 1 large carrot (peeled and cubed)
- 2 white potatoes (peeled and cubed)
- 1/2 package (1.75 oz.) of curry sauce mix
- 1 cup of chicken broth

Directions
1. Preheat your Food on sear/sauté mode.

2. Season the chicken with salt and pepper. Coat each cutlet with flour, egg, and breadcrumbs.
3. Add oil to the preheated Foodi followed by the coated cutlets. Brown each of the sides and transfer them to a towel-lined plate.
4. Add rice to the pot and insert the reversible rack.
5. Put the remaining ingredients to the baking pan and place the pan on the rack.
6. Close the pressure lid and cook the ingredients on high mode for four minutes.
7. Let the accumulated pressure exit naturally for 10 minutes and quick release the rest. Open the lid and stir the veggies until they thicken.
8. Serve your chicken dish with rice and curried veggies.

Portuguese Style Chicken

Preparation time: 10minutes|Cook Time: 30 minutes |Servings: 4
Ingredients
- 2 lbs of chicken thighs (bony and skinny)
- 1 tablespoon of avocado oil
- 1½ cup of diced zucchini
- Frozen chicken
- 4 lemon slices
- 1/4 cup of diced red bell pepper
- water

For the marinade:
- ¼ cup of extra virgin olive oil
- 3 tablespoons of lime juice
- 3 cloves garlic, peeled and minced
- 1 tablespoon of red vinegar
- ¼ teaspoon of crushed red pepper flakes
- 1 teaspoon of dried thyme
- 2 teaspoon of paprika
- ¼ teaspoon of black pepper
- ½ teaspoon of salt

Directions
1. Add all the marinade ingredients to your Ziploc bag. Add chicken and lemon slices and let it marinade for overnight.
2. Pour a half cup of water into the pot and mix it with the remaining marinade, zucchini and red bell pepper.
3. Place the seasoned chicken in the basket and insert it in the Foodi.
4. Seal the pressure lid and cook the contents on high mode for ten minutes. Quick release the accumulated pressure and open the lid.
5. Brush the chicken with oil and close the crisping lid. Set the Foodi to air crisp mode, temperature to 390°F, and cook time to 20 minutes.
6. Bake the seasoned chicken until the internal temperature drops to around 165°F.

7. Transfer it to a bowl and let it cool before serving.

Spicy Thai Chicken Wings

Preparation time: 5 minutes| Cook Time: 27 minutes |Servings: 4-6
Ingredients
- 2 lbs of frozen chicken wings, drums and flats separated
- 1/2 cup of water
- 2 tablespoons of Thai chili sauce
- 2 tablespoons of canola oil
- 2 teaspoons of kosher salt
- 2 teaspoons of sesame seeds (for garnishing)

Directions
1. Pour the water into the Foodi. Put the chicken wings in the basket and insert it in the pot.
2. Lock the pressure lid and cook the wings on high mode for 12 minutes.
3. Conduct a quick release of pressure by turning the release valve to vent. Open the lid.
4. Pat-dry the wings and spray it with oil. Close the crisping lid and press the air crisp button. Set the cooking time to fifteen minutes and temperature to 390°F. Remember to flip the chicken when air-frying.
5. Now, combine the Thai chili sauce and salt in a bowl.
6. After crisping the chicken, toss it over the chilli sauce to coat. Serve while garnished with sesame seeds.

Keto Coq Au Vin

Preparation time: 10 minutes| Cook Time: 25 minutes| Servings: 4
Ingredients
- 4 chicken legs, skinny
- 7 ounces of smoked bacon cubes
- 2/3 cups of pearl onions
- 7 oz of white mushrooms
- ½ cup of dark wine
- ¾ servings of chicken stock
- Some thyme sprigs
- Parsley
- Salt and pepper
- 1/8 teaspoon of Xantham Gum

Directions
1. Preheat your Foodi on sear/sauté mode over medium-high temperature.
2. Fry the bacon until it becomes crispy by flipping.
3. Season the chicken with salt and pepper. Add it to the bacon and sauté them until they turn golden yellow.
4. Add the onions and mushrooms to the pot. Season them with salt, pepper, thyme, and wine.

5. Return the chicken to the Foodi and add chicken stock. Add half of the bacon mixture and let it boil.
6. Lock the pressure lid and cook the ingredients on high mode for 15 minutes.
7. Quick release the pressure and open the cooker's lid. Remove the chicken legs.
8. Sauté the remaining fluid on medium-heat until it starts drying.
9. Add the xantham gum to make it thick.
10. Serve the chicken with the sauce. Garnish it with the crispy bacon and fresh parsley. You can also serve alongside toasted baguettes.

Piripiri Chicken

Preparation time: 7 minutes| Cook Time: 20 minutes |Servings:4
Ingredients
- 1 lb of chicken thighs (boneless and skinless)
- 1 teaspoon of House Seasoning Blend
- Zest and juice extracted from a lemon
- 1 orange, juiced
- 1/4 cup of extra virgin olive oil
- 3 garlic cloves, minced
- 2 teaspoons of paprika
- 1 teaspoon of dried oregano
- 1/2 teaspoon of red pepper flakes, crushed
- 1 tablespoon of fresh parsley, chopped

Directions
1. Pour water into the Foodi and put the chicken in the basket. Insert the basket in the pot.
2. Close the pressure lid and cook the chicken on high mode for 5minutes.
3. After that, release the accumulated vapor naturally for 5 minutes and quick release the rest.
4. Meanwhile, combine the orange juice with the fresh lemon juice, zest, dried oregano, red pepper flakes, extra virgin olive oil, garlic, and paprika in a bowl.
5. Remove the cooked chicken using the silicone-tipped tongs. Toss it in the House seasoning blend and coat it with the orange juice sauce.
6. Return the chicken to the basket and close the crisping lid.
7. Set the Food to air crisp mode, temperature to 400°F, and cooking time to 15 minutes.
8. While crisping, open the lid and pour the remaining spice mixture over the chicken. Resume cooking.
9. When everything is ready, transfer the chicken to a serving platter and garnish it with the chopped parsley.

Shredded Chicken Breast

Preparation time: 2 minutes| Cook Time: 15minutes|Servings: 20
Ingredients
- 4 lb of chicken
- 1/2 teaspoon of sea salt
- 1/2 teaspoon of black pepper
- 1 tablespoon of Italian seasoning
- A cup of chicken broth

Directions
1. Place the chicken in your Foodi pot, and sprinkle it with sea salt, black pepper, and the Italian seasoning. Stir and pour the chicken broth over it.
2. Close the pressure lid and cook the sea salt mixture on high mode for 15 minutes.
3. Allow the pressure to escape naturally for ten minutes and quick release the rest.
4. Open the lid and shred the chicken using two forks.

Teriyaki Chicken with Rice and Broccoli

Preparation time: ten minutes| Cook Time: 32 minutes |Servings: 2
Ingredients
- 1 cup of long-grain white rice
- 1/2 cup of frozen mixed vegetables
- 1 cup of chicken stock
- 2 teaspoons of kosher salt, divided
- 1 tablespoon of Adobo seasoning
- 2 teaspoons of ground black pepper, divided
- 2 raw boneless and skinless chicken breasts (8 oz. each)
- A broccoli head cut in 2-inch pieces
- 1 tablespoon of extra virgin olive oil
- 1/4 cup of teriyaki sauce

Directions
1. Rinse rice and put it into the Foodi. Add chicken stock, frozen veggies, a teaspoon of salt, a teaspoon of pepper, and the Adobo seasoning. Stir.
2. Place the chicken breasts on the reversible rack and fit it above the rice mixture.
3. Secure the pressure lid and cook both meals on high mode for two minutes.
4. Meanwhile, mix broccoli with olive oil, the remaining salt, and pepper.
5. Once the pressure cooking time elapses, release the accumulated pressure naturally for ten minutes and quick release the rest.
6. Open the lid and brush the chicken with the teriyaki sauce.
7. Add broccoli mixture to the rack containing the chicken.
8. Close the crisping lid and select the broil function. Cook for 12 and stop whenever the internal temperature drops to165°F.

9. Subdivide your teriyaki sauce dish between two plates.

Indian Chicken Vindaloo

Preparation time: 15 minutes| Cook Time: 30 minutes |Servings: 4-6

Ingredients
- 1 cup of diced onions
- 5 garlic cloves
- 2-3 slices of ginger, minced
- 1 tablespoon of oil
- 1/4 cup of white vinegar
- 1 cup of tomato, chopped
- A teaspoon of garam Masala
- 1 teaspoon of salt
- 2 teaspoons of cayenne
- 1 teaspoon of smoked paprika
- 1/2 teaspoon of ground coriander
- 1/2 teaspoon of turmeric
- 1/2 teaspoon of ground cumin
- 1 pound of chicken thighs, boneless and skinless
- 1/4 cup of water

Directions
1. Sauté onions, garlic, and ginger in the Foodi until they brown.
2. Transfer the mixture to the blender. Add the remaining ingredients (except the chicken, water, and turmeric) to the blender. Blend to a puree and wash the blender.
3. Place the chicken in a bowl and pour the puree over it.
4. Now add turmeric and allow it to marinate for at least thirty minutes.
5. Transfer the marinated chicken to the Ninja Foodi and close the pressure lid.
6. Cook it on high mode for ten minutes. After that, release the accumulated moisture naturally for 10 minutes.
7. Transfer the chicken pieces to your bowl and sauté its fluid to desired thickness. Enjoy!

Buffalo Chicken Meatballs

Preparation time: 10 minutes |Cook Time: 20 minutes| Servings: 6

Ingredients
- 1 1/2 lbs of ground chicken
- 3/4 cup of almond meal
- 1 teaspoon of sea salt
- 2 garlic cloves, minced
- 2 green onions, thinly sliced
- 2 tablespoons of ghee
- 6 tablespoons of hot sauce
- 4 tablespoons of butter, melted in the microwave
- Chopped green onions, for garnish

Directions
1. Add chicken, almond meal, garlic cloves, green onions, and salt in a large bowl and mix using your hands.
2. Grease your hands with coconut oil and shape the mixture into 1-2 inches wide meatballs.
3. Brown the meatballs by sautéing it in your Foodi with half of the butter. You can brown them in batches.
4. Transfer the browned meatballs to the basket and insert it in the pot.
5. Add the melted butter and hot sauce. Close the crisping lid.
6. Set your Foodi to bake/roast mode over the temperature of 400°F. Roast your meatballs for 15 minutes. Transfer them to a platter and serve alongside noodles or cauliflower rice.

Chicken Lemon Sauce Pasta

Preparation time: 15 minutes |Cook Time: 20 minutes |Servings 6

Ingredients
- 1 package (16 oz.) of halved linguine
- 4 cups of chicken broth, divided
- 1 tablespoon of organic olive oil
- ½ teaspoon of kosher salt
- 3 tablespoons of fresh lemon juice and 1 teaspoon of zest, divided
- 6(4-6 oz. each) uncooked chicken fillets, thinly cut
- Ground black pepper, for seasoning
- 1/2 cup of all-purpose flour
- 1/2 stick (1/4 cup) butter, melted
- 1 cup of Parmesan cheese, grated
- 3 tablespoons of capers
- 3 tablespoons of fresh parsley, chopped

Directions
1. Combine the linguine with three and half glasses of broth, two tablespoons of freshly squeezed lemon juice, oil, and salt. Stir.
2. Close the pressure lid and cook the mixture on high mode for five minutes. Open the lid and season with salt and pepper.
3. Toss the chicken in the flour and shake off excess flour. Brush the tossed chicken with the melted butter and transfer it to a bowl.
4. Put the Parmesan cheese, the remaining chicken broth, capers, the remaining lemon juice, and lemon zest into the pot.
5. Transfer the chicken into the reversible rack and fix it in the Foodi.
6. Seal the crisping lid and press the bake / roast button.
7. Bake the chicken at a temperature of 375°F for 15 minutes.

8. Add parsley, salt, and pepper to the caper sauce.
9. Serve your chicken with the sauce pasta.

Hungarian Chicken Paprikash

Preparation time: 10 minutes| Cook Time: 30 minutes| Servings: 6
Ingredients
- 2 large onions, diced
- 3 cloves garlic, minced
- 1 chicken, cut into pieces
- 1 1/2 teaspoon of Pink Himalayan salt
- 2 teaspoon of Pepper
- 1 tablespoon of Smokey paprika
- 2 teaspoon of Sweet paprika
- Juice of ½ a lemon
- 1 tomato
- 1 tablespoon of tomato paste
- 1 bay leaf
- 3 tablespoons of essential olive oil
- 2 servings of chicken stock

Directions
1. Put all the ingredients into the Foodi. Close the pressure lid and cook them on high mode for fifteen minutes. Quick release the accumulated vapor and open the lid.
2. Turn the chicken parts (skin-side up) and then close the crisping lid.
3. Press the broil button and cook for fifteen minutes or until it brown.
4. Transfer the chicken to a plate and pour its sauce over it.

Tip: whenever the sauce is too light, you can thicken it by adding sour cream and flour.Alternatively, you can sauté the chicken with oil and pressure cook.

Cereal-Crusted Tenders

Preparation time: 15 minutes |Cook Time: 12 minutes |Servings: 4
Ingredients
- 2 chicken breasts, strips
- 3 cups of any cereal, crushed
- 1 cup of rice flour
- 3 teaspoons of kosher salt, divided
- 2 eggs, beaten
- 2 teaspoons of ground black pepper

Directions
1. Combine the rice flour with salt (2 teaspoon) in a plate and stir to blend.
2. Add eggs to a bowl and whisk. Mix the crushed cereal with pepper, and the remaining salt in the third bowl.
3. Toss your chicken in the flour and shake off excess flour. Coat it with the egg and pass it over the cereal mixture to coat well. Do this in batches.
4. Wrap the coated chicken in a Ziploc bag and freeze for five hours.
5. Unwrap the frozen chicken and put it in the crisping basket.
6. Brush the chicken with oil and close the crisping lid.
7. Set the Foodi to air crisp mode, temperature to, 390°F, cooking time to two minutes.
8. Remove the crisped chicken from the basket and let it cool for some minutes before serving.

Keto Chicken Pot Pie

Preparation time:30 minutes |Cook Time: 30 minutes| Servings: 8
Ingredients
Chicken pot pie filling:
- 2 tablespoons of butter
- 1/2 cup of mixed veggies
- 1/4 small onion, diced
- 1/4 teaspoon of pepper
- 1/4 teaspoon of pink salt
- 2 garlic cloves, minced
- 3/4 cup of heavy whipping cream
- 1 cup of chicken broth
- 1 teaspoon of poultry seasoning
- 1/4 teaspoon of rosemary
- 2 1/2 cups of cooked chicken, diced
- Pinch thyme
- 1/4 teaspoon of Xantham Gum

For the crust:
- 4 1/2 tablespoons of butter (melted and then cooled)
- 2 tablespoons of heavy sour cream
- 1/3 cup of coconut flour
- 1/4 teaspoon of salt
- 4 eggs
- 1/4 teaspoon of baking powder
- 1 1/3 cups of cheddar or mozzarella cheese, shredded

Directions
1. Set your Ninja Foodi to sear/sauté mode over medium high.
2. Add 2 tablespoons of butter to the pot followed by onions, mixed vegetables, garlic cloves, pepper, and salt.
3. Sauté the vegetable mixture for 5 minutes or until the onions becomes translucent.
4. Add the chicken broth, heavy cream, thyme, poultry seasoning, and rosemary.
5. Sprinkle it with the Xantham Gum and simmer for 5 minutes to thicken.
6. Add the cooked chicken and stir.

To make the crust:
1. Add the melted butter to sour cream, eggs, and salt in a bowl and whisk thoroughly.

2. Add baking powder and coconut flour and stir. Add the cheese and stir again.
3. Put the dollop of batter in the cooker but do not spread it.
4. Close the crisping lid and select the bake/roast function. Bake the batter for two minutes or until it browns at the temperature of 400°F for fifteen minutes.
5. Sprinkle it with dried parsley and serve with the chicken.

Chicken Enchilada Dish

Preparation time:5minutes|Cook Time: 20minutes| Servings: 4
Ingredients
- 2 tablespoons of coconut oil
- 1 pound of chicken thighs (boneless and skinless)
- 3/4 cup of red enchilada sauce
- 1/4 cup of water
- 1/4 cup of onion, chopped
- 4 oz of diced green chilies

Optional toppings:
- 1 avocado, diced
- 1/4 cup of pickled jalapenos, chopped
- A cup of shredded cheese
- 1 tomato, chopped
- 1/2 cup of sour cream

Directions
1. Set your Foodi to sear/sauté mode and preheat it for 5 minutes.
2. Melt the coconut oil and add the chicken thighs. Sauté the thighs until they turn lightly brown.
3. Pour water, enchilada sauce, green chilies, and onions.
4. Close the pressure lid and cook on high mode for 15 minutes.
5. Quick release the accumulated pressure and open the lid.
6. Place the chicken on a flat surface and shred it using a fork.
7. Return the shreds to the Foodi and set it to sear/sauté mode.
8. Simmer for 3-5 minutes over medium-high.
9. Serve your chicken enchilada with your desired toppings alongside cauliflower rice.

Salsa Chicken

Frozen chicken breasts with taco seasoning and salsa prepared in a Ninja Foodi. The appetizing meal is Mexican-themed.
Preparation time: 5 minutes| Cook Time: 15 minutes| Servings: 6
Ingredients
- 1 lb of frozen chicken (skinless, boneless, and halved)
- 1 (1 oz) packet of taco seasoning mix
- 1/2 cup of salsa
- 1/2 cup of low-sodium chicken broth

Directions
1. Place the chicken breast in the basket and sprinkle it with the taco seasoning.
2. Pour the chicken broth and salsa over it and close the pressure lid.
3. Cook the seasoned chicken on high mode for 15 minutes.
4. After that, quick release the accumulated pressure and open the lid.
5. Splash the chicken with the cooking spray and close the crisping lid.
6. Set the Foodi to air crisp mode, temperature to 400°F, and cooking time to 10 minutes. Confirm that your salsa chicken has attained your desired crispness.

Chicken Puttanesca

Preparation time: 10 minutes |Cook Time: 30 minutes| Servings: 6
Ingredients
- 6 chicken thighs, skinny
- 2 tablespoons of extra virgin olive oil
- 2 cloves garlic, crushed
- Salt and black pepper
- 1/2 teaspoon of red chili flakes
- 14 1/2 oz of chopped tomatoes
- 6 oz of pitted black olives
- 1 tablespoon of capers, rinsed and drained
- 1 tablespoons of chopped fresh basil
- 3/4 cup of water

Directions
1. Add water, chopped tomatoes, olives, capers, garlic, red chili flakes, chopped basil, salt, and pepper in the Foodi.
2. Place the chicken pieces in the basket (skin side down) and fit the basket in the Foodi.
3. Secure the pressure lid and cook the contents for 15 minutes. Quick release the in-built pressure and open the lid.
4. Pat-dry the chicken thighs and brush with oil.
5. Close the crisping lid and set your pot to air crisp mode. Set the cooking time to 15 minutes and temperature to 400°F. Confirm that it has attained your desired crispiness.
6. Serve your chicken puttanesca with vegetables.

Spaghetti Squash Chicken Alfredo

This is a quick and easy Keto-recipe consisting of a creamy sauce and aromatic chicken.
Preparation time: 5 minutes| Cook Time: 35 minutes| Servings:5

Ingredients
- A spaghetti squash
- 16 oz of skinless chicken breasts, 1 " cubed
- 4 oz of reduced-fat cream cheese, softened
- 1/2 cup of low-sodium chicken broth
- 2 cups of chopped broccoli
- 1 cup of shredded parmesan cheese
- 1/4 cup of heavy cream
- 3/4 tablespoon of butter, softened
- 1 tablespoon of flour
- 1 tablespoon of minced garlic
- 2 cups of almond milk
- 1 cup of water
- 1 teaspoon of extra virgin olive oil
- McCormick's seasoning, salt, and pepper

Directions
1. Begin by halving the spaghetti crosswise. Scoop the seeds and discard.
2. Pour a cup of water into the Ninja Foodi pot and add the squash halves. Ensure that the cut sides face up.
3. Close the pressure lid and cook on high mode for 7 minutes. Quick release the in-built vapor and open the lid.
4. Transfer the squash to a flat surface and shred into spaghetti strips using a fork.
5. Discard the excess fluid from the Foodi and preheat it on sauté mode.
6. Season the chicken meat with the McCormick's seasonings.
7. Pour the extra virgin olive oil into the pot and add the seasoned chicken.
8. Brown it by sautéing each of its sides for 3 minutes.
9. Transfer the browned chicken into a bowl.
10. Add the minced garlic into the Foodi and sauté for two minutes.
11. Add the chicken broth and deglaze the pot. Put the heavy cream, almond milk, butter, and cheese into the pot. Stir.
12. Add the chopped broccoli and mozzarella cheese. Let it cook for 3 minutes or until the broccoli softens and the sauce thickens. Add the flour and stir.
13. Return the chicken into the Foodi and season it with salt and pepper.

Chicken Pie Casserole

Preparation time: 15 minutes| Cook Time: 50 minutes| Servings: 8

Ingredients
- 2 pounds of frozen chicken breasts or thighs (boneless and skinless)
- 5 garlic cloves (peeled and minced)
- 1 large onion (peeled and diced)
- 1/2 cup of stock, preferably chicken
- 2 teaspoons of salt
- 1 teaspoon of ground black pepper
- 2 tablespoons of all-purpose flour
- 1 lb of fresh baby spinach
- 8 oz of feta cheese, crumbled
- A bunch of fresh dill, chopped
- 1 bunch of scallions, thinly sliced
- 8 sheets of phyllo dough, thawed
- 1/2 stick (1/4 cup) of butter, melted

Directions
1. Combine the chicken with garlic, onion, stock, salt, and pepper in the Foodi.
2. Close the pressure lid and cook on high mode for 22 minutes.
3. Quick release the accumulated steam and open the lid. Set the unit to sauté and add the spinach leaves. Allow it to soften and add the chicken mixture.
4. Add the flour and stir. Add the scallions, feta, and dill. Stir.
5. Align the chicken dough on a flat surface and brush with the melted butter.
6. Close the crisping lid and set the Foodi to air crisp mode, temperature to 325°F, and cooking time to 20 minutes.
7. Cook until the chicken dough becomes golden crispy. Transfer it into a bowl, cool, and garnish with dill.

Turkey Meatballs with Pasta

Preparation time: 15 minutes| Cook Time: 25minutes|Servings 4

Ingredients
- 1 lb of uncooked ground turkey
- 1/2 cup of basil pesto
- 1/4 cup of panko bread crumbs
- 1 large egg, beaten lightly
- 1 tablespoon of extra-virgin organic olive oil
- A teaspoon of kosher salt, divided
- 1 onion (peeled and chopped finely)
- 3 cloves garlic (peeled and minced)
- 2 cups of the prepared marinara sauce
- 2 1/2 cups (8 oz) of penne pasta
- 2 cups of water
- 1/4 cup of fresh basil leaves, chopped
- Parmesan cheese

Directions
1. Mix the turkey with bread crumbs, pesto, eggs, and half teaspoon of salt in a bowl.
2. Roll about a quarter cup of the mixture into one meatball using your hands. Roll several.
3. Pour oil into the Foodi and sauté it on medium temperature.
4. Once the oil heats add the meatballs and brown each of their sides for ten minutes. Put aside all the balls after browning.

5. Add garlic, onion, and the remaining salt to the Foodi and sauté for 3 minutes or until they soften.
6. Add the marinara sauce, water, and pasta.
7. Place the meatballs over the pasta and close the pressure lid partially. In this, leave the release valve on vent position.
8. Simmer the meatballs for 15 minutes or until they are cooked and the pasta is tender.
9. Turn off the sauté function. Add salt and pepper to your preferred taste. Serve while sprinkled with cheese and basil.

Orange Chicken

Preparation time: 10 minutes| Cook Time: 40 minutes| Servings: 4
Ingredients
- 2 oranges (halved, peeled, and juiced)
- 1 whole chicken (3 lbs or less)
- 1 cup of cream
- 2 tablespoons of kosher salt
- 1 tablespoon of sugar
- 1 cup of chicken broth
- 1 tablespoon of instant flour

Directions
1. Stuff the chicken cavity with the orange halves.
2. Combine the cream, salt, and sugar in a bowl.
3. Put the stuffed chicken in the Ziploc bag together with the cream mixture, orange juice, and zest. Marinate overnight.
4. Pour the chicken broth into the Foodi.
5. Insert the basket in the pot. Transfer chicken from the bag to basket and close the pressure lid.
6. Cook on high mode for 15 minutes. Quick release the accumulated pressure and open the lid.
7. Close the crisping lid and set the multi-cooker to air crisp mode for twenty minutes at 390°F.
8. Remove the chicken from the Foodi. Add flour to the broth and sauté it until it boils.
9. Serve the chicken and ladle sauce over it.

Crack Chicken

Nutritious, creamy, and flavorful!
Preparation time: 5 minutes| Cook Time: 20 minutes| Servings: 8
Ingredients
- 2 slices of chopped bacon
- 2 lbs of chicken breasts, boneless and skinless
- 2 (8 oz.) blocks of cream cheese
- ½ cup of water
- 1½ teaspoons of garlic powder
- 1 tablespoon of dried chives
- A teaspoon of dill, dried
- 1 teaspoon of crushed red pepper flakes
- 1½ teaspoons of onion powder
- ¼ teaspoon of salt
- ¼ teaspoon of black pepper
- ½ cup of cheddar, shredded
- 1 scallion, thinly sliced (green and white parts only)

Directions
1. Put the chicken, chives, water, vinegar, onion powder, garlic powder, dill, crushed red pepper flakes, salt, and pepper into the Foodi.
2. Secure the pressure lid and cook the spiced chicken on high mode for 10 minutes.
3. Quick release the accumulated pressure and unsecure the lid.
4. Place the bacon in the basket and close the crisping lid. Select the air frying option and cook for ten minutes in a temperature of 330°F. Do not preheat.
5. Remove your bacon from the basket and put the shredded chicken in the pot.
6. Add the cheddar cheese and cream cheese and stir to combine.
7. Serve your chicken topped with air fried bacon and scallion.

Chicken and Dumplings

Preparation time: 20 minutes| Cook Time: 35 minutes| Servings: 6
Ingredients
- 1 onion peeled and chopped
- 2 tablespoons of organic olive oil
- 3 stalks celery, chopped
- 2 cloves garlic, peeled and minced
- 2 carrots, peeled and chopped
- 1 teaspoon of dried rosemary
- 1 teaspoon of dried thyme
- 1/2 teaspoon of pepper
- 1 1/2 teaspoons of kosher salt
- 2 pounds of boneless and skinless chicken breasts and thighs, uncooked
- 1 can (10.5oz.) of cream of chicken soup
- 6 cups of chicken stock
- 1/2 cup of milk
- 1 1/2 cups of all-purpose baking mix
- 1 bunch of fresh parsley (chopped finely, stems out)

Directions
1. Put onion, carrots, and celery in the Ninja Foodi and sauté on medium heat for five minutes, while stirring frequently.
2. Add the thyme, garlic, rosemary, pepper, and salt. Stir.
3. Add the chicken, soup, and stock. Stir.
4. Secure the pressure lid and cook on high ode for 15 minutes.

5. Meanwhile, mix milk with baking in a bowl and combine until dough forms. Put aside.
6. Quick release the pressure and transfer the chicken into a bowl. Shred it and return to the Foodi.
7. Simmer the liquid in the pot on sauté mode. Drop some balls formed from the dough and cook for ten minutes. Turn off sauté.
8. Secure the crisping lid and the dish sit for 5 minutes. Garnish your chicken and dumplings with parsley and enjoy.

Bruschetta Chicken

Preparation time: 10 minutes| Cook Time: 35 minutes |Servings: 6
Ingredients
- 2 lbs of chicken white meat (boneless, skinless, and cut into 6-8 pieces)
- 1 tablespoon of extra virgin olive oil
- 1/2 cup of chicken broth
- Salt and pepper

For the Tomato Sauce:
- 1 -15 oz of diced tomatoes
- 1 teaspoon of oregano, dried
- 1/4 cup of balsamic vinegar
- 4 garlic cloves
- 1 teaspoon of dried basil

Directions
1. Combine all the ingredients of the tomato sauce and reserve.
2. Pour the chicken broth and half of the tomato mix into the pot.
3. Place the chicken parts in the basket and insert it in the Foodi.
4. Close the pressure lid and cook it on high mode for 20 minutes.
5. Open the lid and brush the chicken with oil.
6. Close the crisping lid and set the unit to air crisp or bake/roast button.
7. Set the cooking time to 15 minutes and temperature to 375°F.
8. Remember to shake the basket halfway or turn your chicken using tongs for even cooking. Remove the meat when the thermometer shows 160F.
9. Top with all the reserved tomato sauce and garnish with fresh basil.
10. Alternatively, once the chicken is pressure cooked, open the lid and top it with bread crumbs or shredded mozzarella.
11. Secure the crisping lid and broil for 5 minutes. In this, ensure that it does not burn.

Hungarian Paprika Turkey

Preparation time: 5 minutes| Cook Time: 40 minutes |Servings: 4
Ingredients
- 2 turkey legs, bone-in (about 2 lb)
- 2 turkey thighs, bone-in (about 3 lb)
- 4 cloves garlic, peeled
- 1/4 cup of pickled jalapeños brine liquid
- 2 tablespoons of Hungarian paprika
- 1 tablespoon of kosher salt
- 1 cup of sour cream
- 1 cup of beer
- 2 tablespoons of instant flour

Directions
1. Combine all the ingredients in the Food and secure the pressure lid.
2. Cook on high mode for twenty minute and quick release the pressure.
3. Flip the turkey parts (skin side up) and close the crisping lid.
4. Press the broil button and set the cook time to 15 minutes or until it browns.
5. Transfer the chicken to a platter and drizzle the sauce over it.
6. Reset the Foodi to sauté mode and add the sour cream followed by flour. Let them boil while stirring constantly. Ladle the sauce over the turkey and enjoy.

Lemon Rotisserie Chicken

Amazingly tender and moist chicken, perfect for a family dinner!
Preparation time: 5 minutes |Cook Time: 34 minutes| Servings:5
Ingredients
- 1 (21/2 lb.) whole chicken
- 1 lemon, cut into 4 wedges
- 2 tablespoons of olive oil
- 1 teaspoon of garlic powder
- 1 1/2 teaspoons of salt
- 1 teaspoon of paprika
- 1/2 teaspoon of ground black pepper
- 1 cup of chicken broth

Directions
1. Rinse the chicken, and pat dry with a paper towel. Insert the lemon wedges in the chicken cavity.
2. Combine the broth with paprika, salt, pepper, and garlic. Place the lemonade chicken in the basket and fit it in the Foodi.
3. Secure the pressure lid and cook on high mode for 15 minutes. Quick release the pressure and unsecure the lid.
4. Brush the chicken with canola oil and close the crisping lid. Select the air crisp mode and set the temperature to 400°F. Air-crisp the brushed chicken for 15 minutes.
5. Transfer the crisped chicken to a wide bowl and let it cool before serving.

Chicken and Rice Casserole

Preparation time: 10 minutes| Cook Time: 70 minutes| Servings: 8

Ingredients
- ½ cup of sour cream
- 2 large eggs
- ½ tablespoon of onion powder
- ½ tablespoon of garlic powder
- ½ teaspoon of pepper
- ½ teaspoon of salt
- 1 stick of butter
- 2 teaspoons of xantham gum
- 5 cups of cauliflower rice
- 2 glasses of chicken broth
- 3 cups of rotisserie chicken (pre-cooked)
- 3 oz of pork rinds, crushed
- ¼ cup and 2 tablespoons of mozzarella cheese

Directions
1. Combine the eggs with sour cream, onion powder, garlic powder, salt, and pepper in a bowl. Leave aside.
2. Set the multi-cooker to sauté mode over medium heat. Add the butter and melt.
3. Add the xantham gum and stir constantly for 5 minutes or until it turns golden brown. Do not allow it to scotch.
4. Add the chicken broth and allow it to thicken for 5 minutes.
5. Turn off the sauté function and add the cooked chicken, cauliflower, crushed pork rinds, Parmesan, and the sour cream mixture while stirring.
6. Close the crisping lid and se the unit to bake/ roast mode. Set the temperature to 350°F and bake for one hour or until it turns golden brown.

30-Minutes Moroccan Chicken

Preparation time: 10 minutes| Cook Time: 20 minutes |Servings: 4

Ingredients
- 1 teaspoon of turmeric
- A teaspoon of paprika
- 1 teaspoon of ground cumin
- 1/4 teaspoon of black pepper
- 1/2 teaspoon of salt
- 3 tablespoons of olive oil, divided
- 1/2 lb of boneless and skinless chicken thighs
- 11/2 servings of chicken broth
- 2 garlic cloves, minced
- 1/2 cup of onions, finely diced
- 1 teaspoon of minced ginger
- 3/4 cup of uncooked quinoa
- 1/2 cup of dried apricots
- 1 can of chickpeas, drained

Directions
1. Combine turmeric with paprika, cumin, pepper, and salt in a bowl. Coat both sides of the chicken with the mixture.
2. Sauté the chicken with half of the olive oil until it browns. Set aside.
3. Sauté the onions, garlic, and ginger with the remaining oil and stir gently.
4. Add the quinoa, cherries, chickpeas, and the browned chicken.
5. Close the pressure lid and cook on high mode for ten minutes. Quick release the accumulated vapor and open the lid. Subdivide your Moroccan chicken between serving plates and enjoy.

Moroccan Frozen Chicken

Preparation time: 10 minutes| Cook Time: 40 minutes| Servings: 2

Ingredients
- 2 tablespoons of extra virgin olive oil, divided
- 1 small onion, peeled and then diced
- 1 cup of wild rice
- 3 teaspoons of kosher salt, divided
- 3/4 cup of chicken stock
- 1 tablespoon of Moroccan seasoning
- 2 frozen chicken breasts (8 oz each)
- 1 bag (12 oz) of green beans, trimmed
- 1/4 cup of fresh parsley, chopped
- 1 teaspoon of black pepper, divided
- 1/4 cup of honey mustard sauce

Directions
1. Preheat the Foodi on sauté mode and add the onions.
2. Cook while stirring for 3 minutes and add the wild rice, 2 teaspoons of salt, and the Moroccan seasoning.
3. Let it cook and stir until the rice is coated with oil-it will appear shiny.
4. Add the chicken stock and stir.
5. Place the frozen meat on the rack (higher position) and fix it in the Foodi containing the rice mixture. Cook on high mode for 2 minutes.
6. Meanwhile, combine the green beans with oil, pepper, and salt in a bowl. Toss to mix.
7. Natural release the accumulated pressure for 10 minutes and quick release the rest. Remove the rack from the Foodi and add parsley and green beans.
8. Brush the chicken breast with the honey mustard sauce and return the rack to the pot containing the rice mixture.
9. Close the crisping lid and broil the chicken for 10 minutes. Serve your chicken with green beans and rice.

Chicken Thighs

Preparation time: 2 minutes| Cook Time: 22 minutes| Servings: 6

Ingredients

- 6-8 chicken thighs, fresh or frozen thighs
- Pepper
- Water
- 1/2 small onion (optional)
- 2 peeled garlic cloves (optional)

Directions
1. Season the chicken with salt and pepper.
2. Pour one cup of water in the Foodi. Add onion and garlic.
3. Put the chicken thighs on a reversible rack and fix it in the multi-cooker.
4. Secure the pressure lid and cook on high mode for 10 minutes.
5. Quick release the pressure and open the lid. Close the crisping lid and set the Foodi to air fry mode.
6. Close the crisping lid and air crisp the chicken at 375°F for 15 minutes.

Crispy Breaded Air Fried Chicken

Preparation time: 15 minutes | Cook Time: 10 minutes | Servings: 4

Ingredients
- 4 (about 18 oz. total) boneless skinless chicken thighs

Egg Wash:
- 2 large eggs
- 2 tablespoons of heavy cream

For "Breading":
- 2/3 cup of blanched almond flour
- 2/3 cup of parmesan cheese, finely grated
- 1 teaspoon of salt
- 1/2 teaspoon of black pepper
- 1/2 teaspoon of cayenne
- 1/2 teaspoon of paprika

Directions
1. Mix the eggs and cream in a bowl.
2. Combine all the breading ingredients in a separate bowl and set aside.
3. Cut the chicken thigh into 3 equal pieces and pat it dry with paper towels.
4. First, coat each chicken piece with the breading. After that, pass it in the egg wash. Coat it again with the breading mixture.
5. Shake off excess coating and transfer the chicken to the crisping basket. Spray them with the cooking spray or brush with oil.
6. Close the crisping lid and set the Foodi to air crisp mode. Set the temperature to 390°F and cooking time to 20 minutes. Toss or flip halfway during cooking.
7. Serve your air-fried chicken hot and crispy.

Tasty Chicken Ramen

Preparation time: 15 minutes | Cook Time: 25 minutes | Servings: 4

Ingredients
- 2-3 lbs of chicken thighs, bony and skinny
- 1-inch piece of fresh ginger, peeled and quartered
- 4 cloves garlic, peeled and smashed
- 1/2 yellow onion, peeled
- 1/4 cup plus 2 tablespoons of soy sauce, divided
- 1/4 cup of Dijon mustard
- 5 glasses of water
- 1 tablespoon of granulated sugar
- 4 packages (3 oz. each) of instant ramen noodles

Optional Toppings:
- Thinly-sliced fresh scallions
- Soft boiled eggs
- Bamboo shoots
- Corn
- Citrus zest
- Cooked veggies

Directions
1. Add the chicken, garlic, ginger, onion, water, and a quarter cup of soy sauce to the Foodi and stir.
2. Secure the pressure mode and cook the mixture on high mode for 2 minutes. Quick release the in-built pressure and allow the chicken to cool.
3. Remove garlic, ginger, and onion using a slotted spoon and discard.
4. Shred the cool meat and discard its bones.
5. Mix sugar with two tablespoons of soy sauce in a bowl. Combine the mixture with the shredded meat and cover with a plastic wrap.
6. Sauté the mixture and let it boil. Add the Dijon and whisk. Turn off the sauté mode.
7. Break the noodles in a bowl and ladle the broth over them.
8. Cover the bowls using plastic wraps for four minutes or until the noodles softens.
9. Uncover them and add your preferred toppings. Serve!

Turmeric Nutty Chicken

Preparation time: 3 minutes | Cook Time: 15 minutes | Servings: 4

Ingredients:
- 1 can of coconut cream
- 2 pounds of chicken thighs
- 1 tablespoon of turmeric

Directions:
1. Combine all the ingredients in the Foodi and close the pressure lid.
2. Cook the mixture on high mode for fifteen minutes.
3. Allow the pressure to escape naturally and open the lid.
4. Season the chicken with salt and serve.

Roasted Red Pepper Chicken

Preparation time: 15 minutes | Cook Time: 17 minutes | Servings: 4

Ingredients

- 1.5 lb of chicken thighs, boneless and skinless
- 1 teaspoon of Pink Himalayan Salt
- 1 tablespoon of coconut oil
- 1/2 teaspoon of black pepper
- 4 ounces of goat cheese
- 1-2 tablespoons of chopped fresh parsley

Roasted Red Pepper Sauce:
- 4 oz of roasted red peppers (in water)
- 2 cloves garlic
- 2 tablespoons of organic olive oil
- ½ cup of water or chicken broth
- 1/2 cup of heavy cream

Directions
1. Pour the water or chicken broth into the Foodi.
2. Season the chicken thighs with salt and pepper and place them in the crisping. Insert it in the pot and secure the pressure lid.
3. Cook the seasoned thighs on high mode for five minutes.
4. Meanwhile, mix the roasted red peppers with olive oil and garlic cloves to your blender and puree. Add the heavy cream and blend again to make the sauce smooth.
5. Quick release the pressure and open the lid.
6. Pour the sauce over the chicken thighs and flip to coat well. Crumble the goat cheese over the thighs and close the crisping lid.
7. Set the Foodi to bake / roast mode, temperature to 350°F, and cook time to 12 minutes.
8. Garnish your roasted pepper chicken with fresh parsley and enjoy.

Barbeque Pulled Chicken

Preparation time: 5 minutes |Cook Time: 20minutes| Servings: 4
Ingredients:
- 1 (12-16 ounce) bottle of barbeque sauce
- 1 ½ pounds of chicken breasts

Directions:
1. Add a half cup of water and half of the barbecue sauce to the Foodi.
2. Place the chicken in the basket and fix it in the pot. Seal the pressure lid and cook on high mode for fifteen minutes.
3. Quick release the pressure and open the lid. Coat the chicken with the remaining barbecue sauce and close the crisping lid.
4. Broil your chicken breasts for 10 minutes and enjoy.

Air Fried Turkey Breast

Tasty turkey breast ever!
Preparation time: 10 minutes| Cook Time: 35 minutes| Servings: 6
Ingredients
- 1 (1 oz.) package of onion soup mix
- 1 (6 lb.) turkey breast
- 2 ribs celery, cut largely into chunks
- 1 onion, cut largely into chunks
- 1 cup of chicken broth
- 2 tablespoons of water
- 1 tablespoon of cornstarch

Directions
1. Pour the water, chicken broth, onion soup mix, onion chunks, and celery into the Foodi.
2. Place the chicken in the crisping basket and insert it in the pot.
3. Close the pressure lid and cook on high mode for twenty minutes.
4. Quick release the pressure and open the lid. Brush the chunks with oil and season with salt and pepper.
5. Close the crisping lid and set the Foodi to air crisp mode. Set the temperature to 400°F and cook time to fifteen minutes.
6. Once cooked, remove it from the basket. Mix water and cornstarch in a bowl. Pour the mixture into the Foodi and set it to sauté mode. Whisk for 2 -3 minutes or until it thickens.
7. Serve the gravy with the turkey.

Chicken with Cashew Cream and Naan

Preparation time: 25 minutes| Cook Time: 45 minutes| Servings: 4
Ingredients
- 1 1/2-2 lbs of chicken thighs, boneless skinless and cut into pieces
- 2 1/2 tablespoons of garlic (peeled, grated, and divided)
- 1 1/2 tablespoons of fresh ginger (peeled, grated and divided)
- 3 teaspoons of garam Masala, divided
- 1 1/2 tablespoons of sweet paprika
- 1 teaspoon of kosher salt, divided
- 2 tablespoons of avocado oil
- 5 tablespoons of unsalted butter, cold and divided
- 3 dried bay leaves
- 1 teaspoon of whole cumin seeds
- 1 large onion (peeled and finely diced)
- 1/2 teaspoon of turmeric
- 2 teaspoons of paprika
- 2 tablespoons of apple cider vinegar treatment
- 1 can (14.5 oz.) of tomato sauce
- 3/4 cup of water
- 1 teaspoon of white granulated sugar
- 1 teaspoon of dried fenugreek leaves
- 1 package of frozen naan

For the Cashew Cream:
- 3/4 cup of whole raw cashews
- 4 tablespoons of heavy cream
- Hot water

Directions
1. First, season the chicken with paprika, a half tablespoon of ginger, one tablespoon of garlic, an

eighth teaspoon of salt, and two teaspoons of garam Masala.
2. Cover the chicken and allow it to rest for fifteen minutes or refrigerate for 8 hours.
3. *For the cashew cream:* Soak the raw cashes in hot water for fifteen minutes. Puree with a blender and add some water. Add the heavy cream and puree again.
4. Preheat the Foodi and add the oil. Melt the butter and sauté the chicken while stirring frequently until it browns.
5. Add cumin, the remaining garlic, ginger, onions, and bay leaves to the browned chicken.
6. Sauté to soften the onions and add turmeric and paprika, cook for two minutes.
7. Add the apple cider vinegar and stir. Cook until it begins evaporating.
8. Add tomato sauce, sugar, one teaspoon of garam Masala, and the remaining salt.
9. Stir and let it boil. Return the chicken into the Foodi and add three-quarter cup of water. Stir.
5. Secure the pressure lid and cook the chicken for ten minutes. Release the pressure naturally for 10 minutes before performing a quick release.
6. Add the cashew cream and fenugreek leaves. Add the remaining butter and stir to melt.
7. Fix the rack in the Foodi and place naan on it. Close the crisping lid and broil 2 minutes.
8. Serve your chicken and toasted naan garnished with extra fenugreek leaves

Chicken and Brown Rice

Preparation time: 10 minutes| Cook Time: 30 minutes| Servings: 8
Ingredients
- 1 medium onion, diced
- 3 garlic cloves, minced
- 2 cups of carrots, baby
- 2 cups of Crimini mushrooms, chopped
- 2 cups of brown raw rice
- 1 tablespoon of organic olive oil
- 2 1/4 cups of low-sodium chicken broth
- 2 pounds of chicken thighs, boneless and skinless
- 1/8 teaspoon of ground black pepper
- 1/8 teaspoon of salt
- 1 can (10.75 oz.) of chicken cream soup, canned and condensed
- 2 tablespoons of Worcestershire sauce
- 1 tablespoon of fresh thyme

Directions
1. Preheat the Foodi unit. Add oil and sauté the onion. Turn off the sauté mode and rice, vegetables, garlic, and broth.
2. Add the chicken on to and sprinkle the mixture with salt and pepper.
3. Pour chicken soup and Worcestershire sauce over it and top with some thyme springs.
4. Close the pressure lid and cook the mixture on high mode for 25 minutes. Quick release the pressure and open the lid.
5. Remove the thyme sprigs, stir, and serve warm.

Peppered Chicken and Potatoes

Preparation time: 10 minutes| Cook Time: 15 minutes| Servings: 4
Ingredients
- 1½ pounds of boneless and skinless chicken thighs, trimmed
- 1 teaspoon of dried rosemary
- 1 teaspoon of smoked paprika
- ¾ teaspoon of salt, divided
- ¼ teaspoon of ground pepper
- 2 tablespoons of canola organic olive oil
- 2 garlic cloves, sliced
- 1 red bell pepper, sliced
- 1½ lb of baby potatoes, scrubbed
- ½ cup of chicken broth
- 2 teaspoons of vinegar, sherry, or red-wine
- 1 scallion, thinly sliced

Directions
1. Season the chicken with rosemary, paprika, pepper, and a half teaspoon of salt.
2. Sauté the chicken in oil until it browns and transfer it to a platter.
3. Add garlic and bell pepper to the Foodi and cook on sauté mode for two minutes.

BEEF/LAMB

Fall-Apart Pot Roast

Preparation time: 10 minutes |Cook Time: 20 minutes| Servings: 4

Ingredients
- 3 lbs of grass-fed chuck roast
- 1 medium onion, sliced
- 2 tablespoons of coconut oil
- 1 teaspoon of sea salt
- 2 cups of bone broth

Directions
1. Set your Food to sear/sauté mode and add oil.
2. Season both sides of the chunk roast with salt and pepper.
3. Add the roast to the pot and sauté it until it turns golden.
4. Add sea salt and top with onions. Add the bone broth and close the pressure lid.
5. Cook on high mode for 70 minutes.
6. Quick release the accumulated pressure and open the lid. Serve.

Beef Stroganoff with Egg Noodles

A one-pot meal of beef and mushrooms with egg noodles.

Preparation time: 20 minutes| Cook Time: 37 minutes |Servings: 6

Ingredients
- 2 tablespoons of canola oil
- 1/2 onion, diced
- 2 teaspoons of salt, divided
- 2 pounds of beef stew meat, cut into cubes
- 1 teaspoon of ground black pepper
- 3 garlic cloves, diced finely
- 1/2 teaspoon of dried thyme
- 3 cups of mushrooms, chopped
- 2 tablespoons of soy sauce
- 2 tablespoons of all-purpose flour
- 3 glasses of chicken broth
- 1 (16 ounce) package of egg noodles
- 3/4 cup of sour cream

Directions
1. Set your Foodi to sauté mode and add oil.
2. Heat for a minute and add onions and a half teaspoon of salt. Stir.
3. Cook for 3 to 4 minutes or until the onions begin to soften.
4. Season the beef with a teaspoon of salt and pepper and add it to the Foodi.
5. Cook for 2 minutes while stirring frequently until it browns evenly.
6. Add thyme and garlic. Cook for around thirty seconds.
7. Add soy sauce and mushrooms. Stir.
8. Combine the Foodi content with flour. Add the chicken broth and the remaining salt.
9. Close the pressure lid and cook on high mode for fifteen minutes. Quick release the pressure and open the lid.
10. Add the egg noodles and close the crisping lid.
11. Set the temperature to 360°F and set the Foodi to crisp mode for five minutes.
12. When cooking is complete, open the Foodi and add the sour cream. Stir and serve.

Beef Bourguignon

Preparation time: 30 minutes| Cook Time: 50 minutes |Servings: 6

Ingredients
- 11/2 - 2 lbs of beef chuck roast (cut into 3/4-inches cubes)
- 5 strips of bacon, diced
- 1 small onion, chopped
- 10 oz of cremini mushrooms, quartered
- 2 carrots, chopped
- 5 garlic cloves, minced
- 3 bay leaves
- 3/4 cup of dry dark wine
- 1 tablespoon of tomato paste
- 3/4 teaspoon of xantham gum
- 1 teaspoon of dried thyme
- Salt and pepper

Directions
1. Set the Foodi to sear/sauté mode on medium high.
2. Add the diced bacon and cook for five minutes while stirring frequently until it becomes crispy. Transfer everything into a platter.
3. Season the beef with salt and pepper. Brown them in the Foodi and transfer to another plate.
4. Add onions and garlic to the Foodi and sauté them while stirring frequently.
5. Add the dark wine and tomato paste. Stir and turn off the sauté mode.
6. Put the seasoned beef in the pot.
7. Add mushrooms, carrots, and thyme. Stir. Top with bay leaves.
8. Secure the pressure lid and cook on high mode for 40 minutes. Quick release the pressure and unsecure the lid.
9. Remove the bay leaves and sprinkle the mixture with xantham gum. Stir.
10. Boil for 1-2 minutes and stir to thicken.
11. Serve your beef topped with crispy bacon.

Ragù Bolognese

Tenderized meat, flavors, and powdered gelatin make this delightful dish more appealing!
Preparation time: 30minutes|Cook Time: 80minutes| Servings: 8

Ingredients
- 1 cup of low-sodium chicken stock
- 4 packets (1 oz) of powdered gelatin
- 2 tablespoons of extra-virgin organic olive oil
- 1/2 lb of pancetta, finely diced
- 1 large onion (about 1 1/2 cups), minced finely
- 2 large carrots, chopped (about 1 cup)
- 2 large stalks of celery, chopped (about 1 cup)
- 4 medium garlic cloves, minced
- 1/4 cup of fresh sage leaves, minced
- 1/2 cup of parsley leaves, minced and divided
- 1/2 pound of chicken livers, minced
- 2 pounds of ground beef chuck
- 1 pound of ground pork shoulder
- Kosher salt and freshly ground black pepper
- 1 (14-oz) can of crushed tomatoes
- 2 cups of dry red wine
- 1 1/2 cups of heavy cream, divided
- 2 bay leaves
- 3 oz of Parmesan cheese, finely grated
- 1 to 2 tablespoons of Thai fish sauce
- 1/4 cup of fresh basil leaves, minced

To Serve:
- 1 pound of dried penne, cooked
- Finely grated Parmesan cheese

Directions
1. Put the chicken stock in a bowl and sprinkle it with gelatin. Set aside.
2. Sauté the pancetta in extra virgin olive oil for ten minutes or until browned.
3. Add the onions, celery, carrots, sage, garlic, and half of the parsley.
4. Cook the spices until they soften.
5. Add the chicken livers and stir until the pinkness fades.
6. Add beef, pork, salt, and pepper. Cook for 10 minutes or until the beef's redness fades while stirring frequently.
7. Continue to cook-stir for around 25 minutes or until the excess fluid drains and the meat begins to sizzle.
8. Add wine, the reserved mixture, tomatoes, a cup of heavy cream, and the bay leaves. Turn off the sauté function.
9. Secure the pressure lid and cook the sautéed mixture on high mode for 35 minutes. Perform a quick release and open the lid. After that, simmer it on sauté mode to thicken.
10. Add the remaining parsley, half cup of the heavy cream, fish sauce, and basil.
11. Let it boil and season with salt and pepper.
12. Serve your ragu Bolognese alongside the cooked pasta and parmesan.

Air Fried Beef Satay

Preparation time: 35minutes| Cook Time: 8minutes| Serving: 2

Ingredients
- 1 lb of beef flank steak, sliced thinly
- 2 tablespoons of canola oil
- 1 tablespoon of fish sauce
- A tablespoon of soy sauce
- 1 tablespoon of minced ginger,
- A tablespoon of garlic, minced
- 1 teaspoon of Sriracha
- A tablespoon of sugar
- 1 teaspoon of ground coriander
- 1/2 cup of chopped cilantro, divided
- 1/4 cup of roasted peanuts, chopped

Directions
1. Get a Ziploc bag and stuff it with the beef strips, fish sauce, canola oil, ginger, garlic, cilantro(quarter cup,) coriander, Sriracha, soy sauce, and sugar. Toss.
2. Marinate in the refrigerator for at least 30 minutes.
3. Preheat the Foodi on Air Crisp Mode at 400°F.
4. Insert the basket in the multi-cooker and transfer the beef-strip mixture in it (side by side.) Cook for 8 minutes at 400°F (flip once, halfway.)
5. Ladle your air-fried beef into serving plates and top with the roasted peanuts and chopped cilantro.

Keto Indian Kheema

It's an easy meal to prepare and a kid-friendly recipe.
Preparation time: 15 minutes |Cook Time: 10 minutes |Servings: 4

Ingredients
- 1 cup of onions, chopped
- 1 tablespoon of ginger, minced
- 1 tablespoon of garlic
- 4 pods of cardamom pods
- 3 or 4 pieces of Indian cinnamon cassia bark
- 1 pound of lean ground beef
- 1 teaspoon of garam Masala
- A teaspoon of salt
- 1/2 teaspoon of turmeric

- 1/2 teaspoon of cayenne
- 1/2 teaspoon of ground cumin
- 1/2 teaspoon of ground coriander
- 1/4 cup of water

Directions
1. Set the Foodi unit to sear/sauté mode over medium-high temperatures. Let it preheat for 5 minutes.
2. Add your oil and heat. Add the cinnamon sticks and cardamom.
3. After 10 seconds, add the onions, garlic, and ginger. Cook for approximately 5 minutes.
4. Add the ground beef and sauté for some minutes while breaking the clumps.
5. Add the spices and water. Secure the pressure lid.
6. Cook for 5 minutes on high mode and release the in-built pressure naturally.

Un-Stuffed Beef and Cabbage

Preparation time: 5 minutes| Cook Time: 20 minutes| Servings 4

Ingredients
- 2 lbs of organic beef
- 1 cabbage head, chopped
- 1 whole yellow onion
- 2 tablespoons of Italian seasoning
- Salt and pepper
- 2 tablespoons of garlic, minced
- 1 14.5 oz of diced and canned tomatoes, juicy
- 1/2 cup of water
- Shredded cheese

Directions
1. Set the Foodi unit to sear/sauté mode over medium-high temperatures. Add the beef and brown it while breaking up large lumps.
2. Add the onions, seasoning, garlic, pepper, and salt. Cook while stirring for 5 minutes and turn off the sauté mode.
3. Add the chopped cabbage to the beef mixture. Add the canned tomatoes.
4. Secure the pressure lid and cook on high mode for 5 minutes.
5. Quick release the pressure and open the lid.
6. Add the shredded cheese and close the crisping lid. Air-fry it for 3 minutes at a temperature of 390°F.

Mississippi Pot Roast

A delicious dinner!
Preparation time: 20 minutes| Cook Time: 70 minutes| Servings 4

Ingredients
- 1 tablespoon of oil
- 2 lbs of chuck roast
- ½ teaspoon of black pepper
- 2 teaspoons of salt
- ¼ cup of unsalted butter
- 1 small yellow onion, chopped finely
- 1 teaspoon of garlic powder
- 1 teaspoon of onion powder
- ½ teaspoon of thyme, dried
- ½ teaspoon of parsley, dried
- 1½ cups of beef broth
- ½ cup of pepperoncini juice
- 10 pepperoncinis
- 2 bay leaves

Directions
1. Set your Foodi to sauté mode over medium high temperatures.
2. Add oil and heat. Sear the salt and pepper-season the chuck roast until brown on both sides. Set aside.
3. Melt the butter in the Foodi and add the onions. Sauté them until they turn translucent.
4. Add the onion powder, thyme, parsley, and garlic powder. Cook-stir the spices for three minutes and turn off the sauté mode.
5. Add the pepperoncini juice, pepperoncinis, beef broth, and bay leaves into the pot. Stir.
6. Secure the pressure lid and cook on high mode for one hour. Release the pressure naturally.
7. Remove the chuck roast and shred it with two forks. Serve alongside mashed potatoes.

Balsamic Roast Beef

This is a flavorful but an easy meal to prepare.
Preparation time: 45 minutes| Cook Time: 5 minutes| Servings: 6

Ingredients
- 1 (3 lb.) of boneless roast beef
- 1 cup of beef broth
- 1 tablespoon of Worcestershire sauce
- 1/2 cup of balsamic vinegar
- 1 tablespoon of honey
- A tablespoon of soy sauce
- 1/2 teaspoon of red pepper flakes
- 4 garlic cloves, chopped

Directions
1. Put the roast beef in the Foodi.
2. Combine the beef broth with Worcestershire sauce, balsamic vinegar, soy sauce, red pepper flakes, honey, and garlic in a bowl.
3. Secure the pressure lid and cook on high mode for 30 minutes. Release the pressure naturally for 15 minutes and open the lid. Remove the roast from the pot but reserve its gravy.
4. Serve your balsamic roast meat alongside its gravy.

Beef Brisket

Tender brisket done so quickly!
Preparation time: 15 minutes | Cook Time: 90 minutes | Servings: 6-8

Ingredients
- 2 1/2 - 3 1/2 pounds of beef brisket (rinsed, pat-dried, and trimmed)
- 1/2 teaspoon of ground black pepper
- 1 1/2 teaspoons of kosher salt, divided
- 1 tablespoon of extra virgin olive oil
- 3 large garlic cloves, peeled
- 3 medium yellow onions, sliced
- 1/2 cup of dry burgundy or merlot wine
- 1/2 cup of water
- 1/4 cup of ketchup
- A teaspoon of thyme leaves, dried
- 1 teaspoon of rosemary, dried
- A teaspoon of paprika

Directions
1. Season the beef brisket with ground pepper and a teaspoon of salt.
2. Put it in the Foodi. Sauté the beef until all its side browns and transfer it to a platter.
3. Add the onions, garlic, and the remaining salt. Cook-stir the spices until they soften.
4. Add water, wine, ketchup, and other spices into the pot. Stir well.
5. Return the seared brisket to the pot and lock the pressure lid.
6. Cook them on high mode for 50 minutes and release the accumulated pressure naturally.
7. Transfer the brisket to a bowl using tongs. Skim-off the top layer fat and puree the remaining mixture in an immersion blender.
8. Slice the brisket and pour the gravy over it. Serve hot.

Air fryer Lamb Chops

Preparation time: ten minutes | Cook Time: 20 minutes | Servings: 2

Ingredients
- 4 lamb chops
- 2 tablespoons of canola oil
- Garlic herb
- 1/2 tablespoons of finely chopped fresh oregano
- 1 garlic cloves
- Kosher salt

Directions
1. Preheat the Foodi unit on bake/roast at 350°F.
2. Coat the garlic clove with a half teaspoon of oil and place it in the crisping basket.
3. Meanwhile, combine the oregano with half teaspoon of canola oil, salt, and pepper.
4. Coat the lamb chops with the oregano mixture and leave it for 2-3 minutes.
5. Once the garlic bulb browns, remove it and preheat the unit on air crisp mode at 390°F.
6. Put the lamb chops into the basket and set it to 350°F. Air-fry the chops for 5-10 minutes or until they brown. Transfer to a dish.
7. Squeeze the garlic cloves into the remaining oil. Add salt and pepper. Stir well and serve the lamp chops with the garlic sauce.

Steak, Potatoes and Asparagus

Preparation time: 10 minutes | Cook Time: 10 minutes | Servings: 4

Ingredients
- 5 Russet potatoes (peeled and cut in ½" pieces)
- 1/2 cup of water
- 1/2 cup of heavy cream
- 1/4 cup of butter, divided
- 1 cup of cheddar cheese, shredded
- 3 teaspoons of ground black pepper, divided
- 1 tablespoon plus 2 teaspoons of kosher salt, divided
- 2 frozen New York strip steaks (12 oz. each, 1 1/2 inches thick)
- 1 trimmed asparagus
- 1 tablespoon of organic olive oil

Directions
1. Add potatoes and water to the Foodi.
2. Insert the reversible rack in the pot and add the frozen steak (previously seasoned salt and pepper.)
3. Secure the pressure lid and cook the steak strips on high mode for a minute.
4. Add asparagus, oil, a teaspoon of salt, and pepper. Cook the asparagus on high mode for another minute.
5. Quick release the accumulated vapor and open the lid. Remove the rack and transfer the steaks to a bowl. Pat-dry them.
6. Mash the potatoes and add a quarter cup of butter, cheese, cream, a teaspoon of salt, and pepper.
7. Return the dry steak to the Foodi and insert a rack containing asparagus into it.
8. Close the crisping lid and cook on broil mode for 8-12 minutes.
9. Leave the steak to dry for around five minutes and serve it alongside the mashed potatoes and baked asparagus.

Ropa Vieja

Preparation time: 10 minutes | Cook Time: 90 minutes | Servings: 10

Ingredients
- 1 (3 - 3 ½ lb) chuck roast
- 1 onion, sliced

- 4 teaspoons of garlic, minced
- 2 ½ teaspoons of oregano, dried
- 2 teaspoons of paprika
- 2 teaspoons of cumin
- 2 teaspoons of salt
- 1 teaspoon of smoked paprika
- ½ teaspoon of black pepper
- 1/3 teaspoon of ground cloves
- 1 (14.5 oz.) can of diced tomatoes
- 2 bay leaves
- 3 green, red, and yellow bell peppers (sliced)
- Green olives with pimentos

Directions
1. Add all the ingredients in your Foodi (except peppers and olives.)
2. Lock the pressure lid and cook the chunk mixture on high mode for 90 minutes.
3. Natural release the accumulated pressure and open the lid. Transfer the beef to a flat surface and shred it using two forks.
4. Set the Foodi to sear/sauté mode and add the peppers.
5. Simmer for 5minutes or until the pepper tenders.
6. Turn off the sauté mode and then add the green olives. Stir and serve.

Keto Chunky Chili

Preparation time:15 minutes| Cook Time: 30 minutes |Servings: 6
Ingredients
- 1¼ lbs of ground beef
- 1 tablespoon of essential olive oil
- ½ mid-sized yellow onion, chopped
- 2 garlic cloves, peeled and minced
- 2 teaspoons of cumin
- 1½ tablespoons of chili powder
- 1½ teaspoons of sea salt
- 1 teaspoons of garlic powder
- A teaspoon of smoked paprika
- ¼ teaspoon of coriander powder
- 1/8 teaspoon of red pepper cayenne
- 1 cup of beef broth
- 2/3 cup of water
- ¼ cup of canned pumpkin (unsweetened)
- 1 cup of canned diced tomatoes
- 2 tablespoons of tomato paste
- 1 cup of zucchini squash, diced
- 2/3 cup of cauliflower, finely chopped

Optional toppings:
- 2/3 cup of grated cheddar cheese,
- ½ avocado, chopped
- 3 tablespoons of sour cream, optional

Directions:
1. Set the Foodi to sauté mode. Preheat it for a minute and then add the organic olive oil and ground beef.
2. Sauté for 5minutes while splitting up the beef using a wooden spoon.
3. After browning the beef, add the chopped onions and the minced garlic.
4. Sauté until the garlic becomes translucent.
5. Add the remaining ingredients (except the toppings) and stir.
6. Close the pressure lid and cook them on high mode for 25 minutes.
7. Allow the pressure to exit naturally for 10 minutes and quick release the rest.
8. Open the lid and stir. Serve your Keto chunky chilli with the toppings.

Pot Roast

Preparation time: 15 minutes| Cook Time: 65 minutes |Servings: 4
Ingredients
- Kosher salt and pepper
- 3-3 1/2 pounds of boneless chuck roast
- 1/4 cup of flour
- 1 large onion (peeled and chopped)
- 1 tablespoon of essential olive oil
- 3 cloves garlic (peeled and smashed)
- 1 tablespoon of tomato paste
- 1 1/2 cups of beef broth
- 1/2 cup of dark wine
- A sprig of fresh thyme
- 1 bay leaf
- 4 carrots (peeled, cut in 2"pieces)
- 10 whole red baby potatoes
- 2 tablespoons of cornstarch
- 2 tablespoons of water
- Fresh parsley, for garnishing

Directions
1. Preheat your Foodi on sear/sauté mode.
2. Pat-dry the chuck roasts and season with salt and pepper.
3. Coat them with flour and sauté for 5 minutes or until they brown evenly.
4. Add garlic, onion, and tomato paste into the Foodi and cook for 2-3 minutes.
5. Add the broth, wine, carrots, potatoes, thyme, and bay leaves. Close the pressure lid and cook on high mode for 15 minutes.
6. Let the pressure escape naturally for10 minutes and open the lid.
7. Remove the roast and slice it. Transfer the sliced roasts, potatoes, and carrots to a plate. Discard bay leaf and thyme.
8. Mix cornstarch with water and pour the mixture into the Foodi. Simmer it on sauté mode for a minute or until it thicken.

9. Serve your roast and veggies topped with gravy and garnished with fresh parsley.

Beef and Egg Noodles

Preparation time: 15minutes| Cook Time: 45minutes| Servings: 4
Ingredients
- 3 lbs of beef chuck roast, cubed
- 2- 3 cups of water
- 4 cups of beef stock
- 1 1/2 lbs of Crimini mushrooms, quartered
- 1 medium onion (sliced and quartered)
- A dry onion soup mix
- 2 tablespoons of sunflower oil
- 2 garlic cloves, minced
- 2 tablespoons of soy sauce
- 1 teaspoon of marjoram, dried
- A teaspoon of Worcestershire sauce
- 1 teaspoon of garlic powder
- 1 teaspoon of onion powder
- 1/2 teaspoon of thyme
- A tablespoon of kitchen bouquet (optional)
- 1/4 cup of flour
- Salt and pepper

Directions
1. Sauté the beef cubes in sunflower oil for 15 minutes or until they brown.
2. Stir and add onions, spices, garlic, and the onion soup mix.
3. Add the mushrooms, Worcestershire, soy, and stock. Stir.
4. Add some water and lock the pressure lid. Cook the mixture on high mode for 45 minutes.
5. Release the pressure naturally and open the lid. Add flour and the kitchen browning sauce to thicken the gravy.
6. Add salt and pepper, if required. Serve your beef meal alongside egg noodles.

Corned Beef and Cabbage

Preparation time: 15 minutes| Cook Time: 95 minutes| Servings: 8
Ingredients
- 4 lbs of corned beef brisket
- 6 glasses of water
- 2 teaspoons of black peppercorns
- 4 garlic cloves
- 2 teaspoons of dried mustard
- 1 cabbage, cut into wedges
- A cup of carrots, sliced
- 1 cup of onions, sliced
- A cup of celery stalks, chopped

Directions
1. Put the beef brisket into the Foodi. Do not use the spice packet that comes with it.
2. Add water and spices. Stir.
3. Close the pressure lid and cook the spiced brisket on high mode for 60 minutes.
4. After cooking, allow the pressure to release naturally for 10 minutes before performing a quick release.
5. Open the lid and transfer the beef to a plate. Cover it with a foil.
6. Add the sliced carrots and cabbage to the Foodi. Secure the pressure lid.
7. Cook the cabbage mixture on high mode for 15 minutes and quick release the accumulated vapor.
8. Open the lid and add the brisket into the Foodi. Serve it topped with the fiber mustard.

Carbonnade

The tasty meal is perfect for special occasions.
Preparation time: 10minutes|Cook Time: 50minutes| Servings: 4
Ingredients:
- 2 tablespoons of butter
- 2 oz of beef chuck, cubed largely
- 1 onion, chopped finely
- A tablespoon of flour
- 1 cup of beer
- 1 gingerbread or bread slice
- A teaspoon of mustard
- 1 tablespoon of brown sugar

Directions
1. Brown the beef with one and half tablespoons of butter on both sides (on sauté mode.) Remove and set aside.
2. Sauté the onion in the remaining butter for 5 minutes while stirring frequently.
3. Add the browned meat, beer, and flour. Add the bread (spread with brown sugar) and mustard. Stir. Season the beef with salt and pepper.
4. Secure the pressure lid and cook on high mode for 35 minutes. Allow the in-built steam to escape naturally for 10 minutes and quick release the rest.
5. Subdivide your carbonnade between serving bowls and enjoy.

Cheese steak Casserole

Preparation time: 15 minutes |Cook Time: 25 minutes |Servings: 6-8
Ingredients
- 2 tablespoons of canola oil
- 1 large onion (peeled and sliced)
- 1 green bell pepper, sliced thinly
- 1 tablespoon of kosher salt
- 1 package (8 oz) of button mushrooms, sliced thinly
- 1 1/2 pounds of chuck roast or shaved steak (uncooked and thinly sliced)
- 2 teaspoons of garlic powder

- 1/2 teaspoon of ground black pepper
- 2 teaspoons of onion powder
- 1 teaspoon of Worcestershire sauce
- 3 sub rolls, cubed
- 10 slices of American cheese

Directions
1. Sauté the onion and pepper in canola oil for 5 minutes. Add salt and mushrooms. Cook them until the mushrooms tenderizes.
2. Add your steak or roast, the garlic powder, black pepper, and Worcestershire sauce.
3. Cook them for five minutes or until the steak softens.
4. Fold the cubed sub rolls and stuff them with the steak contents.
5. Spread the cheese evenly on the mixture and close the crisping lid.
6. Cook on bake/ roast mode for ten minutes at 375°F. Serve!

Keto Curried Beef

Preparation time: 10 minutes| Cook Time: 30 Minutes| Servings: 4

Ingredients
- 1 tablespoon of coconut oil
- 1.5 lbs of stew beef meat
- 1/2 medium white onion, diced
- 2 teaspoons of curry powder
- 3 teaspoons of minced garlic
- 1 teaspoon of cumin
- 1/2 teaspoon of chili powder
- A teaspoon of Pink Himalayan Salt
- 1 can of coconut milk, refrigerated
- 1/2 cup of Water

Directions
1. Put the coconut milk in the freezer for at least one hour.
2. Set your Foodi to sear/sauté mode and add a half tablespoon of coconut oil.
3. Add the beef and brown it lightly.
4. Add the remaining coconut oil and the diced onion. Cook until the onions become translucent.
5. Add garlic, cumin, curry powder, and chili powder. Stir and cook until they fragrant.
6. Return the stew meat in the Foodi and add some water.
7. Close the pressure lid and cook the beef mixture on high mode for ten minutes.
8. Quick release the accumulated vapor and open the lid.
9. Remove the coconut milk from the freezer and discard the floating liquid.
10. Add the hardened coconut milk to the beef mixture and stir.
11. Simmer the mixture on sauté mode for 10 minutes or until the milk melts and the curry sauce thicken. Enjoy!

Keto Steak Rolls and Asparagus

Preparation time: 5 minutes| Cook Time: 10 minutes |Servings: 4

Ingredients
- 1 yellow bell pepper
- 1 red bell pepper
- 1/2 cup of mushrooms, sliced
- Salt and pepper
- 1 garlic clove, minced
- A bunch of fresh asparagus
- 2 tablespoons of butter
- 1/2 cup of water
- 4 steak, thinly sliced

Directions
1. Season your steaks with salt and pepper. Lay them flat.
2. Add the sliced yellow pepper, red pepper, and some mushrooms.
3. Roll and secure them using a toothpick.
4. Add a cup of water to the Foodi pot. Add the asparagus, garlic, and butter.
5. Put the steak rolls on the reversible rack and fix it in the Foodi.
6. Secure the pressure lid and cook the rolls on high mode for 5 minutes.
7. Allow the pressure to exit naturally for 5 minutes and perform a quick release.

Tex-Mex Meatloaf

Preparation time: fifteen minutes| Cook Time: 30 minutes |Servings: 6

Ingredients
- 1 pound of uncooked ground beef
- 1 bell pepper, diced
- 1 egg
- 1/2 jalapeño pepper (deseeded and minced)
- 1 small onion (peeled and diced)
- 3 corn tortillas, chopped roughly
- 1 tablespoon of garlic powder
- 2 teaspoons of chili powder
- 2 teaspoons of ground cumin
- 1 teaspoon of cayenne pepper
- 2 teaspoons of kosher salt
- Barbecue sauce
- 1/4 cup of fresh cilantro leaves
- A cup of water
- 1 cup of corn chips, crushed

Directions
1. Combine all the ingredients (except the corn cheese and barbecue sauce) in a bowl. Transfer the mixture into a loaf pan of 8 ½" and cover with foil.

2. Pour water in the pot. Put the pan on a reversible rack and fix the rack in the Foodi.
3. Lock the pressure lid and cook the mixture on high mode for 15 minutes. Quick release the accumulated vapor and open the lid.
4. Remove the foil and close the crisping lid. Set your pot to bake/roast mode, temperature to 360°F, and timer to 15 minutes.
5. Meanwhile, mix two tablespoons of barbecue sauce with corn chips in a bowl.
6. Add the barbecue mixture to the pot on the eighth minute and close the lid. Let the mixture cook to completion. Transfer the meat loaf to a serving bowl and enjoy.

Beef Gyros

Preparation time: 15minutes| Cook Time: 30minutes|Servings: 4
Ingredients
- 2 pounds of beef chuck roast, thinly sliced
- ½ teaspoon of freshly ground black pepper
- ¾ teaspoon of salt
- 3 tablespoons of essential olive oil
- 2 teaspoons of oregano leaves, dried
- 2 teaspoons of garlic powder
- 2 tablespoons of freshly-squeezed lemon juice

For the Tzatziki Sauce:
- A garlic clove, minced finely
- 1 cup of plain Greek yogurt
- A tablespoon of fresh-squeezed lemon juice
- 1 tablespoon of essential olive oil
- A teaspoon of dried dill weed
- 1 teaspoon of red vinegar
- Salt and ground black pepper

Directions:
1. Combine all the ingredients of the Tzatziki sauce in a bowl and stir.
2. Refrigerate it until you are ready to serve.
3. Season the beef with salt and pepper. Add the seasoned beef to the Foodi followed by garlic powder, fresh lemon juice, oregano, extra virgin olive oil, pepper, and salt.
4. Pour a third cup of water and close the pressure lid.
5. Cook the beef mixture on high mode for 30 minutes. Let the pressure exit naturally for 15 minutes and quick release the rest.
6. Remove lid and add more seasonings, if necessary.
7. Serve the beef alongside warmed pita. Top it with the Tzatziki sauce, sliced tomatoes, lettuce, cucumbers, and onion.

Peppercinis Pot Roast

Preparation time:15 minutes |Cook Time: 90 minutes| Servings: 4-6
Ingredients
- (1) 3-4 lb roast
- 1 packet of ranch seasoning mix
- 1 stick (1/2 cup) of butter
- ½ jar of Peppercinis, juice inclusive
- ½ cup of water

Directions
1. Put the roast in the Foodi and sprinkle the ranch mix over it.
2. Add butter, peppercinis, and water.
3. Secure the pressure lid and cook on high mode for 90 minutes.
4. Quick release the in-built pressure and open the lid carefully. Shred your pot roast and serve!

Dinner of Beef Short Ribs

Appetizing!
Preparation time: 10minutes| Cook Time: 40minutes| Servings: 4
Ingredients:
- 1 teaspoon of onion salt
- A teaspoon of rosemary
- 1/2 teaspoon of paprika
- 1/2 teaspoon of sage
- 1/2 teaspoon of ground pepper
- 2 lbs of beef short rib
- 2 tablespoons of oil
- 1 (6oz) can of tomato paste
- 1/2 cup of balsamic vinegar
- 1/2 cup of water
- 2 tablespoons of Dijon mustard
- 1 tablespoon of hot chocolate mix, unsweetened
- 6 cloves garlic

Directions
1. Combine sage with rosemary, pepper, paprika, and onion salt in a bowl.
2. Rub the beef short ribs with the mixture. Sauté the ribs with oil and set aside.
3. Add water, tomato paste, balsamic, cocoa, Dijon mustard, and garlic in the Foodi and mix. Add the seasoned short ribs.
4. Secure the pressure lid and cook on high mode for 40 minutes.
5. Quick release the in-built pressure and open the lid.
6. Ladle sauce over the beef ribs and enjoy!

Balsamic Beef Pot Roast

Preparation time: 5 minutes| Cook Time: 25 minutes |Servings:10
Ingredients
- 3 lbs of boneless chuck roast, halved
- 1 tablespoon of kosher salt

- A teaspoon of black ground pepper
- 1 teaspoon of garlic powder
- 1/4 cup of balsamic vinegar
- 2 glasses of water
- 1/2 cup of onion, chopped
- 1/4 teaspoon of xantham gum
- *For garnishing*: Fresh parsley, chopped

Directions
1. Begin by seasoning the meat with garlic powder, salt, and pepper.
2. Preheat your Foodi on sauté mode for 2 minutes. Add the chunk roast and brown them.
3. Add the balsamic vinegar, onion, and a cup of water to the browned roasts.
4. Secure the pressure lid and cook your roast mixture on high mode for 40 minutes.
5. Let the accumulated steam escape naturally for 10 minutes and quick release the rest.
6. Open the pot and transfer the meat to a bowl.
7. Simmer the multi-cooker on sauté mode for 10 minutes or until the Foodi's liquid reduces. Add the xantham gum and return the meat to the pot. Stir.
8. Serve your balsamic beef garnished with chopped parsley. You can serve alongside cauliflower puree.

Shredded Beef Sloppy Joes

A perfect party dish!
Preparation time: 10minutes|Cook Time: 60minutes|Servings: 10

Ingredients
- 6 lbs of boneless chuck, cubed
- 1/2 cup of red chili sauce
- 1 tablespoon of garlic, minced
- 1/2 cup of water
- 2 tablespoons of olive oil
- 1 cup of barbecue sauce
- 1 onion, chopped

Directions
1. Put some oil in the Foodi and add the minced garlic. Sauté the garlic for 30 seconds.
2. Brown the meat and add the barbeque sauce, red chili sauce, onion, and water.
3. Close the pressure lid and cook on high mode for 50 minutes.
4. Quick release the in-built pressure and open the lid.
5. Transfer the beef to a cutting board and shred. Return it and add more barbecue sauce.
6. Serve alongside buns.

Beef and Old-School Calico Beans

Preparation time: 15minutes|Cook Time: 30minutes| Servings: 8

Ingredients

- A pound of ground beef
- 1 pound of bacon or bacon pieces
- 1 large can of pork and beans
- 1 large onion, chopped
- 2 cans (15 ½-oz) of kidney beans, drained
- 2 cans (15 ½- oz) of butter beans, drained
- 3 cups of stewed tomatoes
- ½ cup of sugar
- 1 cup of corn
- ¾ cup of brown sugar
- ½ cup of ketchup
- 1 teaspoon of mustard
- 3 tablespoons of cider vinegar
- A teaspoon of garlic, ground
- 1 tablespoon of water(for smoking)

Directions
1. Brown the bacon on sauté mode. Break it down to form drippings.
2. Add the hamburger and onions. Brown them until all the fats drains.
3. Combine all the ingredients (including the drippings) in the Foodi and pressure cook for 25 minutes.Enjoy.

Sticky St. Louis Ribs

Preparation time: 10minutes| Cook Time: 41minutes| Servings: 4

Ingredients
- 1/4 cup of barbecue spice rub
- 2 tablespoons of brown sugar
- 2 tablespoons of kosher salt
- 1 rack of uncooked St. Louis ribs (3 to three 1/2 lb)
- 1/2 cup of beer
- 1 cup of barbecue sauce

Directions
1. Cut the ribs into three and add them to a bowl. Add the spice rub, brown sugar, and salt.Stir.
2. Pour the beer into the Foodi pot and put your seasoned ribs into the basket.
3. Fix the basket in the pot and close the pressure lid. Cook your ribs on high mode for 20 minutes. Quick release the pressure and open the lid.
4. Close the crisping lid reset the Ninja unit to air crisp mode. Set the cooking temperatures to 400°F and time to 15 minutes.
5. Open the lid after 10minutes and brush the rib mixture with the BBQ sauce. Resume cooking. Cooking ends when the internal temperature drops to 185°F. Serve!

Beef Short Ribs and Vegetables

Preparation time: 15 minutes| Cook Time: 60 minutes |Servings: 4-6

Ingredients

- 6 uncooked beef short ribs (about 3 lb), bony but trimmed
- 2 teaspoons of black pepper, divided
- 2 teaspoons of kosher salt, divided
- 2 tablespoons of olive oil, divided
- 1 onion (peeled and chopped)
- 1/4 cup of beef broth
- 1/4 cup of Masala wine
- 2 tablespoons of brown sugar
- 2 tablespoons of fresh thyme, (minced and divided)
- 3 cloves garlic, (peeled and minced)
- 3 carrots (peeled and cut into 1" pieces)
- 3 parsnips (peeled and cut into 1" pieces)
- 1 cup of pearl onions
- 1/4 cup of fresh minced parsley

Directions

1. Begin by seasoning the short ribs with a teaspoon of salt and pepper. Allow it to sauté for 10 minutes or until both sides turns brown.
2. Add wine, onion, broth, garlic, brown sugar, a tablespoon of thyme, a half teaspoon of salt, and pepper.
3. Secure the pressure lid and cook the mixture on high mode for 40 minutes.
4. Halfway, open the lid and add carrots, pearl onions, parsnips, the remaining thyme, oil, salt, and pepper.
5. After pressure cooking, quick release the accumulated steam and open the lid.
6. Insert the crisping rack and put the vegetables in it. Close the crisping lid and bake at 350°F for fifteen minutes.
7. After that, transfer the baked veggies and ribs to a tray and cover to keep warm.
8. Sauté the remaining liquid for 5 minutes and pour it into another bowl.
9. Spoon off the fatty layer and add the parsley. Stir.
10. Serve your short ribs and veggies alongside the prepared sauce.

PORK

Keto Pulled Pork

Preparation time: 2 minutes| Cook Time: 70 minutes| Servings: 6

Ingredients
- lb of frozen boneless pork loin roast
- 1 cup of chicken bone broth
- 2 teaspoon of sea salt
- 1 teaspoon of smoked paprika
- 1 teaspoon of black pepper
- 1 teaspoon of garlic powder
- 1/2 teaspoon of red pepper flakes
- 3/4 cup of barbecue sauce, sugar-free

Directions
1. Add the pork roast, bone broth, and seasonings to the Foodi.
2. Close the pressure lid and cook the seasoned mixture on high mode for 120 minutes.
3. Quick release the accumulated steam and transfer the roast to a bowl. Shred it using two forks.
4. Sauté the cooking broth until it boils. Add the barbecue sauce and continue cooking for 5 minutes or until the soup reduces to half.
5. Add the shredded roast to the barbeque soup. Stir and sauté for 3 minutes. Enjoy.

BBQ Pork

Preparation time: 10 minutes |Cook time: 20 minutes| Servings: 4

Ingredients
- 3 lbs of baby back pork ribs
- 1 cup of chicken broth
- ½ cup of BBQ sauce
- 1 tablespoon of Worcestershire sauce
- 2 tablespoons of BBQ seasoning

Directions:
1. Clean the pork ribs and cut them into 4 pieces.
2. Add broth, barbeque seasoning, and Worcestershire sauce into the Foodi.
3. Stir and coat the ribs in it. Close the pressure lid and cook the coated pork on high mode for 15 minutes. Let the in-built pressure exit naturally.
4. Place the meat on a board and cut the pork parts into single ribs.
5. Fix the crisping rack in the Foodi and put the single ribs in it.
6. Pour the BBQ sauce over the ribs and broil them until they become crispy and sticky.

Country Style Ribs

Preparation time: ten minutes| Cook Time: 35 minutes |Servings: 5

Ingredients
- 2 lbs of country style pork ribs, boneless
- 1½ cup of beef broth

For the Dry Rub:
- 1 teaspoon of sea salt
- 1½ teaspoon of smoked paprika
- ½ teaspoon of freshly ground pepper
- 1½ teaspoons of onion powder
- 1 teaspoon of cumin
- 1 teaspoon of garlic powder
- A pinch of cayenne pepper

Barbecue Sauce:
- 1 cup of tomato sauce
- 1 tablespoon of apple cider vinegar
- 1½ tablespoons of butter
- ½ tablespoon of water
- ½ tablespoon of Worcestershire sauce
- 2 tablespoon of Erythritol granular sweetener
- 1 teaspoon of garlic powder
- ½ teaspoon of onion powder
- ½ teaspoon of sea salt

Directions:
1. Melt butter on a small sauce pan over medium heat. Add the barbeque sauce and stir. Set aside.
2. Put the beef broth into the Ninja Foodi pot and insert the reversible rack.
3. Mix well all the ingredients of the dry rub in a bowl and add the ribs.
4. Toss the ribs in the dry rub until they are fully coated. Put them in the aligned rack.
5. Pour half of the BBQ sauce over the ribs and close the pressure lid.
6. Cook the coated ribs on high mode for twenty minutes. Let the pressure escape naturally.
7. Close the crisping lid and set your Foodi to air crisp mode, temperature to 400°F, and cooking time to 15 minutes.
8. Open the lid after the sixth minute and brush the ribs with the remaining barbeque sauce.
9. Resume cooking for the remaining time and transfer the ribs to a serving bowl.

Jamaican Jerk Pork Roast

A quick dinner!
Preparation time: 10 minutes| Cook Time: 15 minutes |Servings:12

Ingredients
- 4 lbs of pork shoulder
- 1/4 cup of Jamaican Jerk spice blend
- A tablespoon of olive oil
- 1/2 cup of beef broth

Directions
1. Pour the beef broth into the pot. Coat the pork shoulder with the Jamaican Jerk spice and put it

in the basket. Insert the basket in the Foodi and secure the pressure lid.
2. Cook the spiced pork on high mode for 45 minutes.
3. Quick release the accumulated moisture and open the lid.
4. Brush the pork with olive oil and close the crisping lid.
5. Air-fry it for 15 minutes at a temperature of 375°F. Serve!

Pork and Pinto Bean Nachos

Preparation time: 15minutes| Cook Time: 40minutes| Servings: 10
Ingredients
- 3 lbs of the pork spare ribs, cut into 2-rib sections
- 1 package (4 oz) of beef jerky
- 4 cans (15 oz each) of Pinto beans, rinsed then drained
- 1 cup of onion, chopped
- 6 bacon strips (cooked and crumbled)
- 4 teaspoons of garlic, minced
- 1 teaspoon of red pepper flakes,
- 4 cups of beef broth, divided
- Tortilla chips

For the toppings (optional)
- Shredded cheddar cheese
- Thinly sliced green onions
- Sour cream
- Chopped tomatoes
- Pickled jalapeno slices

Directions
1. Grind the beef jerky using a processor.
2. Add the pork ribs, jerky, beans, onion, bacon strip, garlic, and red pepper flakes into the Foodi. Add the beef broth.
3. Lock the pressure lid and cook the pork ribs mixture on high mode for 40 minutes.
4. Release the accumulated vapor naturally for 10 minutes and quick release the rest.
5. Open the lid, remove the meat, discard all the bones, and shred the meat. Return the shredded meat to the Foodi and sauté for five minutes.
6. Pass the pork mixture through a strainer to squeeze the fluid.
7. Serve your pork and pinto beans nachos with chips and the desired toppings.

Crispy Pork Carnitas

Pressure- cooked and tender crispy carnitas prepared in less time.
Preparation time: 10 minutes| Cook Time: 45 minutes| Servings: 4
Ingredients
- 2 lbs of pork butt, chopped of 2" pieces
- 1/2 teaspoon of oregano
- 1 teaspoon of kosher salt
- 1/2 teaspoon of cumin
- 1 orange, halved
- 6 garlic cloves (peeled and crushed)
- 1 yellow onion (peeled and halved)
- 1/2 cup of chicken broth

Directions
1. Combine pork with cumin, salt, and oregano in the Ninja Foodi pot (ensuring that the seasonings cover the pork.)
2. Squeeze the orange juice over the pork and drop the squeezed orange in the pot.
3. Pour the chicken broth over the Foodi's content and add onion and garlic cloves.
4. Lock the pressure lid and cook the seasoned pork on high mode for 20 minutes.
5. Quick release the accumulated pressure and open the lid. Remove onions, garlic cloves, and the orange.
6. Set the Foodi to sauté mode and simmer the remaining contents on medium high for 10-15 minutes.
7. Secure the air crisp lid and broil the mixture for 8 minutes. Let it cool and serve with cilantro toppings.

Simple Pulled Pork

Preparation time: 10 minutes| Cook time: 75 minutes| Servings: 8
Ingredients
4 pounds of pork shoulder (boneless and halved)
1/2 cup of water
1 - 2 tablespoons of vegetable oil
2 cups of BBQ sauce, divided
Directions:
1. Preheat the unit on sauté mode add oil. Brown the meat.
2. Transfer the browned meat to an empty bowl.
3. Add water and one cup of the sauce to the Foodi pot.
4. Return the meat to the pot containing diluted sauce.
5. Lock the pressure lid and cook for 75 minutes. Quick release the pressure and open the lid.
6. Transfer the pork to a bowl and shred it using two forks.
7. Return the shredded meat to the pot and combine with the pork fluid and the remaining BBQ sauce. Simmer everything on sauté mode. Stir and serve.

Pork Chops with Potato Purée and Gravy

Preparation time: 15minutes| Cook Time: 20minutes|Servings: 3
Ingredients

- 3 tablespoons of essential olive oil
- 2 sprigs thyme (leaves removed and chopped)
- 2 rosemary sprigs (leaves removed and chopped)
- 3 pork chops, cut thickly
- 1 cup of baby Bella mushrooms, chopped
- 4 garlic cloves, minced
- 1 tablespoon of liquid aminos
- 1 cup of chicken broth
- A large sweet potato, chopped
- A teaspoon of cornstarch

Directions
1. Preheat the Foodi on sauté mode. Add 2 tablespoons of olive oil.
2. Add rosemary and thyme. Sear the pork chops until they brown lightly. Set aside.
3. Add mushrooms and garlic to the pot and cook until they tender.
4. Add chicken broth and the liquid aminos.
5. Add the browned chops and insert the reversible rack.
6. Put the sweet potatoes in the cake pan and place it on the rack.
7. Brush the sweet potatoes with a tablespoon of organic olive oil.
8. Close the pressure lid and cook the brushed sweet potatoes on high mode for 10 minutes.
9. Let the pressure escape naturally for 10 minutes and quick release the rest. Remove the rack.
10. Sprinkle cornstarch over the mushroom mixture and stir until they thicken.
11. Add more cornstarches to make the sauce thicker, if desired.
12. Puree the mushroom sauce using an immersion blender and ladle it into a spout.
13. Smash the sweet potatoes.
14. Put the pork chops in a platter and set the smashed sweet potatoes beside them.
15. You can also pour the gravy over the cooked pork chops.

Chipotle Pulled Pork

Preparation time: 5 minutes| Cook time: 45 minutes| Servings: 10

Ingredients
- 12 oz of BBQ sauce
- 4 pounds of pork loin (boneless and quartered)
- 1-2 chipotle peppers in adobo sauce, minced
- 1/2 teaspoon of black pepper
- 1 teaspoon of kosher salt

Directions:
1. Season the pork with pepper and salt. Put the seasoned pork in the pot.
2. Add the chipotle peppers and drizzle the sauce over it.
3. Close the pressure lid and cook for 45 minutes.
4. Release the accumulated vapor naturally for 15 minutes and quick release the rest.
5. Transfer the cooked meat into a bowl and shred with two forks.

Smothered Pork Chops

Preparation time:15minutes| Cook Time:35minutes|Servings: 4

Ingredients
- 4 (4-6 oz) boneless pork loin chops
- 1 teaspoon of garlic powder
- 1 tablespoon of paprika
- 1 teaspoon of onion powder
- 1 teaspoon of salt
- 1 teaspoon of black pepper
- ¼ teaspoon of red pepper cayenne
- ½ medium onion, sliced
- 2 tablespoons of coconut oil
- 6 oz of baby Bella mushrooms, sliced
- 1 tablespoon of butter
- ¼ teaspoon of xantham gum
- ½ cup of almond milk
- 1 tablespoon of fresh parsley, chopped

Directions
1. Combine the garlic powder with paprika, cayenne pepper, black pepper, salt, and onion powder in a bowl.
2. Rinse the pork chops and pat dry them. Sprinkle the chops with a teaspoon of the mixture. Reserve the remaining spice mix.
3. Set your Foodi to sauté mode and preheat it for three minutes.
4. Add the coconut oil and heat it. Add the spiced pork and brown it. Transfer it to a plate.
5. Add the sliced onions, mushrooms, a cup of broth, and the browned pork chops.
6. Close the pressure lid and cook the mixture for 25 minutes.
7. Quick release the accumulated steam and transfer the pork to a plate.
8. Put the remaining spice mix, almond milk, and butter to the pot.
9. Sauté the mixture and add the xantham gum. Let it simmer for 5 minutes or until the butter melts and the gravy thicken.
10. Serve the pot chops topped with onions and mushroom gravy.

Smoky White Beans and Ham

Prep: 15 minutes| Cook: 30 minutes | servings: 10

Ingredients

- 1 lb of dried great northern beans (rinsed and sorted)
- 3 smoked ham hocks (1-1/2 lbs)
- 3 cans (14-1/2 oz each) of chicken or beef broth (reduced-sodium)
- 2 cups of water
- 1 large onion, chopped
- 1 tablespoon of garlic powder
- A tablespoon of onion powder
- 2 teaspoons of pepper
- Thinly sliced green onions, optional

Directions
1. Put the beans into the Foodi. Add the ham hocks and water, broth, onion, and seasonings.
2. Close the pressure lid and cook the beans' mixture on high mode for 30 minutes.
3. Natural release the accumulated steam for 10 minutes and quick release the rest.
4. Let the beans' mixture cool and detach the remove the flesh from the ham hock bones.
5. Cut the ham into pieces and return them to the Foodi. Sauté for two minutes and serve while sprinkled with green onions.

Carnitas

Prep: 10 minutes| Cook: 75 minutes |Servings: 4
Ingredients
- 2½-3 pounds of pork shoulder, boneless
- 1 tablespoon of ghee
- 1 tablespoon of Mexican seasoning
- 1 lemon, juiced
- 2 oranges, juiced
- Freshly ground black pepper
- ¾ teaspoon of sea salt

Directions:
1. Cut the pork shoulder into two-inch chunks and put them in the Crisping basket.
2. Add the seasoning, juices, pepper, salt, and a cup of water to the Foodi.
3. Fix the basket in the Foodi pot and close the pressure lid.
4. Cook the basket contents on high mode for 50 minutes. Allow the accumulated vapor to escape naturally.
5. Shred the pork using two forks. Coat the pork shreds with ghee and brush them with butter. Close the crisping lid and air-fry the pork at 390°F for fifteen minutes.
6. Remove your crisped pork from the basket and juices from the pot. You can serve the carnitas with rice and avocado.

Apples Pork Chops

Preparation time: 10minutes| Cook Time: 12minutes| Servings: 4
Ingredients
- 4 (¾-inch) thick-cut pork chops
- 1 teaspoon of salt
- 1 teaspoon of cumin seeds
- 1 teaspoon of ground black pepper
- 4 apples (peeled, cored, and sliced)
- 1 tablespoon of vegetable oil
- ¾ cup of pork stock

Directions
1. Sprinkle the pork chops with salt, pepper, and cumin. Brown the chops on sauté mode in vegetable oil. Transfer the browned chops to a platter.
2. Add apple slices to the empty pot and arrange the chops overlapping with the apples (brown-sides up).
3. Pour the stock around the edges of the pork.
4. Cook the treated pork on pressure mode for 8 minutes.
5. Quick release the accumulated steam and transfer the pork chops to your serving platter. Serve with applesauce.

Pulled Pork with Crispy Biscuits

Preparation time: 10minutes| Cook Time: 55minutes| Servings: 6
Ingredients
- 2 1/2-3 pounds of boneless pork shoulder (uncooked, trimmed, and cubed)
- 3 tablespoons of BBQ seasoning
- 2 teaspoons of kosher salt
- 1 tablespoon of garlic powder
- 1 cup of apple cider vinegar
- 1 can (6 oz) of tomato paste
- A tube (16.3 oz) of biscuit dough, chilled

Directions
1. Add all the ingredients (except tomato paste and biscuit dough) to the Foodi pot.
2. Cook on pressure mode for 35 minutes and quick release the accumulated steam.
3. Open the lid and set the Foodi to sear/sauté mode.
4. Add the tomato paste and simmer for 10 minutes while stirring frequently. This will shred the pork.
5. Half the biscuits and place the hamburger bun-like biscuit halves on the pork.
6. Close the crisping lid and bake at 350°F for 10 minutes. Serve.

Kalua Pork with Green Cabbage

Preparation time:10minutes|Cook Time:95 minutes| Servings: 8
Ingredients
- 5 pounds of pork butt (bone out and cut largely)
- 1 tablespoon of Hawaiian Sea Salt

- 1 teaspoon of smoked paprika
- 1 cup of water
- 1 head of green cabbage (sliced)

Directions
1. Combine the smoked paprika and salt in a bowl. Rub the pork on the mixture to coat.
2. Add water to the Ninja Foodi pot and put the pork in the basket.
3. Secure the pressure lid and cook the coated pork on high mode for 60 minutes.
4. Quick release the in-built pressure and open the lid.
5. Remove the basket using the roast lifters. Add the sliced cabbage to it and stir.
6. Return the basket into the Foodi and brush the pork with oil.
7. Close the crisping lid and air-fry it at 390°F for 15 minutes.
8. Remove the pork and the cabbages from the pot. Serve with brown rice.

Juicy Kalua Pork

Preparation time: 10 minutes| Cook time: 90 minutes| Servings: 8

Ingredients
- 4 pounds of pork shoulder roast, halved
- ½ cup of water
- 2 teaspoons of coarse kosher salt
- 1-2 tablespoons of oil
- 1 tablespoon of water

Directions:
1. Set your Ninja Foodi to sauté mode. After 5 minutes, add oil and heat. Brown the pork by sautéing and transfer it to a dish.
2. Turn off the sauté function and add water. Return the meat to the pot and season it with salt.
3. Cook the sautéed pork on high mode for 90 minutes.
4. Release the pressure naturally for 20 minutes and quick release the rest.
5. Transfer the pork to a bowl and shred it using two forks.
6. Remove all the visible fats from the pork and mix it with the Foodi's fluid.

Pork Loin, Stuffing, and Gravy

Preparation time: 10 minutes |Cook time: 75 minutes| Servings: 6

Ingredients
- 4 tablespoons of butter, divided
- 24 oz of pork loin (pre-seasoned)
- 1 medium onion, diced
- 6 oz stove top
- 2 1/4 cups of chicken broth
- 2 tablespoons of all-purpose flour

Directions
1. Preheat the Ninja unit on sauté mode. Melt half of the butter and add the pork loin. Sauté the pork for 4 minutes. Add the onions and cook for another 4 minutes.
2. Add the chicken broth and secure the pressure lid. Cook the mixture on high mode for 35 minutes. Let the pressure release naturally and open the lid.
3. Place the pork loin onto a cutting board. Set aside two cups of the cooking liquid.
4. Add the liquid into the Foodi and close the pressure lid. Let it sit for 5 minutes and transfer to a bowl. Cover the bowl.
5. Add the remaining butter and sauté. Once melted, add the flour and whisk for 45 seconds. Add the reserved cooking broth and stir.
6. Let it cook for two minutes or until it thickens. Add salt and pepper.
7. Cut the pork loin and serve with gravy and stuffing.

Ham and Greens

Preparation time:10minutes|Cook Time:10 minutes| Servings: 4

Ingredients
- 8 cups of collard greens, torn in pieces
- 2 cups of cooked ham, chopped
- ¼ cup of stock
- 6 garlic cloves
- 2 bay leaves
- 1 large onion, chopped
- A teaspoon of pepper
- 1 teaspoon of dried thyme
- A tablespoon of apple cider vinegar
- 1 teaspoon of hot sauce
- 1 teaspoon of red pepper flakes
- 1 teaspoon of water
- 1 teaspoon of salt

Directions:
1. Add together all the ingredients (except the hot sauce, vinegar, and water) in the Foodi.
2. Secure the pressure lid and cook the ham mixture on high mode for 4 minutes.
3. Natural release the pressure for 5 minutes and quick release the rest. Open the lid.
4. Add the sauce, water, and vinegar.Subdivide your ham and greens between four bowls and enjoy.

Pork Roast Bacon with Potato Bourbon Mash

Preparation time: 15 minutes| Cook Time: 60 minutes| Servings: 6-8

Ingredients
- 1/8 teaspoon of dried sage
- 1/2 teaspoon of kosher salt
- 1/8 teaspoon of white pepper

- 1/8 teaspoon of granulated garlic
- 1 pork loin roast, center-cut (2 1/2-3 lb)
- A tablespoon of organic olive oil
- 1/2 package (8 oz) of smoked pork bacon
- 3-4 sweet potatoes (peeled and halved lengthwise)
- 1/3 cup of heavy cream
- 1/2 cup of unfiltered apple cider
- 1/3 cup of high-vanilla bourbon
- 1/4 cup of molasses
- 1/4 cup of darkish sugar
- 3 dashes of hot pepper sauce
- Freshly grated nutmeg
- fleur de sel

Directions
1. Combine sage with pepper, garlic, and salt in a bowl. Set aside.
2. Pat-dry the pork loins and brush them with olive oil.
3. Season the brushed pork with the spice mixture.
4. Wrap the bacon around it. Let each bacon overlap with the pork roast until they cover the pork fully.
5. Place the wrapped roast and sweet potatoes on the reversible rack. Pour the apple cider over them.
6. Fix the rack containing the sweet potatoes in the pot and close the pressure lid.
7. Cook them on high mode for 35 minutes and let the pressure escape naturally for 5 minutes before quick releasing the rest.
8. Open the lid and remove the rack. Discard the cooking liquid, leaving a little.
9. Add bourbon, cream, hot sauce, molasses, and brown sugar. Stir.
10. Sauté and cook 5 minutes while stirring frequently.
11. Return the rack containing the sweet potatoes and close the crisping lid.
12. Broil for 6 minutes and open. Let them cool for ten minutes before slicing thickly.
13. Sprinkle with fleur de sel and bourbon mash. Enjoy.

Slow- Cooked Pulled Pork Apple Sliders

Preparation time: 10 minutes| Cook Time: 6 hours| Servings: 6

Ingredients
- 1 pork shoulder roast (3- 4 lb), boneless
- Salt and ground black pepper
- 1/4 cup of spicy brown mustard
- 2 teaspoons of paprika
- 1/4 cup of packed brown sugar
- 3 garlic cloves, minced
- 1 cup of apple juice or apple cider
- 12 mini sandwich buns or 1 package (15 oz) slider

Directions
1. Season the pork with paprika, salt, and black pepper.
2. Put the mustard, garlic, cider, and brown sugar into the pot and stir. Add the seasoned pork and coat with the mustard mixture.
3. Close the pressure lid and cook the coated pork on slow cook mode for 6 hours. Quick release the in-built pressure and open the lid.
4. Shred the cooked pork and spread mustard on the sandwich buns. Subdivide the pork between the buns.

Low-Carb Mexican Pulled Pork

Preparation time: 5 minutes| Cook time: 30 minutes |Servings: 5

Ingredients
- 3-4 pounds of pork roast (boneless, trimmed, and cut)
- 1 cup of orange juice
- ¼ cup of lime juice
- 1/3 cup of taco seasoning
- ½ cup of chicken stock

Directions:
1. Rub the pork roast with the seasoning.
2. Transfer it into the crisping basket.
3. Put the remaining ingredients into the Foodi and stir. Insert the basket into the pot and lock the pressure lid.
4. Cook the pork mixture on high mode for 30 minutes.
5. Let the accumulated vapor escape naturally for 10 minutes and quick release the rest.
6. Close the crisping lid and air-fry the pork at 390°F for ten minutes.

Pepper Jack Pork Chops

Preparation time: 10minutes| Cook time: 12 minutes| Servings: 4

Ingredients
- 6-8 boneless pork Chops
- 2-3 tablespoons of canola oil
- 2 teaspoons of cumin
- 1 teaspoon of onion powder
- 1 teaspoon of garlic powder
- Salt and pepper
- 12 oz of green beans, frozen
- 8 oz of fresh mushrooms, sliced
- 1 bell pepper, sliced thickly
- 1 cup of broth
- 12 slices of pepper jack cheese-toppings

Directions
1. Preheat your Foodi on sear/sauté mode over medium high.

2. Mix cumin with onion powder, garlic powder, salt, and pepper in a Ziploc bag. Toss to coat.
3. Brown the chops in the preheated pot. Add broth and the remaining vegetables and seal the pressure lid.
4. Cook everything on high mode for 10 minutes. Quick release the in-built steam and open the lid.
5. Serve while topped with pepper jack cheese slices.

Puerto Rican Pork Roast

Preparation time: 10minutes| Cook Time: 70minutes|Servings: 6-8

Ingredients
- 4-6 lbs of boneless pork shoulder, cut into 4" chunks
- 3 tablespoons of adobo seasoning
- 2 teaspoons of salt
- 2 tablespoons of garlic powder
- 2 teaspoons of dried basil
- ½ teaspoon of pepper
- ½ teaspoon of cumin
- ½ teaspoon of sage
- ½ teaspoon of turmeric (optional)
- ½ teaspoon of oregano
- 1 bay leaf
- A cup of broth

Directions
1. Combine all the spices (except the bay leaf) in a large bowl. Stir.
2. Coat the pork shoulders with the spice mix.
3. Put the seasoned pork and bay leaf into the Foodi pot.
4. Cover the bay leaf with the broth and close the pressure lid.
5. Cook everything on high mode for 70 minutes and release the in-built pressure naturally.
6. Shred your pork roast and serve.

BBQ Pork Chops

Preparation time: 10 minutes| Cook Time: 15 minutes |Servings:3

Ingredients
- 13 oz (6 small pieces) of fresh pork loin, boneless
- 8 fl oz of barbecue sauce
- 10 onion rings, raw
- 1 tablespoon of organic olive oil
- 2 tablespoons of mozzarella, grated
- 1 teaspoon of garlic powder

Directions
1. Preheat your Ninja Foodi on sear mode over medium-high heat for two minutes.
2. Add the organic olive oil followed by onions and fry until golden.
3. Add the meat and sprinkle it with cheese and garlic powder.
4. Smear the BBQ sauce and turn off the sauté function.
5. Close the crisping lid and air-fry the mixture over 400°F and for 15 minutes. Serve your BBQ pork chops with your favorite main dish.

Braised Pork Belly with Potato and Eggs

Preparation time: 30minutes| Cook Time: 60minutes| Servings: 6

Ingredients:
- 2 lbs of pork belly
- 1 teaspoon of five-spice powder
- 2 glasses of water

Aromatics:
- 1 medium cinnamon stick
- 5 garlic cloves
- 1 star anise

Seasonings:
- 2 tablespoons of dark soy sauce
- 1/3 cup of soy sauce
- 1/3 cup of Chinese rock sugar
- 1/4 teaspoon of white pepper
- 4 hard-boiled eggs
- Potatoes, quartered
- Cilantro leaves, for garnish

Directions
1. Rub the pork belly with the five-spice powder and reserve for 30 minutes.
2. Sear the meat in 1 tablespoon of olive oil until it browns.
3. Add water, seasonings, and aromatics ingredients.Cook the mixture on high mode for 45 minutes.Quick release the accumulated steam
4. Transfer the pork belly onto a chopping board and let it cool. Slice it into smaller pieces. Add potatoes into the remaining cooking liquid and close the pressure lid.
5. Cook on high mode for10 minutes. Quick release the accumulated vapor and add the hard-boiled eggs. Sauté them for 60 minutes or until they turn golden brown.
6. Serve your sliced pork belly with potatoes and hard-boiled eggs. Top the delicacy with the braising liquid and garnish with fresh cilantro leaves.

Bacon Pulled Pork

Preparation time: 5 minutes |Cook time: 30 minutes| Servings: 4

Ingredients
- 2 lbs of pork shoulder
- 1 cup of root beer
- 3-4 raw bacon slices
- 1 cup of BBQ sauce

Directions:
1. Add the pork shoulder into the Foodi's basket and arrange the bacon slices on them
2. Pour the root beer into the pot and insert the basket.

3. Close the pressure lid and cook for 90 minutes. Natural release the in-built vapor and open the lid.
4. Pat the dry meat and coat it with BBQ sauce. Close the crisping lid and air-fry it at 400°F for 15 minutes. Serve your bacon pulled meat with a hamburger bun.

Pork Loin with Vegetables

Preparation time: 15minutes| Cook Time: 40minutes| Servings: 2
Ingredients
- 1 medium zucchini (cut in pieces)
- 1 medium yellow squash (cut in pieces)
- 1 red onion (peeled and cut into 8 pieces)
- 3 teaspoons of kosher salt, divided
- 2 teaspoons of fresh oregano, chopped
- 3 teaspoons of ground black pepper, divided
- A tablespoon of canola oil
- 1 (24 oz) uncooked pork loin roast

Directions:
1. Combine squash with zucchini, onions, and a teaspoon of pepper in a bowl. Add oregano, salt, and canola oil. Toss well.
2. Season the pork loin with the remaining salt and pepper.
3. Place a crisper plate on a basket and insert it in the Foodi. Preheat on air crisp Mode at 325°F for 3 minutes.
4. Add the vegetables into the plate and top it with pork (fat-side down.)
5. Air Fry at 325°F for 40 minutes. Remember to remove the basket and flip its contents on the tenth minute. Resume cooking until the time elapses. Enjoy.

Boneless Pork Chops
Preparation time: 10 minutes| Cook Time: 20minutes|Servings: 4-6
Ingredients
- 1 tablespoon of coconut oil
- 4 boneless pork chops
- A packet of ranch mix
- 1 stick of butter
- 1 cup of water

Directions
1. Pour a half cup of water into the Ninja Foodi. Put the pork chops in the basket. Top it with and sprinkle the ranch mix over it. Fix the basket in the pot and close the pressure lid.
2. Cook the mixture on high mode for 5 minutes and quick release the accumulated moisture.
3. Open the lid and brush the pork chops with oil. Close the crisping lid and air-fry the chops for at 390°F for 15 minutes or until it attain the desired crispness.
4. Remember to toss the chops at the eighth minute as they crisp. Serve with veggies.

Chinese Pork with Ginger Coconut Potatoes

Preparation time: 15 minutes| Cook Time: 20minutes|Servings: 4
Ingredients
- 3 sweet potatoes (peeled and cubed)
- 1/2 cup of coconut milk, unsweetened
- 4 frozen boneless pork chops (8 oz. each), uncooked
- 1/4 cup of hoisin sauce
- 1 1/2 tablespoons of soy sauce
- 1/3 cup of honey
- 1 teaspoon of Chinese five spice powder
- 1/4 cup (1/2 stick) of butter
- 1 tablespoon of fresh ginger (peeled and minced)
- 1/2 teaspoon of white pepper
- A teaspoon of kosher salt

Directions
1. Add coconut milk and potatoes to the Foodi. Fix the rack and put the pork chops on it. Seal the pressure lid and cook on high mode for four minutes.
2. Meanwhile, combine honey with hoisin sauce, Chinese five spice powder, and soy sauce in a bowl.
3. Quick the accumulated steam and unsecure the lid. Also, remove the rack from the pot. Mash potatoes with butter, salt, and ginger.
4. Return the rack to the Foodi and brush the pork with half of the sauce mixture.
5. Close the crisping lid and broil for 15 minutes. Open the lid after 5 minutes to flip the chops and brush them with the remaining sauce.
6. Resume cooking until you get the desired doneness. Let the pork rest for 5 minutes and then serve with mashed potatoes.

Pork and Fennel Sausage Risotto

Preparation time: 10minutes| Cook Time: 30minutes| Servings: 4
Ingredients
- 6 pork and fennel sausages
- 1 tablespoon of olive oil
- 1½ teaspoons of butter
- 1 medium brown onion, finely chopped
- 1 garlic clove, crushed
- 1 medium fennel bulb (trimmed and chopped finely)
- 1½ cups of Arborio rice
- 3 ½cups of chicken stock
- ½ cup of dry white wine
- 2 cups of water
- ½ cup of frozen peas
- ½ cup of cheese, finely grated
- 2 teaspoons of fresh thyme, finely chopped

Directions

1. Sauté the sausages for ten minutes and transfer them to a bowl. Slice thinly.
2. Add oil and butter into the Foodi.
3. Sauté the onion, fennel, and garlic on low heat while stirring frequently until they soften. Add the rice and stir to coat well.
4. Add wine and allow it to simmer before the liquid is absorbed. Add the water and stock.
5. Cook the ingredients on low mode for 15 minutes. Quick release the accumulated steam and open the lid.
6. Add sausages and peas and close the lid. Allow it rest for 5 minutes.
7. Open and add the grated cheese and thyme. Serve your risotto sprinkled with other cheese.

Sweet and Sour Pork

Preparation time: 15minutes| Cook Time: 15minutes| Servings: 4
Ingredients
- 1 pound of pork loin, cut
- ¼ cup of beef stock
- 2 tablespoons of honey
- 2 tablespoons of sweet chili sauce
- 2 tablespoons of soy sauce
- ¼ cup of water
- 2 tablespoons of cornstarch

Directions
1. Combine the beef stock with honey, soy sauce, and sweet chili sauce in the multi-cooker. Stir. Add the pork and stir again to coat.
2. Close the pressure lid and cook the honey mixture on high mode for 5 minutes. Allow the accumulated steam to escape naturally and open the lid.
3. Combine cornstarch with water in a small bowl and whisk to dissolve.
4. Pour the mixture into the Foodi pot and stir. Sauté them for five minutes or until they thicken.

Mexican- styled Pork Pozole

Preparation time: 15minutes| Cook Time: 45minutes| Servings: 6
Ingredients
- 2 lbs of boneless pork shoulder (cut into 2" pieces)
- Salt and black pepper, ground
- 1 tablespoon of olive oil
- A large sweet onion, sliced
- 1½ teaspoons of cumin
- 3 garlic cloves, sliced
- 1 teaspoon of oregano
- ½ teaspoon of smoked paprika
- 2 cups of chicken broth
- 1 (14½ oz) can of diced tomatoes
- 1 (15 oz) can of hominy (rinsed and drained)

Directions
1. Begin by seasoning the pork with salt and pepper. Sauté it for three minutes or until it browns. Transfer them to a bowl and set aside.
2. Add onions and let them soften. Add cumin, garlic, smoked paprika, and oregano. Cook until they fragrant.
3. Return the pork together with its soup into the Foodi and add the tomatoes, chicken broth, and hominy.
4. Close the pressure lid and cook the juicy pork on high mode for 35 minutes.
5. Let the accumulated pressure exit naturally for 10 minutes and quick release the rest.

Hot and Spicy Pork Shoulder

Preparation time: 25minutes|Cook Time: 45minutes| Servings: 10
Ingredients
For the pork:
- 5 garlic cloves, minced
- 2 tablespoons of honey
- A tablespoon of crushed red pepper or Korean Chile
- 1 teaspoon of ground black pepper
- 1 tablespoon of kosher salt
- 5 lbs of boneless pork shoulder, cut into pieces

Sauce:
- 1 tablespoon of peanut oil
- 4 garlic cloves, grated
- 2 tablespoons of grated fresh ginger herb
- ⅓ Cup of Korean Chile paste
- ¼ cup of soy sauce
- 2 tablespoons of mirin
- 2 tablespoons of ketchup
- 2 tablespoons of honey
- 1 teaspoon of Asian fish sauce
- A tablespoon of rice wine vinegar
- 1 teaspoon of sesame oil

Sesame pickled cucumbers:
- 4 cups of cucumbers, sliced
- 1½ tablespoons of rice vinegar
- 2 teaspoons of sesame oil
- 2 teaspoons of brown sugar
- ½ teaspoon of fine sea salt
- ¼ cup of red onion, thinly sliced
- 2 teaspoons of sesame seeds

Directions
1. Combine the brown sugar with garlic, Chile flakes, pepper, and salt. Rub the pork over the seasonings and reserve them for one hour.
2. Sear the pork until it browns. Add three-quarter cup of water and lock the pressure lid. Cook on high mode for 90 minutes.
3. Meanwhile, sauté the ginger and garlic in the peanut oil until the spices produce a sweet smell.
4. Add the remaining ingredients and simmer for ten minutes or until it thickens. Set aside.

5. After pork cooking time elapses, allow the pressure to escape naturally. Transfer your pork to a bowl, allow it to cool, and shred.
6. Remove the cooking liquid from pot and discard the top layer fat.
7. Combine the sesame cucumber ingredients (except the sesame seeds) on a bowl.
8. Toss repeatedly and add the reserved seeds. Stir.
9. Insert the rack in the Foodi and place the pork on it. Toss with sauce and two teaspoons of the cooking liquid.
10. Close the crisping lid and broil your pork for three minutes or until its top crisps. Serve your crisped pork with rice and cucumbers.

Stir-Fried Pork and Noodles

Preparation time: 15minutes| Cook Time: 15minutes|Servings: 4
Ingredients
- 2 teaspoons of canola oil
- 1/4 cup of fresh ginger herb (peeled and chopped roughly)
- 5 garlic cloves, peeled
- 3 tablespoons of soy sauce, low-sodium
- 3 tablespoons of dry sherry or rice wine
- A teaspoon of dark sesame oil
- 1/2 lb of lean pork loin, sliced thinly
- 1/2 lb of cooked angel hair pasta
- 1 green onion, sliced thinly
- Noodles

Directions
1. Pulse the oil, garlic, ginger, soy sauce, sesame oil, and sherry using a mixer.
2. Pour the puree in the Foodi and add the pork slices. Sauté the pork while stirring until it softens and the sauce thickens.
3. Boil the noodles following the package instructions.
4. Serve your air-fried pork with noodles, green onions, and warm pasta.

Mushroom Pork

Tender pork served with creamy sauce.
Preparation time: 5 minutes| Cook time: 5 minutes| Servings: 4
Ingredients
- 1 (13.75-oz) can of cream mushroom soup
- 2 pounds of pork
- ¾ cup of chicken broth
- Salt and Pepper

Directions:
1. Pour the chicken broth into pot and add the pork.
2. Season lightly with salt and pepper. Top with your pork with the mushroom soup.
3. Close the pressure lid and cook the seasoned pork on high mode for 15 minutes.
4. Quick release the accumulated steam and open the lid. Enjoy!

Pork Tenderloin with Gravy

Preparation time: 15minutes| Cook Time: 6minutes| Servings: 4
Ingredients
- 2-3 lbs of pork tenderloin, halved
- 1/2 teaspoon of kosher salt
- 1/2 teaspoon of garlic powder
- 1/4 teaspoon of ground ginger
- 1/4 teaspoon of black pepper
- 1/4 teaspoon of dried thyme
- A tablespoon of essential olive oil
- 2 tablespoons of fresh lemon juice
- 2 cups of chicken broth
- 1 tablespoon of low sodium soy sauce
- 3 tablespoons of cornstarch
- 3 tablespoons of cold water
- Salt and pepper

Directions
1. Mix the garlic powder with ginger, kosher salt, thyme, and pepper in a bowl.
2. Rub the pork tenderloins with the spice mix and sauté in oil to brown.
3. Remove the pork from the Foodi using tongs and place it on a cutting board.
4. Pour the chicken broth in the pot and scrape its base to remove stuck bits.
5. Add soy sauce and the freshly-squeezed lemon juice.
6. Insert the rack and place the pork pieces on it. Secure the pressure lid and cook on high mode for six minutes.
7. Let the pressure release naturally for 15 minutes and quick release the rest. Open the lid and transfer the pork into a platter. Mix cornstarch with water.
8. Sauté the cornstarch mixture while stirring repeatedly. Add salt and pepper. Serve your pork tenderloin with gravy and enjoy.

Hawaiian Pork Roast

Preparation time: 10minutes| Cook Time: 45minutes|Servings: 4
Ingredients
- 4 lbs of pork shoulder (cut into 2-2 ¼ inch cube)
- 2 banana leaves, pieces
- 1 cup of water
- A tablespoon of coarse alaea red Hawaiian sea salt

Directions:
1. Put the pork chunks in a bowl. Add water and sea salt. Marinate for thirty minutes.
2. Pour some water into the Foodi and place a banana leaf on its base.

3. Add the marinated meat and ensure that it's submerged partially in the cooking fluid. Cover the ingredients with a second banana leaf.
4. Close the pressure lid and cook the submerged meat on high meat for 45 minutes.
5. Let the accumulated vapor release naturally for 15 minutes and open the lid.
6. Discard the leaves and shred the pork using two forks.
7. Taste and add more seasoning, if necessary.

Very Tender Pork Roast

Preparation time: 15minutes| Cook Time: 3 hours| Servings: 4
Ingredients
- 3 lbs of pork roast, cut in the top
- 1 onion chopped
- 2 garlic cloves, minced
- 1 tablespoon of salt
- A tablespoon of cayenne
- 1 tablespoon of pepper
- 1 teaspoon of canola oil
- 2 packs of brown gravy mix
- 2 cups of water

Directions
1. Rub the pork roast with all the dry seasonings and stuff with half onion and garlic.
2. Preheat your Ninja Foodi on sauté mode over medium-high heat for two minutes.
3. Sear the pork roast at the top for three minutes and flip its bottom. Sear it also for three minutes. Sprinkle the pork with the remaining onions.
4. Mix two packets of brown gravy mix with water in a bowl and pour it over the roast.
5. Secure the pressure lid and cook the soaked pork on high mode for three hours.
6. Confirm that your pork is tender before transferring it to a serving bowl.

Chinese BBQ Pork with Ginger Almond Sweet Potatoes

Preparation time: 15 minutes| Cook Time: 14-19 minutes |Servings: 4
Ingredients
- 3 sweet potatoes (peeled and cubed)
- 1/2 cup of almond milk
- 4 (8 oz each) frozen boneless pork chops, uncooked
- 1/4 cup of hoisin sauce
- 2 tablespoons of soy sauce
- 1/3 cup of honey
- 1 teaspoon of Chinese five spice powder
- 1 tablespoon of fresh ginger (peeled and minced)
- 1/2 stick (1/4 cup) of butter
- 1 teaspoon of kosher salt
- 1/2 teaspoon of black pepper

Directions
1. Mix milk with potatoes in a Foodi. Insert the reversible rack and place the pork chops on it.
2. Cook the chops on high mode for 4 minutes and quick release the accumulated steam.
3. Meanwhile, combine the hoisin sauce with soy sauce, Chinese five spice powder, and honey in a bowl. Stir.
4. Remove your rack from the pot. Add ginger, butter, and salt into pot and mash the potatoes. Return the rack containing the pork into the pot.
5. Brush it with half of the sauce mixture and close the crisping lid. Broil for fifteen minutes.
6. Flip the pork chops after 5 minutes and brush it with the remaining sauce. Continue to cook until the time elapses and serve.

Air Fryer Pork Taquitos

Preparation time: 10 minutes| Cook Time: 10 minutes |Servings: 5
Ingredients
- 30 oz of cooked shredded pork tenderloin
- 2 1/2 cups of shredded mozzarella
- 10 small flour tortillas
- Juice from a lime
- Cooking spray

Directions
1. Preheat the unit on air crisp at 380°F.
2. Sprinkle the lime juice over the pork.
3. Place a damp paper towel over 5 tortillas and soften for around 10 seconds in the microwave. Repeat the procedure for the remaining 4.
4. Add 3 oz of pork and a quarter-cup cheese to one of the tortillas and roll up gently but tightly.
5. Do the same for the rest and grease a previously foiled pan.
6. Spray a coat of cooking spray evenly over the tortillas.
7. Place the pan on a rack and air-fry for 10 minutes or until they turn golden (flip on the fifth minute.)

FISH AND SEAFOOD

Indian Fish Curry

A mild coconut milk with curry that is quick and easy to produce.
Preparation time: 5 minutes| Cook Time: 10minutes| Servings: 4
Ingredients
- 2 tablespoons of coconut oil
- 10 curry leaves
- 1 cup of onion, chopped
- A tablespoon of ginger
- 1 tablespoon of garlic
- 1/2 jalapeno or Serrano chili pepper, sliced
- 1 cup of tomatoes, chopped
- A teaspoon of ground coriander
- 1/4 teaspoon of ground cumin
- 1/2 teaspoon of turmeric
- 1/2 teaspoon of black pepper
- 1 teaspoon of salt
- 2 tablespoons of water
- 1 cup (1/2 of 14 oz can) of canned coconut milk
- 1 1/2 lbs of fish fillets, cut into 2-inches pieces
- 1 teaspoon of lime juice

Directions
1. Warm up the coconut oil on sauté mode.
2. Add the curry leaves and stir for some seconds. Add the onions, garlic, ginger, and green chilies. Continue cooking until the onions are soft.
3. Add the tomatoes and sauté them until it starts to break.
4. Add cumin, coriander, turmeric, salt, and black pepper. Sauté for some seconds until it starts to burn.
5. Add water to deglaze and add the coconut milk.
6. Insert a reversible rack in the Foodi and put the fish cutlets in it. Close the pressure lid and steam the fish for 2 minutes.
7. Quick release the accumulated vapor and open the lid. Remove the rack containing fish and add lime juice to the curry mixture. Stir.
8. Transfer fish and its gravy into bowl and garnish with fresh tomato slices and chopped cilantro.

Shrimp Chicken Jambalaya

Preparation time: 10 minutes| Cook Time: 15minutes| Servings: 4-6
Ingredients
- 12 ounces of large shrimp (peeled and deveined)
- 2 skinless and boneless chicken (halved and cubed)
- 1 cup of rice, uncooked
- 1 large green pepper, diced
- 1 onion, chopped
- 3 stalks celery, sliced
- 2 garlic cloves, minced
- 1 tablespoon of vegetable oil
- 1 can (8 oz) of tomato sauce
- 1-1/4 cups of chicken broth
- 1/2 teaspoon of dried thyme leaves
- 1/2 teaspoon of salt
- 1 bay leaf
- 1/2 teaspoon of white pepper
- 2 dashes of hot pepper sauce
- 1/4 teaspoon of red pepper cayenne
- 1/2 teaspoon of sage

Directions
1. Preheat the Foodi unit for 5 minutes.
2. Sauté the onion, chicken, garlic green pepper, and celery until they tenderizes.
3. Add the remaining ingredients and close the pressure lid.
4. Cook the mixture on high mode for 9 minutes. Quick release the accumulated pressure.

Mussels and Chorizo

Preparation time: 30 minutes| Cook Time: ten minutes| Servings: 4
Ingredients
- A small French baguette, ½" slices
- 2 tablespoons of organic olive oil
- 2 tablespoons of butter
- 2 shallots (peeled and thinly sliced)
- 2 garlic cloves (peeled and thinly sliced)
- 1 cup of fennel, sliced thinly
- A (6 oz) Spanish-style chorizo (casings off and cut into ¼" pieces)
- 1 cup of diced tomatoes
- 1/4 cup of heavy cream
- 3/4 cup of white wine
- 2 pounds of mussels, cleaned and de-bearded
- 2 tablespoons of fresh parsley, chopped
- Juice from a lemon

Directions
1. Brush the baguette slices with a little organic olive oil.
2. Insert the reversible rack in the pot and put the brushed slices in it.
3. Close the crisping lid and toast the baguette at 400°F for 5 minutes.
4. Once cooked, remove the rack with toasted baguette and set it aside.

5. Preheat the multi-cooker in sauté mode and then add butter, garlic, shallots, and fennel. Sauté the spices for 2 minutes.
6. Add tomatoes, chorizo, heavy cream, wine, and mussels. Seal the pressure lid and cook on low mode for 3 minutes.
7. Quick release the pressure and transfer the mussels with into a platter.
8. Sprinkle them with lemon juice and parsley. Serve with toast.

Garlicky Shrimp Scampi

A delicious low-carb dish prepared within 15 minutes.
Preparation time: 10 minutes| Cook Time: 15 minutes| Servings: 4
Ingredients
- 1 1/4 pounds of shrimp (peeled and de-veined)
- 4 tablespoons of butter
- 3 cloves of garlic, chopped roughly
- 1/4 cup of chardonnay wine
- 1/4 cup of lemon juice
- 1/4 teaspoon of red pepper flakes
- 1/4 cup of chopped parsley
- 2 scallions (white and light green part), sliced
- 1/2 cup of Parmesan cheese, shredded
- Salt and black pepper

Directions
1. Preheat your Foodi by sautéing it over medium high.
2. Add butter to the pot followed by the chopped garlic. Let it cook until the garlic softens. Stir.
3. Add the de-veined shrimp and red pepper flakes. Add the lemon juice and wine.
4. Close the pressure lid and cook the shrimp on high mode for 10 minutes. Quick release the accumulated steam and open the lid.
5. Add the chopped parsley and scallions. Stir. Season the mixture with salt and pepper
6. Serve while topped with Parmesan cheese, if desired.

Creamy Crab

Preparation time: 10 minutes| Cook Time: 14 minutes | Servings: 4
Ingredients
- 1 pound of lump crabmeat (raw)
- ½ cup of heavy cream
- 4 tablespoons of butter
- ¼ cup of chicken broth
- ½ stalk celery, diced finely
- 1 small red onion (peeled and finely diced)
- Salt and freshly ground black pepper

Directions
1. Preheat the unit on Sauté mode for a minute. Add butter and let it melt.
2. Add the celery and cook until it softens. Stir.
3. Add the onions and cook for 3 minutes.
4. Add the chicken broth and crabmeat. Stir and close the pressure lid.
5. Cook on low mode for 3 minutes. Quick release the accumulated pressure and open the lid. Add cream and mix. Add salt and pepper. Stir and set aside.
6. Melt butter over medium heat. Add celery and sauté until it softens.
7. Add the onion and stir. Sauté the mixture for 3 minutes.
8. Add the crabmeat and broth. Stir and secure the lid. Cook them on low mode for 3 minutes and quick release open the lid. Stir.
9. Add the heavy cream followed by salt and pepper. Enjoy.

Paella

Preparation time: 15 minutes| Cook Time: 12 minutes| Servings: 4-6
Ingredients
- 2 tablespoons of extra virgin olive oil
- 3 links of chorizo, sliced
- 3 boneless skinless chicken thighs (cut)
- 1 medium onion (peeled and chopped finely)
- 2 cloves of garlic (peeled and minced)
- 1 small red bell pepper, chopped
- A teaspoon of paprika
- 1/2 teaspoon of oregano, dried
- 1/4 teaspoon of crushed red pepper
- 1/2 teaspoon of pepper
- A teaspoon of kosher salt
- Pinch of saffron threads, crumbled
- A can (14 oz) of diced tomatoes
- 1/2 cup of chicken stock
- 1/4 cup of white wine
- A cup of basmati rice
- 1 pound of mussels (scrubbed and de-bearded)
- 1 bag (12 oz) of frozen jumbo shrimp (peeled and deveined)
- Juice from one lemon
- 2 tablespoons of fresh parsley, for garnishing

Directions
1. Preheat your Foodi on sauté mode for a minute. Add the chicken thighs and sliced chorizos in oil. Cook for 5 minutes.
2. Add the onions, garlic, red pepper, and spices. Sauté for another 5 minutes.
3. Add the wine, stock, rice, tomatoes, shrimp, and mussels. Stir.

4. Close the pressure lid and cook for 2 minutes. Quick release the accumulated pressure and open the lid.
5. Transfer your Paella into a large bowl. Serve while topped with parsley and fresh lemon juice.

Creamy Shrimp Scampi

Preparation time: 5 minutes| Cook Time: 10 minutes| Servings: 6

Ingredients
- 2 tablespoons of butter
- 1lb of shrimp, frozen
- 4 garlic cloves, minced
- 1/4 teaspoons of red pepper flakes
- 1/2 teaspoon of paprika
- 2 cups of uncooked low-carbohydrate pasta (Carbanada)
- 1 cup of chicken broth
- 1/2 cup of half and half
- 1/2 cup of mozzarella cheese
- Pepper

Directions
1. Melt butter on sauté mode. Add the red pepper flakes and garlic and cook until the garlic browns.
2. Add the paprika, frozen shrimp, pepper, and the noodles. Add the chicken broth and close the pressure lid.
3. Cook for 2 minutes and quick release the in-built pressure.
4. Set your Foodi to sauté mode and add the cheese. Add the half and half and stir. Cook the mixture until everything melt.
5. Close the crisping lid and bake at 350°F or until the internal temperature drops to 165° F. Allow it to cool before serving.

Brazilian Fish Stew (Moqueca)

A flavorful coconut milk and tomato-fish stew.
Preparation time: 10 minutes| Cook Time: 25 minutes| Servings: 5

Ingredients
For the Stew:
- 1 red bell pepper, sliced
- 1 onion, diced
- 5 garlic cloves, minced
- 8 oz of fish broth
- 14 oz of canned tomatoes, crushed
- 6 oz of full-fat coconut milk, canned
- 1 tablespoon of ground cumin
- 2 tablespoons of coconut oil
- 1 tablespoon of smoked paprika
- 1/2 teaspoon of black pepper
- A teaspoon of salt
- ¼ and ½ teaspoons of ground cayenne

Finishing:
- 1 1/2 pounds of cod or halibut
- A tablespoon of lime juice
- 2 tablespoons of coconut oil
- 1 tablespoon of fresh cilantro or parsley, chopped

Directions
1. Combine all the ingredients in your Foodi and stir.
2. Seal the pressure lid and cook on high mode for 10 minutes. When the cooking time elapses, quick release the accumulated steam.
3. Open the lid and set the Foodi to sauté mode. Thicken the stew over medium heat for around 10 minutes, while stirring frequently.
4. Meanwhile, prepare the fish by removing its skin and bones and then pat drying it with paper towels. Cut the fish into one inch pieces.
5. Once stew has thickened, add the fish cutlets and stir. Cook for 5 minutes and turn off the sauté function.
6. Add the coconut oil and lime juice. Stir.
7. Serve while topped with chopped parsley or cilantro.

Seared Shrimp and Rice with Fruity Salsa

Preparation time: 10 minutes| Cook Time: 20 minutes| Servings: 4

Ingredients
- A cup of basmati rice
- 1 cup of water
- 1 1/2 teaspoons of sea salt, divided
- 3 tablespoons of canola oil
- 3 tablespoons of fresh lime juice, divided
- 1 lb (31-35) of large shrimp, uncooked
- 1 1/2 teaspoons of crab seasoning
- A teaspoon of garlic powder
- 1 teaspoon of smoked paprika
- 1/2 teaspoon of onion powder
- 1 mango (peeled and chopped)
- 1/2 teaspoon of sugar
- 1/4 cup of red onion (peeled and chopped)
- 1 small bell pepper (red,) chopped
- 1/2 cup of pineapple, chopped
- 3 scallions, finely sliced
- 1 avocado, sliced

Directions
1. Peel the shrimp, devein it and remove its tail. Put it aside. If frozen, thaw it first.
2. Add, water, rice, and a teaspoon of salt in the Foodi. Close the pressure lid and cook on high mode for 2 minutes. Quick release the in-built pressure and open the lid.
3. Meanwhile, toss the shrimp with the crab seasoning, onion powder, garlic powder, sugar, smoked paprika, and 2 tablespoons of oil.

4. Open the pressure lid and add the remaining oil and a teaspoon of lime juice. Stir.
5. Fix the rack in the rice-pot. Place shrimp on the rack and close the crisping lid.
6. Broil it for 7 minutes. Halfway, open the lid and flip the shrimp.
7. Meanwhile, add the mango, pineapple, bell pepper, red onion, the remaining salt and the lime juice.
8. After the cooking time elapses, serve the broiled shrimp with rice. Top with avocado slices, scallions, and salsa.

Keto Clam Chowder

Preparation time: 10 minutes| Cook Time: 15 minutes| Servings: 6

Ingredients
- 4 slices (4.2 oz) of bacon, chopped
- 4 tablespoons of unsalted butter
- 1 white onion, diced
- 2 celery stalks, diced
- 2 garlic cloves, minced
- 3 cups of diced turnips
- 1 teaspoon of sea salt
- Few sprigs of fresh thyme
- 1/4 teaspoon of black pepper
- A cup of clam juice
- 1 lb of clams

Optional
- 1/4 teaspoon of cayenne
- 2 (10 oz) cans of baby clams, boiled (reserve juice)
- 1 1/2 glasses of heavy cream

Directions
1. Preheat your Foodi on sauté mode for a minute. Add the bacon and butter and allow it to fry for 5 minutes or until its crispy.
2. Add onions, celery, garlic, and spices. Sauté for another 3 minutes or until the spices tenderize.
3. Add the diced turnips and clam juice. Close the pressure lid and cook on low mode for a minute.
4. Once cooked quick release the pressure and open the lid carefully.
5. Add your littleneck clams and cream. Stir. Sauté the mixture on high mode for 4 minutes. Mash half of the turnips using a tomato masher.
6. Let the turnips simmer for 5- 7 minutes while stirring frequently.
7. Serve your Keto clam chowder while garnished with thyme.

Hot Prawns with Cocktail Sauce

Preparation time: 10 minutes | Cook Time: 6 minutes | Servings: 4

Ingredients
- 1 teaspoon of chili powder
- ½ teaspoon of sea salt
- 1 teaspoon of chili flakes
- ½ teaspoon of fresh ground black pepper
- 8 fresh king prawns
- 1 tablespoon of ketchup
- 3 tablespoons of mayonnaise
- 1 tablespoons of wine

Directions
1. Preheat the Foodi unit on air crisp mode at 300°F.
2. Combine all spices in a bowl.
3. Add the prawns and toss with the spices to coat.
4. Put the prawns in the basket and cook crisp for 6 minutes.
5. Combine the sauce ingredients in a bowl. Serve the hot spicy prawns with the sauce.

Garlic Shrimp with Risotto Primavera

Preparation time: 15 minutes| Cook Time: 24 minutes| Servings: 4

Directions
- 2 tablespoons of organic olive oil, divided
- 1 small onion (peeled and diced finely)
- 4 cloves garlic (peeled, minced, and divided)
- 3 teaspoons of sea salt, divided
- 5 1/2 cups of chicken stock
- 2 glasses of short- grained rice
- 16 uncooked jumbo shrimp (peeled and deveined)
- 2 teaspoons of garlic powder
- 1 teaspoon of ground black pepper
- 2 tablespoons of butter
- Juice from a lemon
- 1 bunch of asparagus (trimmed and cut)
- 1 1/2 cups of grated Parmesan cheese

Directions
1. Set your Foodi to sauté mode. Add a tablespoon of oil.
2. Add the onion and cook until it softens.
3. Add half of the garlic and cook for 1 minute or until its fragrant.
4. Add 2 teaspoons of salt, stock, and rice. Close the pressure lid.
5. Toss the shrimp in the oil and add the remaining garlic, garlic powder, salt, and black pepper.
6. Let the pressure release naturally for 10 minutes before quick releasing the rest.
7. Open the lid and add butter, fresh lemon juice, and asparagus into it.
8. Fix the reversible rack over the risotto and add the shrimp into the rack.
9. Close the crisping lid and broil for 8 minutes.

10. Remove the rack and add Parmesan into the risotto. Stir.
11. Serve your meal while topped with shrimp and Parmesan.

Catfish with French Sauce

Preparation time: 10 minutes | Cook Time: 5 minutes | Servings: 4
Ingredients
- 1½ pounds of catfish fillets (rinse, pat-dry, and cut)
- 1 (14½-ounce) can of diced tomatoes
- 2 teaspoons of dried minced onion
- ¼ teaspoon of onion powder
- 1 teaspoon of dried minced garlic
- ¼ teaspoon of garlic powder
- 1 teaspoon of hot paprika
- 1 medium green bell pepper (seeded and diced)
- ¼ teaspoon of dried tarragon
- 1 celery stalk, diced finely
- Salt and freshly ground pepper
- ½ cup of chili sauce
- ¼ teaspoon of sugar

Directions
1. Add all the ingredients (except the fish fillets) to the pot and mix thoroughly.
2. Add the fillets and stir.
3. Close the pressure lid and cook the fillets mixture on low mode for five minutes.
4. Quick release the accumulated pressure and open the lid.
5. Stir gently and add more seasonings, if required.

Orange Roughy with Black Olive Sauce

Preparation time: 10 minutes | Cook Time: 5 minutes | Servings: 4
Ingredients
- 2 (8-oz) orange roughy, sliced
- 3 tablespoons of butter, melted
- 4 teaspoons of lime juice, freshly squeezed
- 6 sprigs of fresh dill or ¼ teaspoon of dried dill
- 6 Kalamata olives (pitted and chopped)
- 4 thin slices of white onion
- ¼ cup of dry white wine
- ¼ cup of water
- Sea salt

Directions
1. Mix wine with water in your Foodi pot. Insert the reversible rack.
2. Wash the fish and pat dry. Sprinkle with salt.
3. Place 2 slices of onions in the rack and top with a sprig of dill.
4. Place the orange fish over the dill and top each with a sprig of dill.
5. Place the remaining slices of onions over the dill and close the pressure lid.
6. Cook the combination on high mode for 5 minutes. Let the pressure escape naturally for five minutes and quick release the rest.
7. Make a sauce by whisking lime juice, ½ tablespoon of cooking liquid, butter, and olives. Stir. Garnish with the remaining dill.

Salmon with Orange Ginger Sauce

A sure family-pleaser!
Preparation time: 15 minutes| Cook Time: 15 minutes| Servings: 4
Ingredients
- 1 pound of salmon
- 2 teaspoons of minced ginger
- 1 tablespoon of dark soy sauce
- 1 teaspoon of garlic, minced
- ½ teaspoon of salt
- 1-11/2 teaspoon of ground pepper
- 2 tablespoons of marmalade, low sugar

Directions
1. Put salmon in a Ziploc bag. Add the minced ginger, dark soy sauce, garlic, marmalade, salt, and pepper. Let it marinate for 30 minutes.
2. Add 2 glasses of water in the Foodi. Fix a reversible rack over it and add the seasoned salmon with sauce.
3. Close the pressure lid and cook on low mode for 3 minutes. Allow the in-built pressure to escape naturally.
4. Close the crisping lid and broil the contents for 3 minutes.
5. Alternatively, bake the seasoned fish at a temperature of 350°F for 5 minutes.

Country Grouper

Preparation time: 15 minutes| Cook Time: 15 minutes| Servings: 4
Ingredients
- 2 tablespoons of vegetable oil
- 4 grouper fillets
- 1 small onion (peeled and diced)
- A tablespoon of tomato paste
- 1 green bell pepper (seeded and diced)
- 1 celery stick, diced
- 1 can (14½-ounce) of diced tomatoes
- 1 teaspoon of sugar
- Pinch basil
- ¼ cup of water
- ½ teaspoon of chili powder
- Salt and pepper

Directions

1. Sauté the green pepper, onion, and celery in oil for 3 minutes.
2. Add the tomato paste, un-drained tomatoes, water, basil, sugar and chili powder. Stir.
3. Add the rinsed, pat-dry, and cut fish pieces in the Foodi.
4. Secure the pressure lid and cook on high mode for 5 minutes.
5. Quick release the in-built pressure and open the lid. Enjoy.

Thai Shrimp Soup

Lime, lemongrass, red curry, ginger, and coconut are included in this dish. Our intention is to serve the creamy dish with the Thai flavor.

Preparation time: 6 minutes| Cook Time: 5 minutes| Servings: 6

Ingredients
- 2 tablespoons of unsalted butter, divided
- ½ lb of medium shrimp (uncooked, peeled, and deveined)
- ½ yellow onion, diced
- 2 cloves of garlic, minced
- 2 tablespoons of fish sauce
- 4 servings of chicken broth
- 2 tablespoons of lime juice
- 1 tablespoon of coconut aminos or tamari sauce
- 2½ teaspoons of red curry paste
- 1 stalk of lemongrass (bruised and chopped)
- 1 cup of fresh white mushrooms, sliced
- 1 tablespoon of fresh cinnamon, grated
- ½ teaspoon of freshly ground black pepper
- 1 teaspoon of sea salt
- 1 can(13.66-oz) of unsweetened, full-fat coconut milk
- 3 tablespoons of fresh cilantro, chopped

Directions
1. Set your Foodi to sauté mode. Add a tablespoon of butter and allow it to melt.
2. Add the shrimp and stir until it turns pink. Transfer it into a bowl and set aside.
3. Add the remaining butter into the pot and let it melt.
4. Add onion and the garlic. Sauté for 3 minutes or until it turns translucent.
5. Add the chicken broth, fish sauce, lime juice, tamari sauce or coconut aminos, red curry paste, grated cinnamon, mushrooms, lemongrass, sea salt, and black pepper. Mix well.
6. Close the pressure lid and cook on high mode for 5 minutes.
7. When cooking time elapses, let the pressure to escape naturally for 5 minutes.
8. Quick release the remaining pressure and open the lid.
9. Add the coconut shrimp and milk. Stir to combine.
10. Boil the soup on sauté mode for around 5 minutes. Let the soup rest for two minutes before serving. Serve with cilantro toppings.

Shrimp with Tomatoes and Feta

Preparation time: 10 minutes| Cook Time: 12 minutes| Servings: 6

Ingredients
- 2 tablespoons of butter
- 1/2 teaspoon of red pepper flakes
- A tablespoon of garlic
- 11/2 cups of onions, chopped
- A (14.5oz) canned tomatoes
- 1 teaspoon of salt
- 1 teaspoon of dried oregano
- 1 lb of frozen shrimp, shelled

For serving:
- 1 cup of crumbled feta cheese
- 1/2 cup of black olives, sliced
- 1/4 cup of parsley, chopped

Directions
1. Set your Foodi to sauté mode. Add butter to melt.
2. Add garlic, red pepper flakes, tomatoes, onions, salt, and oregano.
3. Add the frozen shrimps and close the pressure lid. Cook the shrimp mixture on low mode for one minute. Quick release the in-built pressure and open the lid.
4. Cool and serve it sprinkled with feta cheese, sliced olives, and chopped parsley.
5. Enjoy your tomato shrimp with cauliflower rice or as dipping for buttered French bread.

Shrimp and Cheesy Butter Grits

Preparation time: 10 minutes| Cook Time: 14 minutes| Servings: 4

Ingredients
- 3 cups of water, divided
- 1 cup of grits
- 3 teaspoons of kosher salt, divided
- 16 uncooked jumbo shrimps, frozen
- Juice from a lemon
- 1 teaspoon of extra virgin olive oil
- 2 garlic cloves (peeled and minced)
- 1 teaspoon of chili powder
- A teaspoon of black pepper
- 1 teaspoon of garlic powder
- 1/4 cup of butter, cut into 8 pieces
- 1/4 cup of grated Parmesan cheese, grated
- 2 tablespoons of fresh parsley, chopped
- 2 scallions, thinly sliced

Directions
1. Peel the shrimps, devein and pat dry.

2. Pour a half cup of water into the Foodi. Put the remaining water in an 8" baking pan and add grits and two teaspoons of salt. Stir.
3. Fix the pan in the reversible rack and insert it in the Foodi.
4. Cook the ingredients on high mode for four minutes. Allow the in-built pressure to escape naturally for ten minutes and quick release the rest.
5. Meanwhile, put shrimp in a bowl and toss with extra virgin olive oil, lemon juice, garlic, garlic powder, chili powder, pepper, and the remaining salt. Coat well and set aside.
6. Add cheese and butter in the Foodi and sir to melt.
7. Spread the coated shrimps on the grits and close the crisping lid. Bake them at 375°F for 10 minutes.
8. Serve while garnished with scallions and parsley.

Low Town Shrimp Boil

Preparation time: 5minutes| Cook Time: 6minutes| Servings: 6
Ingredients
- 1/2 pound of smoked shrimp sausages, sliced
- 1 lb of large fresh shrimp, in shells
- 1 can (14.5 oz) of chicken broth
- 1/3 cup of white wine
- 4 whole black peppercorns
- 1/4 teaspoon of dried crushed red pepper
- 1 bay leaf
- 6 red potatoes
- 2 ears corn, cut into thirds
- 3/4 cup of water

Directions
1. Combine all the ingredients in the Foodi (except the sausages).
2. Close the pressure lid and cook on high mode for four minutes. Quick release the in-built pressure and open the lid.
3. Add the shrimp sausages and cook on low mode for 2 minutes. Quick release the pressure and open the lid. Serve hot.

Red Snapper with miso

Preparation time: 10 minutes| Cook Time: 14 minutes| Servings: 4
Ingredients
- 2 pounds of red snapper fillets
- 1 tablespoon of red miso paste
- A tablespoon of rice wine
- 1 (2-inch) fresh ginger, peeled and cut long
- 4 green onions (halved lengthwise and cut into 2"pieces)
- 2 teaspoons of sesame oil
- A teaspoon of dark soy sauce
- 2 teaspoons of fermented black beans
- 2 garlic cloves (peeled and minced)
- ½ teaspoon of Asian chili paste
- Salt
- Water

Directions
1. Insert a rack in the Foodi. Pour some water into the pot.
2. Mix miso with rice wine, black beans, sesame oil, chili paste, and soy sauce in a bowl. Sprinkle salt over the mixture and rub the snapper fillets with it.
3. Put half of the peeled ginger on the pan. Add half of the garlic.
4. Pour half of the green onions over the garlic and ginger.
5. Place the fillets in the pan and sprinkle them with the ginger mixture. Transfer them to the fitted rack.
6. Close the pressure lid and cook on low mode for 3 minutes. Quick release the accumulated steam and serve.

Wild Salmon Tagine

Preparation time: 10 minutes| Cook Time: 14 minutes| Servings: 4
Ingredients
Spice Paste:
- 4 1/2 oz of coriander leaves and stems
- 4 cloves of garlic
- Juice from a lemon
- Orange zest (one orange)
- 1 lemon zest
- A tablespoon of ground paprika
- 1 tablespoon of apple cider vinegar
- 1 red chili (seeded and stem off)
- A tablespoon of ground cumin
- 1/4 teaspoon of red pepper cayenne
- 1/4 teaspoon of sea salt

Tagine:
- 4 frozen salmon fillets
- 4 tablespoon of extra virgin organic olive oil
- 1 red onion
- 10 oz of sweet potatoes (peeled and diced)
- 2 carrots, diced
- 14 oz of chopped tomatoes (tinned)
- A cup of stock, vegetable or fish
- 1.5 oz of dried cherries
- 2 oz of pitted olives
- 2 oranges (peeled and chopped)

Directions
1. Preheat the Foodi pot.
2. Puree all the spice paste ingredients. Spread a tablespoon of the paste on the fish.

3. Melt butter in the Foodi and add the red onion, carrots, sweet potatoes, and the remaining spice mix.
4. Sauté and stir for 5 minutes. Add the stock, tinned tomatoes, oranges, olives, and dried cherries.
5. Place the frozen fish on top and seal the pressure lid.
6. Cook on high mode for 4 minutes. Quick release the in-built vapor and open the lid.
7. Serve your wild salmon tagine garnished with fresh herbs (preferably parsley and mint leaves.)

Calamari with Tomato Stew

Preparation time: 10 minutes| Cook Time: 15 minutes| Servings: 4
Ingredients
- 2½ pounds of calamari
- 2 tablespoons of essential olive oil
- 1 small white onion (peeled and diced)
- 1 small stalk celery, finely diced
- 1 small carrot (peeled and grated)
- 3 cloves garlic (peeled and minced)
- 1 can (28-oz) of diced tomatoes
- Salt and freshly ground black pepper
- ½ cup of white wine
- 1/3 of cup water
- 1 tablespoon of fresh parsley
- A tablespoon of fresh basil

Directions
1. Sauté the celery stalk and carrots in oil for two minutes.
2. Add onions and cook for 3 minutes. Add the garlic and cook for thirty seconds.
3. Clean and pat-dry the calamari and add it to the Foodi.
4. Add the remaining ingredients and close the pressure lid.
5. Cook the mixture on low mode for 10 minutes and quick release the in-built steam.
6. Open the lid and add the fresh herbs. Serve your calamari dish hot.

Fish Steaks with Olive Sauce and Tomato

Preparation time: 10 minutes| Cook Time: 14 minutes| Servings: 2
Ingredients
- 2 firm fish steaks (cut thickly into ½ inches)
- 2/3 cup of sliced mushrooms
- 2 tablespoons of extra virgin olive oil
- 1/2 cup of chopped onion
- 2 garlic cloves, minced
- 4 Roma tomatoes, chopped
- 2 tablespoons of capers, drained
- 1/4 cup of chopped and pitted kalamata olives
- 2 tablespoons of fresh parsley, minced
- 1/8 teaspoon of crushed red pepper, dried
- 1/4 cup of white wine
- 1/4 teaspoon of salt

Directions
1. Preheat the Foodi unit on sauté mode. Add garlic and onion in oil and cook for 3 minutes. Add the remaining ingredients (except the fish) and stir.
2. Put the fish steaks in the basket and insert it in the Foodi.
3. Close the pressure lid and steam the fish for five minutes. Enjoy!

SOUPS/ STEWS/ SAUCES/ BROTHS

Double Bean and Ham Soup

Preparation time: 10minutes| Cook Time: 45minutes| Servings:6

Ingredients
- 2 cups of dry navy beans
- 2 cups of chicken broth
- 2 cups of water
- 1 can (14.5 ounce) of diced tomatoes, undrained
- 2 carrots, chopped
- 1 onion, chopped
- 2 celery stalks, chopped
- 1 can (16 ounce) of pork and beans, undrained
- A cup of chopped ham
- Salt and ground black pepper

Directions
1. Put the chicken broth, navy beans, water carrots, tomatoes, celery, and onion in the Foodi.
2. Close the pressure lid and cook on high mode for 45 minutes.
3. Allow the in-built pressure to exit naturally for 10 minutes and quick release the rest. Open the lid.
4. Add ham, pork, and beans. Stir and season with salt.

Chicken Thigh Soup

A simple savory soup cooked in one hour.
Preparation time: 10 minutes| Cook Time: 30 minutes| Servings: 6

Ingredients
- 4 celery stalks, chopped
- 10 oz of radishes
- 1/2 small onion, chopped
- 1 tablespoon of fresh basil, chopped
- A tablespoon of fresh rosemary, chopped
- 3 cloves of garlic, minced
- 1/2 teaspoon of salt
- 1/4 teaspoon of ground black pepper
- 4 glasses of chicken broth
- 2 pounds of chicken thighs (skin and bones on)
- 2 bay leaves
- Fresh parsley for garnish

Directions
1. Add the chopped celery stalks, rosemary, radishes, garlic, basil, onion, salt, and pepper in your Foodi pot.
2. Pour the chicken broth over the vegetables and stir. Add the chicken thighs and bay leaves.
3. Close the pressure lid and cook on high mode for 30 minutes.
4. Allow the in-built steam to escape naturally for 15 minutes and quick release the rest.
5. Remove the chicken using tongs and separate fresh parts from the bones and skins.
6. Subdivide it into pieces and return them to the Foodi.
7. Add more seasonings if necessary. Subdivide your chicken thigh soup into bowls and serve. Top with fresh parsley and enjoy.

Kale Chicken Soup

Preparation time: 5 minutes| Cook time: 15 minutes| Servings: 4

Ingredients
- 12 ounces of frozen kale
- 4 cups of chicken broth
- 2 glasses of cooked chicken
- 1 onion, chopped
- 2 teaspoons of garlic, minced
- 1 tablespoon of bouillon chicken mix
- ½ teaspoon of ground cinnamon
- 1/16 teaspoon of ground cloves
- 1 teaspoon of salt
- 1 teaspoon of pepper

Directions:
Combine all the ingredients in your Foodi and cook on high mode for 5 minutes.
Let the pressure escape naturally for 10 minutes and quick release the rest.
You can add more seasonings to your chicken soup if necessary.

North African Lentil and Spinach Soup

Preparation time: 5 minutes| Cook time: 20 minutes| Servings: 4-6

Ingredients
- 1 tablespoon of organic olive oil
- 2 tablespoons of unsalted butter
- 1 medium red onion, finely chopped
- 2 teaspoons of ground coriander
- 1 teaspoon of garlic powder
- ½ teaspoon of cinnamon powder
- ¼ teaspoon of clove powder
- ½ teaspoon of turmeric powder
- ¼ teaspoon of red pepper cayenne
- ¼ teaspoon of fresh grated nutmeg
- ¼ teaspoon of cardamom powder
- 2 cups of lentils
- 8 cups of water
- ¼ teaspoon of pepper
- 2 teaspoons of salt
- 6 oz of fresh spinach (about 4 packed cups)
- 4 tablespoons of freshly squeezed lemon juice

Directions
1. Sauté the red onion, ground coriander, garlic powder, cinnamon powder, clove powder, turmeric powder, cayenne pepper, grated nutmeg, and cardamom powder in the melted butter and oil for 2-3 minutes.
2. Add the water and lentils. Close the pressure lid and cook on high mode for 10 minutes.
3. Let the in-built vapor exit naturally and open the lid.
4. Add salt, pepper, and the spinach leaves.
5. Stir to wilt and t add the fresh lemon juice.

Barley and Mushroom Soup

Preparation time: 10 minutes| Cook time: 30 minutes| Servings: 6
Ingredients
- 2 tablespoons of butter
- 2 carrots (peeled and diced)
- 1 yellow onion, chopped
- 3 celery stalks, chopped
- 2 garlic cloves, minced
- 1/2 cup of dried mushroom
- 8 ounces of fresh mushrooms, sliced
- 6 cups of chicken broth
- 1/2 cup of pearl barley
- 2 bay leaves
- Salt and pepper

Directions:
1. Sear your Foodi on medium high heat for a minute.
2. Add butter and melt it. Add carrots and celery and sauté for 2 minutes.
3. Add onion and garlic. Sauté the spice mix for 3 minutes and add the sliced mushrooms. Sauté again for 5 minutes and add the vegetable broth. Stir.
4. Add the barley and bay leaves.
5. Close the pressure lid and cook the ingredients on high mode for 20 minutes.
6. Let the pressure exit naturally and open the lid.
7. Remove the bay leaves and discard. Season your mushroom soup with salt and pepper.

White Chicken Chili

Preparation time: 10minutes| Cook Time: 20minutes| Servings: 4
Ingredients
- 1 1/2 lbs of chicken white meat
- 2 garlic cloves
- 1 cup of celery, chopped
- A cup of onion, chopped
- 1 cup of heavy cream
- 1 tablespoon of Poblano pepper
- 3 glasses of chicken broth
- 1 cup of water
- A tablespoon of cumin
- 1 tablespoon of turmeric
- Salt and pepper
- Coconut or avocado oil

Directions
1. Pour water into the Foodi pot.
2. Put the chicken in the basket and fix it into the pot.
3. Close the pressure lid and cook it on high pressure for 12 minutes.
4. Allow the pressure to escape naturally and open the lid.
5. Remove the chicken using tongs and shred it into pieces.
6. Sauté the avocado oil in your Foodi on medium high heat for one minute.
7. Add the diced onions, poblano pepper, garlic, and celery. Sauté them until the onion turns light brown.
8. Add broth and water to the mixture. Allow it to simmer and add the chicken spices followed by heavy cream. Mix them well.
9. Close the pressure lid and cook the mixture on high mode for 3 minutes. Quick release the in-built pressure and serve.

Leek, Potato, and Pea Soup

Preparation time: 15 minutes| Cook time: 22 minutes| Servings: 4
Ingredients
- 2 tablespoons of vegetable oil
- 1 pound of leeks (washed and chopped finely)
- A pound of potatoes, cubed
- 1 cup of peas
- A pinch of dried mint leaves, crumbled
- 2 tablespoons of fresh parsley, minced
- 1 cup of coconut milk
- 4 cups of vegetable stock
- Salt and pepper

Directions:
1. Sauté the leeks in vegetable oil for ten minutes or until they tender.
2. Add the potatoes, peas, parsley, and mint.
3. Add the coconut milk and the vegetable stock.
4. Add salt and pepper. Close the pressure lid and cook the mixture on high mode for 12 minutes.
5. Quick release the in-built pressure and transfer everything to a mixer.
6. Puree the ingredients and pour your pea soup into bowls.

Ground Beef Cabbage Soup

A delicious cabbage soup recipe for anyone!

Preparation time: 15 minutes| Cook Time: 30 minutes| Servings: 14

Ingredients
- A tablespoon of avocado oil
- 1 large onion, chopped
- 1 lb of ground beef
- A teaspoon of sea salt
- 1/4 teaspoon of black pepper
- 1 lb of coleslaw mix, shredded
- 1 (15-oz) can of diced tomatoes (liquid inclusive)
- 6 cups of beef bone broth
- 1 tablespoon of Italian seasoning
- 1/2 teaspoon of garlic powder
- 2 medium bay leaves (optional)

Directions
1. Sauté the chopped onions in oil for two minutes or until the onions turn translucent while stirring occasionally.
2. Add the ground beef into the Foodi.
3. Add salt and pepper. Sauté on high temperature for 10 minutes while breaking the beef.
4. Add the remaining ingredients and stir. Season the beef with salt and pepper.
5. Close the pressure lid and cook on high mode for 20 minutes
6. Let the pressure release naturally for ten minutes and quick release the rest.
7. Remove the bay leaves and serve.

Kimchi Beef Stew

Preparation time: 10 minutes| Cook Time: 15 minutes| Servings: 6

Ingredients
- 1 pound of beef cubes, cut
- 2 glasses of kimchi
- 2 cups of water
- 1 cup of chopped firm tofu, optional
- 1 cup of dried shiitake mushrooms
- 1 cup of chopped onion
- ½ cup of chopped green onion(optional)
- 1 tablespoon of dark soy sauce
- A tablespoon of crushed ginger
- 1 tablespoon of crushed garlic
- 1 tablespoon of Gochujang
- A tablespoon of sesame oil
- 1 tablespoon of Gochugaru Korean chili paste
- ½ teaspoon of sugar
- Salt

Directions:
1. Mix all the ingredients in the Foodi and cook on high mode for 15 minutes. Let the pressure release naturally for 5 minutes.
2. Add the tofu and green onions. Serve hot.

Oxtails Stew

Preparation time: 10minutes| Cook Time: 15| Servings: 4

Ingredients
- 5 pounds of oxtails
- 2 glasses of red
- 1 large onion (peeled and chopped)
- 3 carrots, chopped
- 3 celery stalks, chopped
- 1 cup of chopped tomatoes
- 1 small parsley, chopped
- A garlic clove (peeled and chopped)
- 1 cup of water
- Sugar
- Salt and pepper

Directions
1. Begin by seasoning the oxtails with salt and pepper. Put them into the Ninja Foodi.
2. Add the remaining ingredients (except wine and water) into the oxtails.
3. Add the wine and water.
4. Cook the ingredients on high mode for 10 minutes.
5. Allow the pressure to escape naturally and open the lid.
6. Add more seasonings, if required. Enjoy!

Chicken Taco Soup

Bursting with flavor and so tasty; this soup makes a great weeknight meal!
Preparation time: 15minutes| Cook Time: 20minutes| Servings: 4

Ingredients
- 1 lb of chicken breasts
- 1/2 cup of onion, diced
- A tablespoon of chipotles in adobo sauce, minced
- 4 garlic cloves, minced
- ½ teaspoon of chili powder
- 1 tablespoon of cumin
- ½ teaspoon of salt
- ½ teaspoon of paprika
- 1 tablespoon of lime juice
- 2 tablespoons of freshly squeezed lemon juice
- 2 cups of chicken broth
- 8 ounces of cream cheese
- ½ cup cilantro, chopped

Directions
1. Mix all the ingredients (except the cream cheese and cilantro) in the Foodi.
2. Secure the pressure lid and cook on high mode for 18 minutes.

3. Allow the pressure to exit naturally release for ten minutes and quick release the rest. Remove the chicken with tongs and shred.
4. Set your Foodi to sauté mode and add the cream cheese. Whisk and cook until the cheese dissolves.
5. Turn off the cook function and return the shredded chicken into the pot.
6. Add the cilantro and stir. Serve while topped with cilantro, grated cheddar cheese, diced tomatoes, and sour cream.

Beef and Wheat Berry Soup

Preparation time: 10 minutes| Cook Time: 30 minutes| Servings: 6
Ingredients
- 2 tablespoon of canola oil
- 1 onion, chopped finely
- A can (6-oz) of tomato paste
- 4 cups of broth, beef or chicken
- 1 lb of beef stew or leftover roast, cubed
- 1/2 cup of wheat berries or barley/brown rice
- 1 1/2 teaspoon of coarse salt
- 2 cups of spinach or kale, finely chopped

Directions
1. Set your Foodi to sauté mode. Add oil and brown the onions for ten minutes.
2. Add tomato paste and cook-stir for 3 minutes.
3. Add broth, wheat berries, and salt. Cook on high mode for 30 minutes.
4. Quick release the in-built pressure and open the lid.
5. Add the chopped greens and stir.

Minestrone Soup

Preparation time: 15 minutes| Cook Time: 6 minutes| servings: 6
Ingredients
- 2 tablespoons of canola oil
- 4 cloves garlic (peeled and sliced thinly)
- 2 celery stalks, chopped
- 1 medium yellow onion (peeled and chopped)
- Pinch red pepper, crushed
- 1 teaspoon of ground black pepper
- 2 teaspoons of kosher salt
- 2 medium carrots (peeled and chopped)
- 2 Yukon Gold potatoes (peeled and diced)
- 1/2 teaspoon of dried thyme
- 1 can (14.5 oz) of diced tomatoes
- 1/2 teaspoon of dried oregano
- 2 bay leaves
- 4 cups of broth (chicken or vegetable)
- 2 cups of water
- 1 can (15 oz.) of red kidney beans (rinsed and drained)
- 2 cups of baby spinach
- 2 teaspoons of lemon juice
- Fresh Parmesan cheese, grated

Directions
1. Preheat the Ninja unit for 5 minutes. Sauté oil, garlic, celery, crushed red pepper, pepper, and salt. Stir and cook until everything softens.
2. Add the remaining ingredients (except Parmesan) and cook for a minute on high mode.
3. Quick release the in-built pressure and open the lid. Serve while topped with Parmesan Cheese.

Butternut Squash and Apple Soup

Preparation time: 20 minutes| Cook time: 10 minutes| Servings: 8
Ingredients
- 1 tablespoon of extra-virgin essential olive oil
- 3 shallots (peeled and quartered)
- 1 teaspoon of kosher salt
- 2 butternut squash-4 lb (peeled, cut, and seeds removed)
- 2 apples (peeled, cored, and chopped)
- 1 cup of heavy cream
- 4 cups of vegetable broth, divided
- 2 tablespoons of maple syrup
- 2 teaspoons of apple cider vinegar
- Ground black pepper

Directions
1. Sauté the shallots in oil for 3 minutes.
2. Add salt and cook until it turns brown. Add apples, butternut squash, and a cup of broth. Stir.
3. Close the pressure lid and cook on high mode for 5 minutes.
4. Quick release the in-built pressure and open the lid. Add cream and the reserved broth. Puree the ingredients using an immersion blender.
5. Add maple syrup and vinegar.
6. Sauté on low mode until the soup is well-heated. Add salt and pepper.

Potato Leek Soup

Preparation time 10 minutes| Cook Time: 45 minutes| Servings: 6
Ingredients
- 2 tablespoon of butter
- 2 leeks (white and green,) sliced
- 1/2 teaspoon of kosher salt
- 3 garlic cloves, minced
- 1/2 teaspoon of dried thyme
- 1 bay leaf
- 1 1/2 lb of yellow potatoes (peeled and diced)

- 5 cups of low sodium stock (vegetable or chicken)
- 1 cup of half and half
- Kosher salt and black pepper

Optional toppings:
- chives
- croutons
- cream
- bacon

Directions
1. Set your Ninja Foodi to sauté mode. Let it preheat for two minutes.
2. Add butter and melt. Add the leeks and sauté it for 8 minutes.
3. Add the garlic and cook for a minute.
4. Add the potatoes, thyme, bay leaf, and stock. Close the pressure lid and cook on high mode for 7 minutes
5. Let the pressure release naturally for 10 minutes and quick release the rest.
6. Open the lid and remove the bay leaf. Puree everything using a blender.
7. Add the half and half and more seasonings if required.
8. Serve your soup with the optional toppings.

Chicken and Kale Stew

Tender chicken stew with power-packed kale and diced tomatoes. Enjoy!
Preparation time: 10 minutes| Cook Time: 30 minutes| Servings: 4

Ingredients
- 1 tablespoon of butter
- ½ of a medium chopped onion
- 2 boneless chicken breasts, diced
- 3 cups of kale, chopped
- 1 can (14.5 oz.) of diced tomatoes
- A cup of chicken broth
- 1/2 teaspoon of garlic powder
- 1/2 teaspoon of salt
- 1/2 teaspoon of oregano
- 1/4 teaspoon of ground black pepper

Directions
1. Set your Foodi to sauté mode. Add butter and melt.
2. Add the onion and cook for 3 minutes or until tender.
3. Now, add the chicken and cook until crispy.
4. Add the chicken broth, kale, diced tomatoes, garlic powder, oregano, salt, and black pepper into the pot contents.
5. Close the pressure lid and cook on high mode for ten minutes.
6. Quick release the in-built pressure and open the lid.

Chinese Hot and Sour Soup

Preparation time: 10 minutes| Cook time: 10 minutes| Servings: 8

Ingredients
- 1 lb of pork tenderloin, sliced thinly
- 1 lb of extra firm tofu
- 5 cups of chicken broth
- 1 cup of dried mushrooms
- 4 eggs, lightly beaten
- 3 tablespoons of soy sauce
- 3 tablespoons of water
- 2 tablespoons of Chinese rice vinegar or white vinegar
- 1 tablespoon of Chinese black vinegar
- 1 teaspoon of salt
- 2 teaspoons of ground pepper
- ½ teaspoon of xantham gum

Directions:
1. Mix all the ingredients (except tofu and eggs) in the pot.
2. Close the pressure lid and cook on high mode for ten minutes.
3. Let the pressure release naturally for 10 minutes and quick release the rest.
4. Reset the Foodi to sauté mode and remove the mushroom. Slice it thinly and return it to the Foodi.
5. Add the tofu and stir. Add the eggs gently and stir thrice, preferably with chopsticks.
6. Close the pressure lid and cook for a minute. Serve.

Belize Chicken Stew

Preparation time: 10 minutes| Cook time: 30 minutes| Servings: 8

Ingredients
- 4 whole chicken legs (cut into 8 pieces)
- 2 glasses of chicken stock
- 1 cup of yellow onions, sliced
- 2 tablespoons of white wine vinegar
- 3 tablespoons of Worcestershire sauce
- 2 tablespoons of achiote paste
- 1 tablespoon of coconut oil
- 1 tablespoon of granulated sugar substitute
- 3 cloves of garlic, sliced
- 1 teaspoon of Mexican dried oregano
- ½ teaspoon of ground black pepper

Directions:
1. Combine the achiote with vinegar, cumin, oregano, sweetener, Worcestershire sauce, and pepper in a bowl.
2. Rub the chicken with the achiote mixture and marinate it overnight.

3. Preheat the Foodi pot on sauté mode and brown the chicken in oil. Transfer it to a bowl and reserve the marinade.
4. Sauté the onions and garlic until tender. Return the chicken to the pot.
5. Combine the broth and the reversed marinade and pour into the Foodi.
6. Close the pressure lid and cook on high mode for 20 minutes. Release the in-built pressure and open the lid.

Tomato Basil Soup

Preparation time: 30 minutes| Cook time: 15 minutes| Servings: 8
Ingredients
- 3 tablespoons of olive oil
- 3 garlic cloves, minced
- 2 yellow onions, chopped
- 3 1/2 cups of vegetable broth
- 3 pounds of tomatoes, quartered
- 1 tablespoon of tomato paste
- 2 cups of fresh basil leaves, lightly packed
- 1 teaspoon of fresh thyme leaves
- 1/2 teaspoon of freshly ground black pepper
- 1/2 teaspoon of salt
- 1/4 cups of grated cheese

Directions:
1. Preheat the Foodi unit on Sauté mode. Add the essential olive oil and sauté the onions until they tenderize.
2. Add the garlic and cook for a minute. Add the vegetable broth, tomato paste, tomatoes, thyme, basil, salt, and pepper.
3. Close the pressure lid and cook on high mode for 5 minutes. Quick release the remaining pressure and open the lid.
4. Puree the ingredients using an immersion. Add Parmesan and simmer on sauté mode for 4 minutes.

African Lamb Stew

Preparation time: 15minutes| Cook time: 35 minutes| Servings: 6
Ingredients
- 2 pounds of boneless lamb shoulder
- 1 tablespoon of canola oil
- 1 cup of dried apricots, cut into four
- 2 cloves of garlic (peeled and minced)
- 1 large onion (peeled and diced)
- 1/3 cup of raisins
- 1 tablespoon of minced fresh ginger
- 1/3 cup of blanched almonds
- ½ teaspoon of ground cinnamon
- 1/3 cup of fresh mint leaves, packed
- ¾ cup of red wine
- ¼ cup of fresh orange juice
- Fresh mint leaves, optional for garnish
- Salt and freshly ground pepper

Directions
1. Preheat the Foodi unit on sauté mode. Trim the lamb of fat and cut it into pieces.
2. Brown the lamb pieces in oil and set aside.
3. Add the onion and sauté for 3 minutes. Add the garlic and sauté for 30 seconds.
4. Add the browned lamb and stir.
5. Add the raisins, apricots, ginger, almonds, wine, cinnamon, mint leaves, and orange juice.
6. Close the pressure lid and cook on high mode for 20 minutes. Quick release the in-built pressure and garnish if desired. Serve your lamb stew alongside couscous.

Keto No- Beans Chili

Preparation time: 15 minutes| Cook Time: 50 minutes| Servings: 10
Ingredients
- 2 1/2 lbs of ground beef
- 1/2 large onion, chopped
- 8 garlic cloves, minced
- 2 cans (15-oz) of diced tomatoes (liquid inclusive)
- 1 can (6-oz) of tomato paste
- 1 can (4-oz) of green chilies (liquid inclusive)
- 2 tablespoons of Worcestershire sauce
- 2 tablespoons of cumin
- 1/4 cup of chili powder
- 1 tablespoons of dried oregano
- 1 teaspoon of black pepper
- 2 teaspoons of sea salt
- 1 cup water or broth

Directions
1. Set your Ninja Foodi to sauté mode. Add a little oil and the chopped onion and cook until they become translucent.
2. Add the garlic and cook until fragrant.
3. Add the ground beef and cook-stir until they turn brown.
4. Add the remaining ingredients (except bay leaf) and close the pressure lid.
5. Cook on high mode for 30 minutes. When the cooking duration elapses, let the in-built steam escape naturally and open the lid.

French Onion Soup

Preparation time: 15 minutes| Cook time: 45 minutes| Servings: 4
Ingredients:
- 2 tablespoons of butter
- 2 large white onions, (peeled and sliced, 1/4-inches)

- 1 tablespoon of soy sauce
- A tablespoon of tomato paste
- 1 tablespoon of Worcestershire sauce
- A box (32 oz) of beef stock
- 1 teaspoon of ground black pepper
- A teaspoon of kosher salt
- 4 cups of crusty French bread (cubed into 1" pieces)
- 2 cups of Mozzarella cheese, shredded

Directions
1. Preheat the Foodi unit for 5 minutes on sauté mode.
2. Add onions and butter. Cook-stir the onions for ten minutes.
3. Add the soy sauce, tomato paste, and Worcestershire sauce. Cook for 5 minutes and add stock, pepper, and salt.
4. Close the pressure lid and cook on high mode for 15 minutes.
5. Quick release the in-built pressure and open the lid.
6. Sprinkle the bread cubes over the soup, squeeze the cheese in the bread.
7. Close the crisping lid and broil for 8 minutes.

Chinese Pork Soup

Preparation time: 10 minutes| Cook time: 35 minutes| Servings: 6
Ingredients
- 1 pound of pork shoulder, chunked
- 3 cups of chopped bok Choy
- ¼ cup of cilantro
- 3 cups of water
- 6 garlic cloves, crushed
- 3-inch crushed ginger
- 2 tablespoons of black vinegar
- 2 tablespoons of peanut oil
- 2 tablespoons of doban Jiang paste
- 2 tablespoons of soy sauce
- ½ onion, sliced
- 2 teaspoons of Szechuan pepper, coarsely crushed
- 11/2 teaspoons of sugar
- 11/2 teaspoons of salt

Directions:
1. Sauté the garlic and ginger on your Foodi. Add the onion, vinegar, soy sauce, pork, doban Jiang paste, water, sugar, salt, and pepper.
2. Seal the pressure lid and cook on high mode for 10 minutes.
3. Quick release the in-built steam and open the lid.
4. Add the bok Choy and cover. Let your pork soup sit for ten minutes. Serve while garnished with cilantro.

Vegetable Soup

Preparation time: 10 minutes| Cook Time: 45 minutes| Servings: 6
Ingredients
- 1 tablespoon of extra-virgin organic olive oil
- 4 garlic cloves, minced
- 1 medium onion, chopped
- Kosher salt
- Freshly ground black pepper
- 1 tablespoon of tomato paste
- 2 cups of chopped cabbage
- 2 cups of small cauliflower florets
- 2 celery stalks, thinly sliced
- 2 carrots (peeled and thinly sliced)
- 1 red bell pepper, chopped
- 1 medium zucchini, chopped
- A can (15-oz) of kidney beans (rinsed and drained)
- 1 can (15-oz) of diced tomatoes
- 4 cups of vegetable broth, low-sodium
- 3/4 teaspoon of paprika
- 2 teaspoons of Italian seasoning
- Freshly parsley, chopped for serving

Directions
1. Sauté the chopped onion and garlic in oil. Add some salt and pepper.
2. Cook-stir for 5 minutes or until the onion softens. Add tomato paste and cook for a minute while stirring. Add the remaining ingredients and stir to mix.
3. Close the pressure lid and cook for 12 minutes.
4. Quick release the in-built pressure and open the lid. Season with salt and pepper.
5. Add parsley and essential olive oil.

Zuppa Toscana Soup

Preparation time: 10 minutes| Cook Time: 30 minutes| Servings:10
Ingredients
- 1 lb of mild Italian sausage
- A bag (16 oz) of whole radishes
- 1 medium onion, diced
- 2 teaspoons of garlic, minced
- 32 oz of broth, chicken or vegetable
- ⅓ Cup of heavy cream
- 4 cups of kale leaves

Directions
1. Cut the radishes into small chunks.
2. Add the sausage to your Ninja Foodi pot and sauté until browned.
3. Pour the broth, diced onions, garlic, and radishes.

4. Close the pressure lid and cook on high mode for fifteen minutes.
5. Let the accumulated pressure release naturally and open the lid. Add the heavy cream and the torn kale leaves. Sauté the mixture for 3 minutes to soften the kale.

Italian Chicken, Lentil, and Bacon Stew

Preparation time: 20 minutes| Cook Time: 10 minutes| Servings: 4
Ingredients
- 2 1/2 pounds of chicken pieces (bone and skin-on)
- 8 oz of pancetta, cut into 1/2-inch
- 2 tablespoons of canola oil
- 2 medium carrots (peeled and chopped)
- 1 medium onion, diced (about 1 cup)
- 2 bay leaves
- 2 teaspoons of sherry vinegar
- 8 oz of dried French lentils
- 12 sprigs of parsley
- 4 cups of chicken stock
- Kosher salt and freshly ground black pepper

Directions
1. Chop the leaves and parsley roughly and tie their stems using a twine.
2. Sauté the bacon until crispy and then add the onions.
3. Cook until they soften and add the chicken stock, lentils, carrots, stems, bay leaves, parsley and the chicken legs.
4. Season the legs mix with salt and pepper. Stir.
5. Close the pressure lid and cook on high mode for 20 minutes.
6. Quick release the in-built pressure and open the lid. Transfer your chicken into a bowl and discard the parsley stems. Sauté the lentil mixture until it thickens.
7. Shred the chicken and discard the bones and skin. Add chicken and vinegar to the beans and stir. Season the boneless and skinless chicken pieces with salt and pepper.
8. Add half of the chopped parsley and stir. Serve while topped with olive oil, parsley, and sherry vinegar.

Carrot Ginger and Turmeric Soup

Preparation time: 5 minutes| Cook Time: 10 minutes| Servings: 6
Ingredients
- A teaspoon of canola oil
- 1 large yellow onion, diced
- 3 garlic cloves, minced
- 1 ginger piece, (about an inch,) peeled and chopped
- 2 celery stalks, chopped
- 3 cups of carrots (peeled and chopped)
- 1/4 teaspoon of ground turmeric
- 3 cups of chicken stock
- 1 teaspoon of sea salt
- 1/3 cup of heavy cream
- 2 tablespoon of chopped cilantro
- Freshly ground pepper, for serving

Directions
1. Set your Ninja Foodi to sauté mode and heat it for 5 minutes.
2. Add oil and brown the onions. Add the garlic and cook for a minute.
3. Add the carrots, ginger, celery, and turmeric. Stir.
4. Close the pressure lid and cook on high mode for 6 minutes. Quick release the in-built pressure and open the lid.
5. Puree the soup ingredients and add cream and black pepper. Blend again.
6. Serve with cream and cilantro.

Beef Taco Soup

Preparation time: 10 minutes| Cook Time: 15 minutes| Servings:8
Ingredients
- 2 lbs of ground beef
- 1 tablespoon of onion flakes, optional
- 4 garlic cloves, minced
- 2 tablespoons of chili powder
- 2 teaspoons of cumin
- 20 oz of diced tomatoes with chilies (Rotel)
- 32 oz of beef broth
- Salt and pepper
- 8 oz of creamy cheese
- 1/2 cup of heavy cream

Optional Toppings:
- Sliced black olives
- Sour cream
- Cheddar cheese, shredded
- Sliced jalapeño peppers

Directions
1. Set your Foodi to sauté mode.
2. Add the ground beef and brown it for 5 minutes.
3. Add the diced tomatoes with chili, onion flakes, chili powder, garlic, beef broth, cumin, salt, and pepper.
4. Close the pressure lid and cook on high mode for 5 minutes. Let the pressure escape naturally for 10 minutes and quick release the rest.
5. Open the lid and add the creamy cheese and cheese. You can serve with the optional toppings.

Mexican Pork Soup

Preparation time: 10 minutes| Cook Time: 30 minutes| Servings: 12

Ingredients
- 36 oz of shredded pork shoulder
- 2 cups of cooked pumpkin
- 6 tablespoons of pork lard
- 6 cups of chicken broth
- 1 cup of cilantro, chopped
- 1 lime, cut
- A cup of canned green chili, chopped
- 4 avocados, diced
- 2 teaspoons of ground cumin
- 1 teaspoon of paprika, smoked
- 2 teaspoons of garlic powder
- 1 teaspoon of sea salt
- 1 onion, diced
- 4 cups of kale, chopped

Directions
1. Mix the cumin with garlic powder, paprika, and salt in a bowl.
2. Preheat the Foodi unit and add the pork lard, onion, pork shoulder, green chili, pumpkin, broth, and the spice mix.
3. Close the pressure lid and cook on high mode for 30 minutes.
4. Let the accumulated vapor exit naturally and open the lid.
5. Add the kale and serve with avocado and cilantro toppings. You can garnish with lime.

Zucchini Pasta Sauce

Preparation time: 3 minutes| Cook Time: 10minutes| Servings: 5

Ingredients
- 3 medium zucchinis, chopped
- 1 tablespoon of olive oil
- 2 garlic cloves, minced finely
- Pinch of crushed red pepper
- 3/4 cup of water
- 1/4 cup of fresh basil leaves
- 2 tablespoons of pine nuts
- Salt and black pepper
- 16 oz of pasta, cooked
- 1 tablespoon of vegetable essential olive oil

Directions:
1. Preheat your Foodi by sautéing it on medium high for 5 minutes.
2. Heat the oil and add garlic and the crushed red pepper. Sauté for 2 minutes and add the zucchini.
3. Pour water into the Foodi and add salt and pepper.
4. Close the pressure lid and cook on high mode for 3 minutes. Quick release the in-built pressure and open the lid. Add the pine nuts and basil leaves. Stir.
5. Transfer everything into a blender and puree. Serve your zucchini pasta sauce with cooked pasta swirled with vegetable oil.

Vegetable Stock

Preparation time: 5 minutes| Cook Time: 20 minutes| Servings: 20

Ingredients
- 1 large onion, chopped roughly
- 3 garlic cloves, minced
- 3 celery stalks, chopped roughly
- 2 large carrots, chopped roughly
- 20 peppercorns
- 5 sprigs of rosemary
- 1 bay leaf
- 1/2 small bunch of fresh thyme
- Water

Directions
1. Combine all the ingredients in the Foodi unit. Pour the water over the mixture until it fills three-quarters of the pot.
2. Close the pressure lid and cook the mixture on high mode for 20 minutes.
3. Let the pressure escape naturally and open the lid.
4. Use a strainer to squeeze the stock over a large sauce pan.
5. You can use it immediately or refrigerate for later usage.

Chicken and Vegetable Noodle Soup

Preparation time: 5 minutes| Cook Time: 25 minutes| Servings:4

Ingredients
- 2 tablespoons of coconut oil
- 1 pound of boneless and skinless chicken thighs
- 1 cup of diced carrots
- 1 cup of diced celery
- ¾ cup of green onions, chopped
- 6 cups of chicken stock
- ½ teaspoon of dried oregano
- ½ teaspoon of dried basil
- 1/8 teaspoon of fresh ground pepper
- 1 teaspoon of grey sea salt
- 2 cups of spiralized daikon noodles

Directions
1. Preheat your Ninja Foodi on sauté mode for two minutes.
2. Add some coconut oil into the pot and brown the chicken thighs.
3. Shred the chicken using a fork and then add the carrots, celery, and onions.
4. Let it cook for two minutes and add the remaining ingredients.
5. Close the pressure lid and cook on high mode for 15 minutes.
6. Quick release the in-built pressure and open the lid.

7. Add the add daikon noodles and serve.

Bacon Cheeseburger Soup

Preparation time: 5 minutes| Cook Time: 15 minutes| Servings: 6

Ingredients
- 1 pound of lean ground beef
- 1/2 can of fire-roasted tomatoes
- 3 glasses of beef broth
- 1/4 cup of cooked and crumbled bacon
- 1 tablespoon of pickled jalapenos, chopped
- 2 teaspoons of Worcestershire sauce
- 4 oz of cream cheese
- 1 cup of sharp cheddar cheese, shredded
- 1/2 medium onion, diced
- 1 teaspoon of salt
- 1/2 teaspoon of pepper
- 1/2 teaspoon of garlic powder
- A pickled spear, diced

Directions
1. Preheat your Ninja Foodi on medium high for two minutes.
2. Sauté the ground beef and onion for 5 minutes.
3. Add the tomatoes, bacon, broth, garlic powder, Worcestershire sauce, the jalapenos, salt, and pepper. Add cream cheese and stir.
4. Close the pressure lid and cook the mixture on high mode for 15 minutes.
5. Quick release the in-built pressure and open the lid.
6. Serve your cheese-burger soup while garnished with diced shredded cheddar and pickles.

Chicken Zoodle Soup

Preparation time: 5 minutes| Cook Time: 20 minutes| Servings:6

Ingredients
- 3 celery stalks, diced
- 2 tablespoons of pickled jalapeño, diced
- 1 cup bok Choy, sliced
- 3 zucchinis, spiralized
- ½ cup of fresh spinach
- 1 tablespoon of coconut oil
- ¼ medium onion, diced
- ¼ cup of button mushrooms, diced
- 2 cups of cooked chicken, diced
- 3 cups of chicken broth
- 1 bay leaf
- ½ teaspoon of garlic powder
- 1 teaspoon of salt
- ⅛ teaspoon of cayenne

Directions
1. Preheat your Foodi by sautéing it on medium heat for two minutes.
2. Add coconut oil, onions, and mushrooms. Sauté the mixture for 5 minutes or until it produce a sweet smell.
3. Add the celery, spinach, jalapeños, and bok Choy. Cook for 4 minutes and switch off the sauté mode.
4. Add mushrooms and onion. Sauté for 3 to 4 minutes or until the onion becomes translucent and fragrant.
5. Add celery and spinach. Cook for 4 minutes and open the lid.
6. Add the cooked chicken, broth, seasonings, and bay leaf. Close the pressure lid and cook on high mode for 20 minutes.
7. Release the inbuilt pressure naturally for ten minutes and quick release the rest.
8. Open the lid and add the spiralised zucchini. Sauté the zucchini mixture on low mode for 3 minutes or until they tenderize. Enjoy warm!

Homemade Hot Sauce

Preparation time: 10 minutes| Cook Time: 5 minutes| Servings: Yields 2 cups

Ingredients
- 12 oz of fresh hot peppers, chopped
- 1 medium onion, minced
- 3 garlic cloves, minced
- A teaspoon of extra virgin olive oil
- 1 teaspoon of kosher salt
- A cup of apple cider vinegar
- 1/2 cup of water

Directions:
1. Sauté the garlic, onion, vinegar, and salt for three minutes in your Foodi pot.
2. Add water and close the pressure lid. Cook for on high mode for one minute and let the pressure exit naturally.
3. Transfer the mixture into an immersion blender and Puree.
4. Add more seasonings if necessary and puree again.
5. Pour the mixture into a glass jar and let it rest for 3 days before using. You can refrigerate your hot sauce for months.

Wild Rice Soup

Preparation time: 15 minutes| Cook Time: 65 minutes| Servings: 8

Ingredients
- 1/2 cup of raw cashews
- 1 medium yellow onion
- 4 medium carrots
- 2 celery stalks
- 8 oz of baby Bella mushrooms
- 6 cloves of garlic
- 2 tablespoons of extra virgin olive oil
- 2 tablespoons of dried oregano
- 1 tablespoon of dried thyme
- 8 cups of vegetable broth
- 1 cup of wild rice
- A cup of dried great northern white beans
- 1/2 teaspoon of black pepper

- 2 1/2 teaspoons of kosher salt, divided
- 2 teaspoons of dried sage
- 1 tablespoon of soy sauce, tamari, or liquid aminos

Directions
1. Soak the cashews in water. Dice the onion, slice the celery and mushrooms, cut the carrots roundly, and mince the garlic.
2. Sauté the onion, celery, and carrot in oil for 5 minutes.
3. Add mushrooms and cook for 2 minutes. Add the garlic, oregano, and thyme. Cook and stir for 2 minutes.
4. Add the broth, dried white beans, wild rice, black pepper, and kosher salt. Close the pressure lid and cook on high mode for 50 minutes.
5. Quick release the in-built pressure and transfer 2 cups of the pot's content into a blender.
6. Drain the soaked cashews and add them into the blender. Add the dried sage.
7. Puree and repeat the procedure with the remaining beans mixture.
8. Add the soy sauce and ½ teaspoon of kosher salt. Garnish with the essential olive oil and ground pepper. Enjoy!

Chili Queso Chicken Soup

Preparation time: 5 minutes| Cook Time: 30 minutes| Servings: 6

Ingredients
- 2 chicken breast pieces (boneless and skinless)
- 28 oz of diced tomatoes
- 1/4 teaspoon of salt
- 1 cup of green salsa
- 2 cups of chicken broth
- 2 tablespoons of taco seasoning
- 8 ounces of softened cream cheese

Directions
1. Mix the chicken with juicy tomatoes, green salsa, taco seasoning, chicken broth, and salt in the Foodi.
2. Close the pressure lid and cook for 10 minutes.
3. Let the pressure escape naturally for 15 minutes. Remove the chicken pieces and transfer them on a platter.
4. Add the creamy cheese and stir until it's heated. Add the chicken pieces and serve with avocado and cheese.

Tortellini Soup

Preparation time: 5 minutes| Cook Time: 17 minutes| Servings: 4

Ingredients
- A tablespoon of garlic, minced
- 1 tablespoon of dried onion, minced
- A tablespoon of chicken base
- ½ teaspoon of pepper, coarsely ground
- 1 ½ pounds of fresh carrots (peeled and cut into ¼ inch coins)
- 6 ounces of dried cheese tortellini
- ¼ cup of dry white wine
- 6 cups of chicken stock
- 7 oz of fresh baby spinach (cleaned and stem removed)
- Parmesan cheese for garnishing

Directions
1. Combine the onions with garlic, chicken base, and ground pepper in your Foodi pot.
2. Add the carrots and spread the tortellini on top.
3. Pour the chicken broth and white wine in the Pot. Close the pressure lid and cook on high mode for two minutes.
4. Quick release the in-built steam and open the Foodi.
5. Add the spinach and stir. Allow it to rest for two minutes. Enjoy your soup with the parmesan cheese.

Cauliflower Soup

Preparation time: 15 minutes| Cook Time: 25 minutes| Servings: 6

Ingredients
- 6 slices of bacon, chopped
- 3 glasses of chicken broth
- 1½ glasses of cheese -cheddar or Monterey, shredded
- ¼ cup of onion, chopped
- ¾ cup of sour cream
- 1 green onion
- 2 garlic cloves, crushed
- A cauliflower head, cut into pieces
- 1 celery stalk, chopped
- Salt and Pepper

Directions:
1. Sauté the bacon slices while stirring frequently and transfer them to a paper-lined plate, once crispy.
2. Add the onion, garlic, celery, salt, and pepper. Cook until they soften and turn off the sauté mode.
3. Add broth and the cauliflower florets. Close the pressure lid and cook on high mode for 5 minutes.
4. Let the accumulated steam escape naturally for ten minutes and quick release the rest.
5. Add a cup of cheese and cream. Pour everything into an immersion blender and puree.
6. Add the bacon, green onion, and cheese for the topping.

Creamy Tomato Feta Soup

Preparation time:5 minutes| Cook Time: 15 minutes| Servings: 6

Ingredients
- 2 tablespoons of organic olive oil or butter
- 1/4 cup of onion, chopped

- 2 garlic cloves
- 1/8 teaspoon of black pepper
- 1/2 teaspoon of salt
- A teaspoon of pesto sauce, optional
- 1/2 teaspoon of dried oregano
- A teaspoon of dried basil
- 1 tablespoon of tomato paste, optional
- 10 tomatoes (skinned, seeded, and chopped)
- 3 glasses of water
- 1/3 cup of almond milk
- 2/3 cup of feta cheese, crumbled

Directions
1. Preheat your Foodi by sautéing it over medium high heat for 5 minutes.
2. Heat the olive oil and add the onion. Stir and cook for a minute.
3. Add the garlic and cook for another minute. Add the tomatoes, pepper, salt, optional pesto, oregano, tomato paste, basil, and water.
4. Close the pressure lid and cook on high mode for 15 minutes.
5. Let the pressure exit naturally and open the lid. Pour everything into an immersion blender and puree.
6. Add the feta cheese and almond milk and simmer on low mode for three minutes minute.
7. Serve your feta soup warm.

Spicy Cranberry Sauce

Preparation time: 2 minutes| Cook Time: 15 minutes| Servings: 21/4 cups

Ingredients
- 1 bag (12-ounce) of cranberries (rinsed and drained)
- 2-3 jalapeno peppers (seeded and minced)
- 1 teaspoons of freshly squeezed lemon juice
- 1/4 cup of dark wine
- A cup of water
- 3/4 cup of sugar

Directions:
1. Mix all the ingredients in your Foodi and stir to dissolve the sugar.
2. Close the pressure lid and cook on high mode for 10 minutes.
3. Let the accumulated vapor exit naturally for 10 minutes and quick release the rest.
4. Puree the contents partially and simmer on sauté mode until it thickens.
5. Cool and serve. You can refrigerate the leftovers for two weeks.

Silky Creamy Chicken Mulligatawny Soup

Preparation time: 15 minutes| Cook Time: 30 minutes| Servings:8

Ingredients
- 4 tablespoons of unsalted butter
- 1 small onion, chopped
- 1" fresh ginger herb, minced
- 1 celery stalk, chopped
- 2 small carrots, diced
- 2 teaspoons of curry powder
- ½ teaspoons of black pepper, freshly ground
- 1 teaspoon of sea salt
- 1/8 teaspoon of ground nutmeg
- 1/8 teaspoon of dried thyme
- 8 chicken thighs (bony but skinless)
- 3 cups of chicken broth
- 2 cups of cauliflower florets, minced
- 2 cups of coconut milk full fat
- ¼ cup of fresh cilantro chopped, plus more for garnishing

Directions
1. Preheat the unit on sauté mode. Melt the butter and add the onions and garlic.
2. Cook the onions until they soften. Add the carrots and celery and cook while stirring for a minute.
3. Add the remaining ingredients (except cilantro and coconut milk) and close the pressure lid.
4. Cook the mixture on high mode for fifteen minutes. Quick release the in-built steam and open the lid.
5. Add the coconut milk and cilantro. Stir. Serve your soup while garnished with cilantro.

Spicy Pasta Sauce

Preparation time: 10 minutes| Cook Time: 15 minutes| Servings: 4

Ingredients
- 3 tablespoons of canola oil
- 1 medium onion, chopped
- 4 garlic cloves, chopped
- 1 can (28-oz) of crushed tomatoes
- A tablespoon of dried dill
- 2 tablespoons of dried basil
- 1 tablespoon of dried thyme
- 1/4 teaspoon of crushed red pepper flakes
- 2 teaspoons of dried oregano
- 1/3 cup of dry dark wine
- 1/2 cup of water
- 1 bay leaf

Directions:
1. Preheat your Ninja Foodi on sauté mode over medium high for 5 minutes.
2. Sauté the onions and garlic.
3. Add the remaining ingredients and stir.
4. Close the pressure lid and cook for 10 minutes.
5. Quick release the in-built pressure and open the lid. Serve the spicy pasta with cooked pasta.

Ethiopian Spinach Lentil Soup

Preparation time: 5 minutes| Cook Time: 20 minutes| Servings: 5

Ingredients
- 6 ounces of spinach
- 2 cups of lentils

- 8 glasses of water
- 1 medium red onion, chopped finely
- 4 tablespoons of lemon juice
- 1 tablespoon of essential olive oil
- 2 tablespoons of unsalted butter
- 2 teaspoons of ground coriander
- 2 teaspoons of salt
- ½ teaspoon of turmeric powder
- 1 teaspoon of garlic powder
- ½ teaspoon of cinnamon powder
- ¼ teaspoon of cayenne pepper
- ¼ teaspoon of pepper
- ¼ teaspoon of fresh nutmeg, grated
- ¼ teaspoon of cardamom powder
- ¼ teaspoon of clove powder

Directions
1. Preheat the unit on sauté mode.
2. Heat the oil and butter. Add all the herbs and spices (except the fresh lemon juice, salt, and pepper) and cook for 3 minutes.
3. Add water and lentils. Stir and close the pressure lid. Cook everything on high mode for 10 minutes.
4. Let the in-built vapor exit naturally for 10 minutes and quick release the rest.
5. Season your lentil soup with salt and pepper. Add spinach and the fresh lemon juice. Stir and serve hot.

Beans Chicken Chili

Preparation time: 5 minutes| Cook Time: 8 minutes |Servings: 4
Ingredients
- 2 cans (15-oz) of great Northern beans, drained
- 4 cups of cooked and shredded chicken
- 2 cups of Salsa Verde
- 6 glasses of chicken stock
- 2 teaspoons of ground cumin

Directions:
1. Add all the ingredients (except the beans) in the pot.
2. Close the pressure lid and cook the mixture on high mode for 8 minutes.
3. Quick release the in-built vapor and open the lid. Add beans and stir.

Bacon Potato Soup

Preparation time: 10 minutes| Cook Time: 20 minutes |Servings: 4
Ingredients
- 5 pounds of Yukon gold potatoes (peeled and chopped)
- 2 glasses of water
- 2 cups of chicken broth
- 1 cup of bacon, chopped
- ½ cup of cheese

Directions:
1. Mix water with broth and potatoes. Stir.
2. Close the pressure lid and cook the potatoes on high mode for 20 minutes.
3. Quick release the accumulated steam and open the lid.
4. Add three-quarter cup of bacon and puree everything using an immersion blender.
5. Serve your bacon potato soup topped with bacon and cheese.

Matzo Ball Soup

Preparation time: 15 minutes| Cook Time: 65 minutes| Servings: 6
Ingredients
- 2 1/4 chicken thighs, bone-in
- 1 1/2 yellow onions, diced
- 3 celery stalks
- 2 1/4 carrots, diced
- 3 cloves of garlic
- 2 fresh parsley sprigs, cut
- 1 bay leaf
- Salt and ground black pepper
- 1/3 cup of matzo meal
- 1 1/2 tablespoons of essential olive oil
- 1 1/2 eggs, slightly whisked
- 3/4 teaspoon of baking powder

Directions
1. Put the chicken, onions, celery, carrots, parsley, garlic, and bay leaf in the Foodi pot.
2. Add salt and pepper to the mixture. Stir and add some water. Secure the pressure lid and cook on high mode for 35 minutes. Let the pressure release naturally and open the lid.
3. Mix the matzo meal with beaten eggs, oil, baking powder, salt, and pepper in a bowl.
4. Cover the matzo mix using a plastic wrap and leave it for fifteen minutes.
5. Reset the Foodi pot to sauté mode. Roll the matzo mixture into balls and drop them in the soup.
6. Cook-stir gently for 30 minutes or until the ball soup is well-cooked.

Homemade Marinara Sauce

Preparation time: 10 minutes| Cook Time: 35 minutes| Servings: 6
Ingredients
- 4 tablespoons of olive oil
- 3 garlic cloves, minced
- 1/3 cup of onions, diced
- 2 large carrots, diced
- 3 tablespoons of chopped fresh parsley
- 1 can (28-oz) of whole tomatoes, crushed
- A teaspoon of dried oregano
- 1/4 teaspoon of ground black pepper
- 1/2 teaspoon of dried thyme
- 1/2 teaspoon of salt

Directions:
1. Preheat the Foodi unit on sauté mode. Add the onion and garlic in oil. Cook for two minutes and add the carrots.

2. Cook for two minutes and add the crushed tomatoes (juice inclusive,) parsley, thyme, oregano, pepper, and salt.
3. Secure the pressure lid and cook on high mode for 30 minutes. Quick release the in-built pressure and open the lid. Serve.

Cabbage Roll Soup

Preparation time: 15 minutes| Cook Time: 45 minutes| Servings: 5

Ingredients
- 3 tablespoons of canola oil
- 1 1/2 pound of ground pork
- 4 cloves of garlic (peeled and minced)
- 1 medium onion, chopped
- 5 cups of beef broth
- 1 can (6 oz) of tomato paste
- A can (28 oz,) of tomatoes (crushed or diced)
- 1 medium cabbage (cored and chopped)
- A tablespoon of dried oregano
- 1/4 cup of chopped fresh parsley
- 2 teaspoons of chopped fresh thyme
- Salt and pepper

Directions
1. Brown the ground pork and onions on sauté mode. Add the garlic and stir. Cook for 2 minutes.
2. Add the remaining ingredients and stir.
3. Close the pressure lid and cook on high mode for 35 minutes.
4. Let the in-built vapor exit naturally for 20 minutes and quick release the rest.
5. Serve your roll soup with sour cream and sprinkle it with thyme leaves.

Pot Roast Soup

Preparation time: ten minutes| Cook Time: 40 minutes| Servings: 6

Ingredients
- 2 lbs of chuck roast, cubed
- ½ teaspoon of black pepper
- ½ teaspoon of kosher salt
- 2 tablespoons of organic olive oil
- 3 carrots (peeled and chopped)
- 1 white onion, chopped
- 2 celery stalks, chopped
- 1 green pepper, chopped
- 4 garlic cloves
- 1/3 cup of farro
- 4 glasses of beef stock
- ¼ cup of tomato paste
- Salt and pepper
- A teaspoon of dried thyme

Directions
1. Season the cubed roast with salt and pepper. Brown the seasoned roast on sauté mode. Remove and set aside.
2. Add the vegetables and cook for 6-7 minutes. Remove and set aside.
3. Return the browned beef into the Foodi and add the farro, tomato paste, thyme, and beef stock.
4. Close the pressure lid and cook on high mode for twenty minutes.
5. Let the pressure exit naturally for 5 minutes and quick release the rest.
6. Open lid and return the cooked veggies.
7. Simmer on sauté for three minutes and serve hot.

Sweet Tomato Chutney

Preparation time: 5 minutes| Cook Time: 15 minutes| Servings: 5 cups

Ingredients
- 2 pounds (about 2 /1/2 cups) of tomatoes, chopped
- 1 red onion, sliced thinly
- 1 apple (peeled, cored, and sliced)
- A tablespoon of ginger, finely chopped
- 3/4 cup of red wine vinegar
- 1/4 cup of organic brown sugar
- 1/2 cup of maple syrup
- Dried red chili flakes

Directions:
1. Combine all the ingredients in the Foodi pot and stir well.
2. Close the pressure lid and cook on high mode for 10 minutes.
3. Allow the pressure to exit naturally for 10 minutes and quick release the rest.
4. Sauté and simmer the mixture until it thickens.
5. Let it relax overnight before using. Store covered in the refrigerator for a month.

VEGETARIAN AND VEGAN

Mushroom Rice Pilaf

Preparation time: 20 minutes| Cook Time: 5 minutes| Servings: 6

Ingredients
- 1/4 cup of butter
- 1 cup of medium grain rice
- 1/2 pound of baby Portobello mushrooms, sliced
- 2 garlic cloves, minced
- 6 green onions, chopped
- 1 cup of water
- 4 teaspoons of beef base

Directions
1. Preheat your Ninja pot for two minutes on sauté mode.
2. Add the butter and heat it. Add the rice and cook for about 5 minutes or until lightly browned.
3. Add the mushrooms, the green onions, and garlic.
4. Combine the beef base and water. Stir and pour over the rice mixture.
5. Close the pressure lid and cook on high mode for four minutes.
6. Let the in-built steam exit naturally. Serve your rice pilaf with green onions.

Spaghetti Squash with Tomatoes

Enjoy a simple and tasty squash as a vegetarian side dish. You can top it with canned tuna to make it a main dish.

Preparation time: 15minutes| Cook Time: 10 minutes |Servings: 10

Ingredients
- 1 medium spaghetti squash (halved lengthwise and deseeded)
- 1/4 cup of green olives with pimientos, sliced
- 1 can (14 oz) of diced tomatoes, drained
- A teaspoon of dried oregano
- 1/2 teaspoon of pepper
- 1/2 teaspoon of salt
- 1/2 cup of cheddar cheese, shredded
- 1/4 cup of fresh basil, minced

Directions:
1. Insert the reversible rack in the Foodi pot and add cup of water.
2. Add the squash into the rack and close the pressure lid.
3. Cook the squash on high mode for 7 minutes. Quick release the in-built steam and open the lid. Remove the rack containing the cooked squash.
4. Drain the liquid in the Ninja Foodi pot. Use a fork to separate the squash into spaghetti-like strands.
5. Throw away the skin and return the squash back into the pot.
6. Add the tomatoes, olives, oregano, salt, and pepper. Stir.
7. Select the Sauté function and cook the mixture on low heat for 3 minutes.
8. Serve your spaghetti squash topped with basil and cheese.

Sweet Potato and Black-Eyed Peas

Preparation time: 15 minutes| Cook time: 20 minutes| servings: 4-6

Ingredients
- 3 medium sweet potatoes (cut)
- 1 medium red onion, chopped
- A tablespoon of olive oil
- 3 garlic cloves, crushed
- 1/2 red bell pepper, diced
- 1 celery stalk, chopped
- 1/2 teaspoon of ground coriander
- 1 tablespoon of dried oregano
- A teaspoon of ground cumin
- 1 teaspoon of ground cinnamon
- 2 tablespoons of chili powder
- 1 lb of kale, chopped
- 1 can (15 ounce) of black-eyed peas (drained and rinsed)
- 3 fresh tomatoes, chopped
- A cup of vegetable broth
- 1/2 cup of water
- 1/2 teaspoon of sea salt
- 3 tablespoons of balsamic vinegar

Directions:
1. Preheat your Foodi pot on sauté mode and add oil, onions, and garlic. Cook for two minutes and add the bell pepper and celery. Stir and let it cook for two-3 minutes.
2. Add the coriander, the cumin, cinnamon, oregano, and chili powder. Let it cook for two minutes.
3. Add the black-eyed peas and stir. Add some water, tomatoes, and broth. Insert the reversible rack and add the potato chunks.
4. Close the pressure lid and cook on high mode for 12 minutes.
5. Let the accumulated pressure escape naturally for ten minutes and quick release the rest.
6. Open the lid and remove the rack. Season peas with salt and drizzle the potatoes with balsamic vinegar.

Vegetable Biryani

A colorful and healthy Indian vegetable dish!
Preparation time: 15minutes| Cook Time: 15 minutes |Servings: 8

Ingredients
- 1 1/2 cups of coconut milk
- 2 cups of rice
- 1 1/2 cups of water
- A medium onion, thinly sliced
- 1 tablespoon of coconut oil
- 1 inch of ginger, grated
- 5 cloves of garlic, grated
- 1 small cauliflower head, separated into florets
- A large carrot (cut into 1" pieces)
- 2 large potatoes (cut into 1" chunks)
- 1 cup of green beans
- 1/4 cup of mint leaves, chopped
- 1/4 cup of coriander leaves, chopped
- 1/4 cup of fried onions
- A teaspoon of black cumin, shah jeera or regular cumin
- 5 green cardamom pods
- 3 cloves
- 2-3 dry bay leaves
- 1 star anise
- 2 teaspoon of Biryani Masala
- Juice extracted from one lemon

Directions
1. Preheat your Ninja Foodi on sauté mode over medium heat for two minutes.
2. Add the cloves, black cumin, star anise, cardamom, and bay leaves and cook in oil for one minute while stirring constantly.
3. Add the onions and cook until slightly browned. Add the ginger and garlic and let it cook for another minute.
4. Add the carrots, potatoes, green beans, and cauliflower.
5. Combine and cook while stirring occasionally for 3 minutes.
6. Add fried onions, Biryani Masala, and coconut milk.
7. Add the mint and coriander leaves. Stir thoroughly to mix well.
8. Add water and salt.
9. Add the fresh lemon juice to the rice and stir. Close the pressure lid and cook on high mode for 10 minutes.
10. Let the in-built steam release naturally and open the lid. Fluff the rice using a spoon and serve with raita.

Chicory and Carrots Salad

Preparation time: 10 minutes| Cook time: 10 minutes| Servings: 4

Ingredients
- A bunch of chicory
- 1 large peeled and grated carrot
- 1 garlic herb, minced
- A cup of vegetable broth
- 1 sprig of thyme
- Salt and pepper
- 3 tablespoons of olive oil
- 2 tablespoons of fresh lemon juice
- 1 tablespoon of balsamic vinegar

Directions:
1. Rinse the chicory, dry, and tear them into pieces.
2. Sauté the carrots in oil and cook for two minutes.
3. Add garlic and thyme. Stir and add the chicory.
4. Add the vegetable broth and season with salt and pepper. Close the pressure lid and cook on high mode for 5 minutes.
5. Let the in-built vapor escape naturally and open the lid. Discard thyme and transfer chicory and carrots into a bowl.
6. Add an olive oil, freshly squeezed lemon juice, and vinegar. Toss and serve.

Sweet Potatoes with Thai Peanut Butter Sauce

Preparation time: 10 minutes| Cook Time: 25 minutes |Servings: 4

Sweet potatoes and slaw:
- 4 medium sweet potatoes (10 -12 oz each)
- 1/4 red cabbage, shredded (3 cups)
- 1/2 yellow bell pepper, sliced thinly
- 1/2 red bell pepper, sliced thinly
- A green onion, sliced thinly
- 1/4 cup of cilantro, chopped
- 2 tablespoons of fresh lime juice
- 1/4 teaspoon of kosher salt
- Crushed peanuts, for garnishing

Thai peanut butter sauce:
- 2 tablespoons of soy sauce
- 1/3 cup of peanut butter
- 2 tablespoons of lime juice
- A teaspoon of maple syrup
- 2 tablespoons of water

Directions
1. Begin by preheating the Foodi unit for 5 minutes on roast mode at 375°F.
2. Half the potatoes and rub its sides with extra virgin olive oil.
3. Place the potatoes on a lined tray and close the crisping lid. Bake for 25 minutes or until they tenderize.

4. Combine the cabbage with green onion, peppers, and cilantro in a large bowl. Add the lime juice and salt. Stir.
5. Combine the soy sauce, peanut butter, maple syrup, lime juice, and water in a small bowl to make the sauce. Season the butter sauce with salt.
6. Slice sweet potatoes by half and top it with top with all the slaw. Serve your sweet potatoes with the Thai peanut butter sauce, sprinkled with chopped peanuts.

Curried Peppers Stuffed With Lentil

Preparation time: 10 Minutes| Cook Time: 30 Minutes| Servings: 4
Directions
- 4 large green sweet peppers (cored and diced)
- 1 yellow onion, diced
- 8 oz of Cremini mushrooms, diced
- A cup of dry brown rice
- 1 cup of dry lentils
- 3 cups of vegetable broth
- 1½ tablespoons of curry powder, salt-free
- 1 teaspoon of garlic powder
- 2 tablespoons of fresh ginger, minced
- 3/4 cup of raw cashews, chopped roughly
- 3 tablespoons of tamari

Directions
1. Add all the ingredients into the pot (except the cored peppers, tamari, and cashews.)Stir. Close the pressure lid and cook on high mode for fifteen minutes.
2. Let the pressure exit naturally for 10 minutes before quick releasing the rest.
3. Open the lid and add cashews and tamari into the Foodi. Stir and stuff them in the cored peppers and top with the reserved cashews.
4. Rinse the pot and transfer the peppers into the basket. Insert it in the Foodi and close the crisping lid.
5. Roast your curried peppers at 360°F for fifteen minutes and enjoy.

Spinach Chana Dal

Preparation time: 20 minutes| Cook time: 18 minutes| Servings: 6
Ingredients
- 1/2 cup of yellow split chickpeas (channa dal)
- 2 tablespoons of essential olive oil
- 1 (8-oz) package of frozen spinach, thawed
- A teaspoon of cumin seeds
- 1 garlic herb, minced
- 1 medium onion, finely chopped
- 1 tablespoon of fresh ginger (peeled and minced)
- 1 large tomato, finely chopped
- Pinch salt
- 1/2 teaspoon of cayenne
- 1 small potato (peeled and finely chopped)
- A small carrot (peeled and finely chopped)
- 1/2 bunch of fresh dill, finely chopped
- A cup of water

Directions:
1. Sort the chickpeas and wash. Chop the vegetables.
2. Sauté the garlic, cumin seeds, onion and ginger in oil. Cook and stir until golden.
3. Add the yellow split chickpeas and cook for five minutes while stirring occasionally.
4. Add tomatoes, cayenne pepper, and salt. Let it cook for two minutes.
5. Add the chopped potatoes, carrot, dill, and thawed spinach. Cook and stir for 5 minutes.
6. Add some water and close the pressure lid.
7. Cook on high mode for 1 minute.
8. Let the pressure exit naturally and open the lid.
9. Mash the vegetables and chickpeas. Serve. Garnish with cilantro and enjoy with naan or steamed rice.

Smoky Lentils and Rice

Preparation time: 3 minutes| Cook Time: 37 minutes| Servings: 8
Ingredients
- 4 cups of vegetable broth
- 2 cups of long grain brown rice
- 2 cups of French green lentils
- 2 tablespoons of smoked paprika
- 2 teaspoons of onion powder
- 2 teaspoons of fennel seeds
- 1 teaspoon of granulated garlic powder
- A teaspoon of kosher salt
- 1 teaspoon of black pepper
- A tablespoon of apple cider vinegar

Directions
1. Put all the ingredients (except vinegar) in the pot.
2. Stir close the pressure lid. Cook the mixture on high mode for 16 minutes and let the in-built vapor exit naturally.
3. Open the lid and add the vinegar. Confirm the salt taste and serve warm.

Zucchini Tomato Medley

Preparation time: 3 minutes| Cook time: 15 minutes| Servings: 4
Ingredients
- A tablespoon of extra virgin olive oil
- 1 lb of cherry tomatoes
- 1 onion, chopped roughly

- 4 medium zucchini, chopped
- 2 tablespoons of tomato paste
- 3/4 cup of water
- 1/2 teaspoon of basil, dried
- 1/2 teaspoon of oregano, dried
- 1 teaspoon of salt
- 2 garlic cloves, minced
- 1 basil
- Olive oil

Directions:
1. Sauté the onion in olive oil until it tenderizes.
2. Add cherry tomatoes, chopped zucchini, tomato paste, water, basil, oregano, and salt.
3. Close the lid and cook your zucchini mixture on high mode for 6 minutes. Quick release the accumulated steam and open the lid. Add garlic and stir.
4. Use the slotted spoon to strain the veggies and serve with fresh basil and extra virgin olive oil.
5. You can refrigerate the cooking liquid and use it as stock for other recipes.

Millet, Beans, and Quinoa

Preparation time: 10 minutes| Cook time: 10 minutes |Servings: 4

Ingredients
- 1/2 cup of kidney or Great Northern beans (dried and soaked overnight)
- 1 cup of quinoa (rinsed and drained)
- 1/2 cup of millet (rinsed and drained)
- 2 celery stalks, chopped
- 2 carrots, sliced
- 1 small onion, diced
- 1 cup of water
- 2 cups of vegetable broth
- 1 teaspoon of thyme
- Salt

Directions:
1. Rinse and drain the beans and pour them into your Foodi.
2. Add the remaining ingredients (except salt) and stir.
3. Secure the pressure lid and cook the bean mix on high mode for ten minutes.
4. Let the in-built pressure exit naturally and open the lid.
5. Stir and season with salt.
6. Fluff the mixture with a fork and cook again for 5 minutes.

Millet and Pinto Bean Chili

Preparation time: 3 hours| Cook time: 40 minutes| Servings: 6

Ingredients
- 1 tablespoon of essential olive oil
- 1/2 onion, chopped
- 1 bell pepper, chopped
- 2 garlic cloves, minced
- 2 tablespoons of chili powder
- 2 teaspoons of powered cocoa
- 1 teaspoon of garlic powder
- A teaspoon of paprika
- 1/2 teaspoon of red chili flakes
- 1/2 teaspoon of ground cinnamon
- 1 bay leaf
- 2 cups of pinto beans (soaked 5 hours)
- A cup of millet (uncooked)
- 1 cup of sweet corn kernels
- 1/4 cup of chopped fresh parsley
- 1/4 cup of chopped fresh cilantro
- 2 cups of fire-roasted and diced tomatoes
- 7 cups of vegetable stock
- 1 tablespoon of coconut sugar
- A cup of fresh mixed greens
- 1 teaspoon of apple cider vinegar treatment
- Sea salt
- Fresh cilantro or parsley, optional garnish

Directions
1. Soak the dried pinto beans for 3 hours.
2. Sauté the chopped onion, garlic, and the bell pepper in oil while stirring frequently.
3. Cook for 5 minutes and add the spices including bay leaf.
4. Sauté for a minute and add the pinto beans, corn, millet, cilantro, and parsley.
5. Cook while stirring for another minute.
6. Add tomatoes and stock. Close the pressure lid and cook for 33 minutes.
7. Quick release the in-built vapor and open the lid.
8. Add vinegar, sugar, and the greens. Stir and season with salt.
9. You can serve with the optional garnishing.

Buffalo Wing Potatoes

Prep: 15 minute |Cook: 5 minutes |servings: 6

Ingredients
- water
- 2 pounds of Yukon Gold potatoes, cubed
- 1/2 small red onion, chopped
- 1 small sweet-yellow pepper, chopped
- 1/4 cup of buffalo wing sauce
- 1/2 cup of cheddar cheese, shredded

Directions
1. Pour a cup of water into the Foodi.
2. Add the cubed potatoes, onions, and yellow pepper.
3. Close the pressure lid and cook on high mode for three minutes.
4. Quick release the accumulated vapor and transfer the potato mixture to a bowl.

5. Discard the cooking liquid and add the buffalo wing sauce into the potatoes.
6. Ensure that they are well coated and sprinkle them with cheese.
7. Cover for 1-2 minutes or until the cheese melts.
8. Top with crumbled bacon, green onions, and sour cream.

Vegan Bread

Preparation time: ten minutes| Cook time: 25 minutes| Servings: 1
Ingredients
1 1/2 cups of whole-wheat flour
1 1/2 cups of all- purpose flour
A teaspoon of salt
1 1/4 cup of almond milk
1/2 teaspoon of baking soda
1 tablespoon of organic olive oil
A tablespoon of sesame seeds
1/2 teaspoon of baking soda
Directions:
1. Coat a 1-quart metal pan with organic olive oil.
2. Combine the flour with baking soda and salt in a bowl.
3. Add the almond milk and stir. Knead the dough for two minutes using your hands. You can also add more water if necessary.
4. Put the dough in a greased metal pan and smear it with oil. Sprinkle with sesame seeds and cover the pan loosely with an oiled aluminum foil.
5. Insert the reversible rack in the Foodi add hot water up to 1" above the rack.
6. Place the pan on the rack and close the pressure lid. Cook the dough on high mode for 25 minutes.
7. Let the pressure escape naturally and open the lid. Leave it to cool for 10 minutes and serve in slices.

Chickpea Tagine

A great Moroccan dish!
Preparation time: 30 minutes| Cook Time: 5 minutes| Servings: 12
Ingredients
- 2 garlic cloves, minced
- 2 tablespoons of olive oil
- 2 teaspoons of paprika
- 1 teaspoon of ground cumin
- A teaspoon of ground ginger
- 1/4 teaspoon of pepper
- 1/2 teaspoon of salt
- 1/4 teaspoon of ground cinnamon
- Butternut squash-about 2 lb (peeled and cubed)
- 2 medium zucchini, cut into pieces
- 1 can (15 oz) of chickpeas (rinsed and drained)
- 1 medium sweet red pepper, chopped coarsely
- 1 medium onion, coarsely chopped
- 12 dried apricots, halved
- 1/2 cup of water
- 2 teaspoons of harissa chili paste
- 2 teaspoons of honey
- 1 can (14.5 oz) of crushed tomatoes, undrained
- 1/4 cup of fresh mint leaves, chopped
- Plain Greek yogurt, optional

Directions
1. Preheat your Ninja Foodi by sautéing it over medium high heat.
2. Add oil and heat it. Add the garlic, ginger, cumin, cinnamon, paprika, salt, and pepper.
3. Cook and stir for a minute or until it turns fragrant.
4. Add the zucchini, squash, chickpeas, onion, red pepper, water, apricots, harissa, and honey. Close the pressure lid and cook on high mode for 3 minutes.
5. Quick release the in-built pressure and open the lid.
6. Add the tomatoes and mint. Once heated, serve while topped with extra mint, yoghurt, honey, and extra virgin olive oil.

Pressure-Cooked Summer Squash

Preparation time: 20 minutes| Cook Time: 5 minutes |Servings: 8
Ingredients
- 1 lb of medium yellow summer squash
- 2 medium tomatoes, chopped
- 1 lb of medium zucchini
- A cup of vegetable broth
- 1/4 cup of green onions, thinly sliced
- 1/4 teaspoon of pepper
- 1/2 teaspoon of salt
- 1-1/2 cups of Caesar salad croutons, crushed coarsely
- 1/2 cup of cheddar cheese, shredded
- 4 bacon strips (cooked and crumbled)

Directions
1. Begin by cutting the squash into thick slices (approximately 1/4-inches) and put them in your Foodi.
2. Add the broth, tomatoes, green onions, salt, and pepper.
3. Close the pressure lid and cook on high mode for a minute. Quick release the accumulated vapor and open the lid.
4. Remove the squash from the Foodi using a slotted spoon.

5. Serve your summer squash topped with croutons, bacons, and cheese.

Bean Pasta

Preparation time 10 minutes |Cook Time 40 minutes |Servings: 6

Ingredients
- 1/2 bag of Goya 16 bean soup mix
- 1 teaspoon of canola oil
- 1 small onion, diced
- 1 teaspoon of garlic, minced
- 14 oz of canned tomatoes, crushed
- 2-3 glasses of vegetable stock
- Salt and pepper
- 1/2 cup of your preferred pasta
- 1/4 cup of mozzarella
- Parsley for garnishing

Directions
1. Soak the beans in water overnight. Rinse then drain them.
2. Set your Foodi to sauté mode and add oil and garlic.
3. Add the tomatoes, stock, salt, and pepper. Add the soaked beans and close the pressure lid.
4. Cook the bean mixture on high mode for 15 minutes and quick release the in-built steam.
5. Open the lid and add the pasta. Cover for around ten minutes to soften the pasta.
6. Transfer a cup of the mixture to an immersion blender and puree it.
7. Add it to the remaining mixture and stir to thicken the soup. Enjoy!

Sicilian Steamed Leeks

Preparation time: 10 minutes |Cook Time: 5 minutes| Servings: 6

Ingredients
- 1 large tomato
- 1 small navel orange
- 2 tablespoons of fresh parsley, minced
- 2 tablespoons of Greek olives, sliced
- 1 teaspoon of capers, drained
- A teaspoon of organic olive oil
- 1 teaspoon of dark wine vinegar
- 1/2 teaspoon of orange zest, grated
- 1/2 teaspoon of pepper
- 6 medium leeks (white part only), halved lengthwise and cleaned
- Crumbled feta cheese

Directions
1. Begin by preparing the ingredients. Chop the tomato, peel, and chop the orange.
2. Cut the white portion of the leeks into two across the length then wash it.
3. Add all the ingredients (except the leeks and cheese) in a bowl.
4. Insert the reversible rack in Foodi and a cup of water.
5. Place the leeks on the rack and close the pressure lid.
6. Steam the leeks on low mode for two minutes.
7. Quick release the accumulated vapor and open the lid carefully.
8. Transfer the steamed leeks to a platter and ladle the tomato mixture. Sprinkle the dish with cheese.

Lemony Broccoli

Enjoy as a meal or side dish!
Preparation time: 5 minutes |Cook time: 2 minutes |Servings: 4

Ingredients
- 2 lbs of broccoli
- 4 lemon slices
- 3/4 cup of water
- Salt and pepper

Directions:
1. Remove the broccoli stalks and discard. Slice the remaining stem and the florets.
2. Pour water into the Foodi and insert the basket.
3. Add the broccoli, lemon slices, salt, and pepper.
4. Secure the pressure lid and cook on high mode for two minutes.
5. Quick release the in-built steam and serve.

Risotto with Lima Beans

Preparation time: 15 minutes| Cook time: 10 minutes| Servings: 4

Ingredients
- A tablespoon of butter
- 1 small onion, diced
- 3 garlic cloves, minced
- A cup of fresh lima beans
- 1 cup of Arborio rice
- 8 oz of mushrooms, diced
- 1 1/4 cups of water
- 2 cups of vegetable broth
- 3 tablespoons of grated parmesan cheese
- 1/2 teaspoon of salt

Directions:
1. Melt the butter and add onions and garlic.
2. Sauté the ingredients for 3 minutes or until the onion soften.
3. Add the mushrooms, lima beans, and rice. Stir. Add water and broth.
4. Close the pressure lid and cook the mushroom mixture on high mode for 7 minutes. Quick release the in-built pressure and open the lid.

5. Add the parmesan cheese and salt. Stir and enjoy.

Vegetable Mélange

Preparation time: 20 minutes| Cook time: 10 minutes| Servings: 4
Ingredients
- 1/2 cup of vegetable oil
- 1 medium onion, chopped
- A teaspoon of dried dill
- 1 garlic herb, chopped
- 1/4 cup of parsley, diced thinly
- 1 cup of vegetable broth
- 3/4 cup of red split lentils
- 3 large tomatoes (sliced and deseeded)
- 2 cups of frozen peas, thawed
- 1 teaspoon of fresh chopped basil
- 2 large carrots, sliced
- 4 medium potatoes (skinned and sliced)
- 2 zucchini, cut largely
- 3 stalks of celery, sliced
- 1 green pepper (deseeded and sliced)
- Salt and pepper

Directions:
1. Preheat your Ninja Foodi by sautéing it on medium high heat for two minutes.
2. Add oil and heat it. Sauté the onions for two minutes and add the dill, garlic, and parsley.
3. Add the broth followed by tomatoes, frozen peas, carrots, basil, celery, zucchini, and green pepper.
4. Add salt and pepper. Close the pressure lid and cook on high mode for 6 minutes.
5. When the cooking time elapses, natural release the accumulated steam.
6. Open the lid and stir. Drain the excess liquid and serve.

Black Beans and Potato

Preparation time: 10 minutes| Cook time: 8 minutes| Servings: 2-3
Ingredients
- A (14-oz) can of beans (drained and rinsed)
- 2 carrots, cubed
- 3 potatoes, diced
- 1 cup of vegetable broth
- 1/2 cup of salsa
- A pound of baby arugula (washed and drained)

Directions
1. Add all the ingredients (except arugula) into your Foodi pot.
2. Close the pressure lid and cook the mixture on high mode for 4 minutes.
3. Quick release the in-built pressure and open the lid.
4. Add the arugula and stir. Cover and allow it to rest for 5 minutes.

Hearty Ratatouille

Preparation time: 20 minutes| Cook time: 25 minutes| Servings: 4
Ingredients
- 4 tablespoons of essential olive oil
- 1 potato, diced
- 2 sweet peppers (seeded and sliced)
- 1 small eggplant (peeled and cubed)
- 2 medium zucchini, sliced
- 2 garlic cloves, minced
- 1 large onion, chopped
- 1/4 cup of vegetable stock
- 2 tablespoons of minced parsley
- 2 medium tomatoes, chopped
- Salt and pepper

Directions
1. Sauté the bell pepper, potato, eggplant, zucchini with half of the olive oil in your Foodi. You can cook these in batches.
2. Transfer the potato mixture into a platter and clean the pot.
3. Add the remaining oil, garlic, and onion into the Foodi and sauté them until the onion tenders.
4. Return the stir-fried vegetables to the pot and add the remaining ingredients.
5. Close the pressure lid and cook on high mode for 4 minutes.
6. Quick release the accumulated steam and open the lid. Simmer for three minutes to thicken the sauce.

Stuffed Acorn Squash with Pecans

Preparation time: 20 minutes| Cook time: 15 minutes| Servings: 4
Ingredients
- 1 cup of white basmati rice
- 1/2 teaspoon of dried sage
- 1/2 teaspoon of kosher salt, divided
- 2 small acorn squash
- 2 cloves of garlic
- 1 small yellow onion
- 2 celery stalks
- 1 tablespoon of organic olive oil
- A teaspoon of dried thyme
- 1 teaspoon of dried oregano
- 3 tablespoons of unsalted butter
- Fresh ground black pepper
- 3/4 cup of raw pecan pieces

Directions
1. Put the rice, sage, a cup of water, and a quarter teaspoon of kosher salt into a Ninja Foodi.

2. Cook the mixture on high mode for 3 minutes. Let the accumulated pressure exit naturally for 10 minutes and quick release the rest.
3. Meanwhile, half the squash and extract the seeds. Half it again to obtain quarter pieces. Dice the celery and onions and mince the garlic.
4. Transfer the cooked rice into a bowl and cover it. Rinse the pot.
5. Pour a cup of water into the rinsed Foodi and insert the basket. Rub the squash with olive oil and sprinkle it with oregano. Put it into the basket and close the crisping lid.
6. Bake/roast the squash at 375°F for 30 minutes
7. Meanwhile, toast the pecans in the skillet for 3 minutes while stirring.
8. Remove and add the organic olive oil. Sauté the onions and celery until they tenderize.
9. Add the garlic, oregano, and thyme. Cook the spices for 2 minutes.
10. Transfer the cooked rice into the skillet and add the black pepper, pecans, butter and ¼ teaspoon kosher salt.
11. Serve your stuffed squash with pecans.

RICE/PASTA

Mac 'N' Cheese

Preparation time: 10 minutes |Cook Time: 31 minutes| Servings: 5

Ingredients
- 1 can (15 oz) of butternut squash puree
- 1 package (12 oz) of frozen cauliflower rice
- 5 cups of water, divided
- A cup of heavy cream
- 1 box (16 ounces) of dry pasta, cavatappi
- 1 teaspoon of kosher salt, plus more
- 2 cups of cheddar cheese, grated
- 3/4 package (6 oz) of creamy cheese
- Ground black pepper
- 1/4 cup (1/2 stick) of unsalted butter, melted
- 3/4 cup of panko bread crumbs
- 1/2 cup of parmesan cheese, shredded
- 1 tablespoon of fresh parsley, minced

Directions
1. Put the cauliflower rice, butternut squash puree, heavy cream, pasta, 4 cups of water, and salt in a Ninja Foodi.
2. Close the pressure lid and cook on high mode for 2 minutes. Let the pressure exit naturally for ten minutes and open the lid.
3. Add the cream cheese, cheddar, and the remaining water. Stir. Season the cauliflower mixture with salt and pepper.
4. Add the bread crumbs, butter, parmesan, and parsley in a bowl. Stir. Sprinkle your Mac and cheese with the bread crumb mixture.
5. Close the crisping lid and broil for 9 minutes. Serve!

Cabbage Risotto

Preparation time: 10 minutes |Cook time: 15 minutes| Servings: 4

Ingredients
- 2 garlic cloves, minced
- 1 tablespoon of essential olive oil
- A medium yellow onion, diced
- 3 cups of vegetable broth
- 2 cups of Arborio rice
- 1/2 cup of white grape juice
- A teaspoon of saffron (about 1 large pinch)
- 1/4 cup of fresh thyme or parsley
- 2 cups of green cabbage, finely chopped
- Salt and pepper
- 1 or 2 tablespoons of vegan butter
- 1/4 cup of freshly squeezed lemon juice

Directions:
1. Sauté the onions and garlic for around 3 minutes.
2. Add the rice and cook-stir for 3 minutes. Add the broth, grape juice, cabbage, thyme, saffron, salt, and pepper.
3. Cook the cabbage mixture on high mode for 6 minutes. Quick release the in-built pressure and open the lid.
4. Add the butter and lemon juice. Stir and enjoy warm.

Vegetarian Chili Mac

Preparation time: 10 minutes| Cook Time: 25 minutes| Servings: 6

Ingredients
- A medium yellow onion, diced
- 1 tablespoon of organic olive oil
- 1 red bell pepper, diced
- 1 jalapeno pepper, minced
- 2 tablespoons of chili powder
- 2 teaspoons of cumin
- A teaspoon of chipotle powder
- 1 1/2 teaspoons of salt
- 1 clove of garlic, minced
- A can (15 oz) of tomato sauce
- 1 can (15 ounce) of diced tomatoes
- A can (15 oz) of kidney beans, drained and rinsed
- 1 (15 oz) can of black beans, drained and rinsed
- 8 oz of whole-wheat elbow pasta
- 2 cups of vegetable broth
- A cup of shredded Monterey jack cheese
- 1 cup of shredded sharp cheddar cheese
- Greek yogurt, cilantro (optional toppings)

Directions
1. Sauté the onion, jalapeno pepper, bell pepper, cumin, chili powder, chipotle powder, and salt in oil for 5 minutes. Stir. Add the garlic and cook for 1 minute.
2. Add the tomatoes, tomato sauce, kidney beans, black beans, elbow pasta, and broth.
3. Cook on high mode for 5 minutes and quick release the accumulated steam.
4. Open lid the lid and add the cheeses. Stir.
5. Serve your vegetarian chili Mac with cilantro and Greek yoghurt.

Steamed White Rice

Preparation time: 2 minutes| Cook Time: 3 minutes| Servings: 5

Ingredients
- 1 cup of long grain white rice
- 1 1/2 cups of vegetable broth
- A cup of water

Directions:

1. Combine rice with 1 1/2 cups of broth in a metal bowl.
2. Add water into the Foodi and insert the reversible rack. Place the metal bowl on the rack and close the pressure lid.
3. Steam the ingredients for 3 minutes and let the accumulated pressure release naturally for 10 minutes before quick releasing the rest.
4. Open the lid, fluff the steamed rice, and serve.

Saffron Rice

Preparation time: 5 minutes| Cook Time: 10 minutes| Servings: 4
Ingredients
- 1 large pinch of saffron, crushed
- 2 teaspoons of hot water
- 2 tablespoons of butter
- 2 cups of long grain white rice
- 3 1/2 glasses of vegetable broth
- Salt to taste

Directions:
1. Dissolve the saffron in hot water.
2. Melt the butter on sauté mode.
3. Add the rice, broth, a teaspoon of salt, and saffron (including its water.)
4. Close the pressure lid and cook the mixture on low mode for 5 minutes.
5. Quick release the accumulated steam, fluff, and serve.

Rice Pilaf with Veggies

Preparation time: 5 minutes| Cook Time: 12 minutes| Servings: 4
Ingredients
- 2 tablespoons of extra-virgin olive oil
- 1 onion, diced
- 1 cup of long grain white rice
- 2 glasses of vegetable stock
- 1 carrot, chopped
- 1/2 teaspoon of ground cinnamon
- A teaspoon of salt
- 1 tablespoon of fresh parsley, chopped
- 2 tablespoons of frozen peas

Directions:
1. Sauté the onions in oil for 5 minutes. Add the rice and cook-stir for two minutes.
2. Add the stock and stir. Add the carrots, cinnamon, peas, and salt.
3. Close the pressure lid and cook on high mode for 5 minutes.
4. Quick release the accumulated pressure and open the lid. Stir your rice pilaf and serve hot.

Cheesy White Wine Risotto

Preparation time: 5 minutes |Cook Time: 15 minutes| Servings: 4
Ingredients
- 2 tablespoons of butter, preferably vegan
- 1 1/2 cups of Arborio rice
- 1 medium onion, chopped finely
- 2 garlic cloves, minced
- 3 cups of vegetable broth
- 1 cup of dry white wine
- Salt and pepper
- 3/4 cup of grated vegan parmesan cheese

Directions:
1. Sauté the onion in butter for 3 minutes. Add the garlic and cook while stirring constantly for one minute.
2. Add the rice and cook-stir for two minutes.
3. Add the wine and cook-stir until its drained and then add the broth.
4. Close the pressure lid and cook on high mode for ten minutes.
5. Quick release the accumulated pressure and open the lid. Add the parmesan cheese and stir. Add the salt and pepper and stir to melt the cheese. Serve hot!

Asparagus and Mushroom Risotto

Preparation time: 5 minutes| Cook Time: 15 minutes| Servings: 4
Ingredients
- A pound of asparagus (trimmed and cut into pieces)
- 4 cups of vegetable broth
- 1 medium onion, chopped
- 2 tablespoons of olive oil
- 3 cups of sliced mushrooms
- Fresh-ground black pepper
- 2 teaspoons of salt
- 2 cups of Arborio rice
- 1/4 cup of dry white wine
- 1/2 teaspoon of grated lemon zest
- *For garnishing*: Extra-virgin essential olive oil or grated vegan Parmesan

Directions:
1. Add vegetable broth and asparagus into the Foodi pot.
2. Seal the pressure lid and cook on high mode for 2 minutes. Quick release the accumulated steam and transfer the cooked asparagus into a bowl.
3. Sauté the onion in oil for two minutes and add the mushroom, salt, and pepper. Cook the mushroom mixture while stirring constantly for 3 minutes.
4. Add the rice and cook-stir for two minutes.
5. Add the wine and cook until it drains.
6. Return the asparagus and broth into the pot and stir.

7. Close the pressure lid and cook the asparagus mixture on high mode for 6 minutes.
8. Add the lemon zest and let it heat. Spray your asparagus and mushroom risotto with oil and parmesan.

Lentil Vegetable Risotto

Preparation time: 5 minutes| Cook Time: 15 minutes |Servings:
Ingredients
- 1 1/2 tablespoons of organic olive oil
- 10-12 sage leaves
- 2 garlic cloves, minced
- 1/2 yellow onion, diced
- 2 small carrots, grated
- 1/2 jalapeno (seeded and diced)
- 1 1/2 cups of Arborio rice
- A cup of dry lentils (brown or green), soaked overnight
- 4 cups of vegetable stock
- 1 teaspoon of salt

Directions:
1. Sauté the sage leaves in olive oil for a minute and transfer them into a bowl.
2. Add the remaining essential olive oil and sauté the onion, garlic, carrots, and jalapeno until they tenderize.
3. Add the rice and cook for a minute while stirring constantly.
4. Add the lentils and stir. Add the stock and salt. Close the pressure lid and cook for 7 minutes.
5. Quick release the in-built steam and serve the risotto garnished with garnish dish with sage leaves and drizzled with olive oil.

Mexican Rice

Preparation time: 5 minutes| Cook Time: 5 minutes| Servings: 6
Ingredients
- A cup of rice (long grain)
- 1 cup of chopped tomatoes plus juice
- 2 1/4 cups of vegetable broth
- 2 tablespoons of vegan butter
- 1 medium onion, finely diced
- A teaspoon of oregano
- 1 garlic herb, minced
- 1/8 teaspoon of cayenne pepper
- A tablespoon of chopped fresh parsley

Directions:
1. Mix all the ingredients in your Foodi and close the pressure lid.
2. Cook the rice mixture on high mode for 5 minutes.
3. Let the accumulated pressure exit naturally for 10 minutes and quick release the rest.
4. Open the lid and leave your Mexican rice for 3 minutes. Stir and serve.

Pasta with Arugula Pesto

Preparation time: 5 minutes| Cook Time: 10minutes| Servings:
Ingredients
- A pound of fusilli or rotini pasta
- Water
- Olive oil
- 2 teaspoons of sea salt
- 4 garlic cloves, smashed
- 5 ounces of baby arugula
- 1 tablespoon of freshly squeezed lemon juice
- Ground pepper
- 2 teaspoons of grated lemon zest
- 2 tablespoons of extra virgin essential olive oil

Directions:
1. Preheat the Foodi unit on sauté mode for 5 minutes.
2. Add the oil and garlic and cook for a minute.
3. Add the pasta, salt, and enough water. Stir and seal the pressure lid and cook on low mode for 7 minutes.
4. Combine the arugula with freshly squeezed lemon juice, zest, pepper, organic olive oil, and cheese in a bowl. Add pasta and toss to coat.

Rich Spaghetti Dish

Preparation time: 10minutes| Cook Time: 15minutes| Servings: 6
Ingredients
- 1/2 lb of lean ground beef
- 1/2 lb of ground Italian sausage
- Salt and pepper
- 1 small yellow onion, chopped
- 2 cloves of garlic, minced
- 1 tablespoon of red wine vinegar
- 3 tablespoons of fresh basil leaves, chopped
- 1/2 teaspoon of garlic powder, sugar
- A teaspoon of Italian seasoning
- 28 oz of tomatoes, crushed
- 8 oz of spaghetti noodles
- 2 tablespoons of tomato paste
- 1/3 cup of cheese, freshly grated
- Fresh parsley leaves, chopped
- A cup of water

Directions
1. Set your Foodi pot to sauté mode. Add the ground beef and sausage. Brown them and add salt and pepper.
2. Drain the grease and add onions. Cook until they tenderize.

3. Add the garlic, garlic powder, Italian seasonings, sugar, and burgundy or merlot wine vinegar.
4. Break noodles in two and add them to the meat mixture.
5. Combine the tomato paste with the crushed tomatoes in a bowl and stir.
6. Pour the tomato mix over the spaghetti noodles.
7. Add some water and ensure that you spaghetti gets submerged.
8. Close the pressure lid and cook on high mode for 5 minutes.
9. Let the in-built pressure escape naturally for 5 minutes and quick release the rest.
10. Open the pressure lid and stir. Serve the rich spaghetti dish topped with chopped parsley, crushed red pepper flakes, and fresh parmesan.

Pineapple and Cauliflower Rice

Preparation time: 5 minutes| Cook Time: 12 minutes |Servings: 2
Ingredients
- 1 cauliflower, minced
- 1 teaspoon of salt
- 2 cups of rice
- 2 teaspoons of oil
- 1/2 pineapple or ½ can of minced pineapples

Directions
1. Combine all the ingredients in your Foodi pot.
2. Close the pressure lid and cook on low mode for 5 minutes.
3. Let the accumulated vapor exit naturally and open the pot. Serve Hot.

Mushroom Stroganoff

Preparation time: 10minutes| Cook Time: 20minutes| Servings: 4
Ingredients
- 3 tablespoons of extra virgin olive oil
- ½ red onion, diced
- 3 garlic cloves, chopped roughly
- 16 ounces of mushrooms, sliced
- ½ teaspoon of pepper
- ¾ teaspoon of salt
- ¼ cup of white wine
- 2 cups of veggie broth
- 2 tablespoons of Dijon mustard
- 1 tablespoon of flour
- 8 ounces of penne pasta
- ½ to ¾ cup of sour cream

Directions
1. Set your Foodi pot to sauté mode and add oil. Heat it and add the onions, garlic, mushrooms, salt, and pepper.
2. Add the wine, mustard, broth, and flour. Stir
3. Add the pasta and stir. Close the pressure lid and cook on high mode for 3 minutes.
4. Let the in-built pressure exit naturally and open the lid.
5. Add the sour cream and let it rest for ten minutes to thicken.

Spicy Farfalle Pasta

Preparation time: 5 minutes Cook time: 12 minutes| Servings: 4-6
Ingredients
- 1 tablespoon of olive oil
- 2 garlic cloves, crushed
- 1/2 red onion, chopped
- A teaspoon of red pepper flakes
- 1 pinch of dried basil
- A pinch of dried parsley
- 1 pinch of dried thyme
- 1can (14.5-oz) of tomato puree
- A pound of farfalle pasta
- Salt

Directions:
1. Preheat the Foodi on sauté mode for 5 minutes.
2. Sauté the onions and add garlic, pepper flakes, thyme, basil, and parsley.
3. Cook the spices for one minute and add the tomato puree and pasta.
4. Pour some water into the Foodi until it covers the pasta.
5. Season the content with salt and stir. Close the pressure lid and cook on low mode for 5 minutes.
6. Quick release the accumulated vapor and open the lid. Stir your spicy farfalle pasta and let it cool before using.

Vegan Pasta Puttanesca

Preparation time: 25minutes|Cook Time: 5minutes| Servings: 4
Ingredients
- 3 cloves of garlic, minced
- 4 cups of pasta sauce
- 3 glasses of water
- 4 cups of penne or fusilli pasta
- 1/4 teaspoon of red pepper flakes, crushed
- A tablespoon of capers
- 1/2 cup of Kalamata olives, sliced
- Salt and pepper

Directions
1. Preheat the unit on sauté mode. Add garlic and a little water and cook for 30 seconds.

2. Mix the remaining ingredients and close the pressure lid.
3. Cook for 5 minutes and quick release the in-built steam. Open the lid and stir. Season your pasta with salt and pepper.

Kimchi Fried Rice

Preparation time: 15 minutes| Cook Time: 12 minutes |Servings: 4
Ingredients
- 2 tablespoons of sesame oil
- 1/2 onion, finely minced
- A clove of garlic, finely minced
- 1/2 cup of kimchi, chopped
- 1 cup of basmati rice
- 3/4 cup of frozen green peas and carrots
- 1 1/2 cups of chicken stock
- 2 tablespoons of reduced- sodium soy sauce
- 4 eggs, lightly beaten
- 2 scallions, chopped green parts

Directions
1. Sauté the onion and garlic in oil for three minutes. Add the rice, kimchi, soy sauce, frozen veggies, the chicken stock.
2. Close the pressure lid and cook on high mode for 4 minutes.
3. Fluff the rice and push it to one corner of the Foodi. Whisk the eggs on the space and fry it. Mix the whisked eggs with rice.
4. Close the crisping lid and air-fry 400°F for 6 minutes.
5. Remember to check the cooking progress after the third minute. Serve the rice while topped with scallions.

Creamy Spaghetti in Pesto Sauce

Preparation time: 5minutes| Cook Time: 15minutes| Servings: 3
Ingredients
- 8 oz of spaghetti
- 1 tablespoon of organic olive oil
- 2 glasses of water
- 3/4 cup of pesto
- 1/3 cup of sundried tomatoes
- A tablespoon of freshly squeezed lemon juice
- Heavy cream
- Optional: red chili flakes, parmesan cheese
- Basil leaves to garnish

Directions
1. Break the spaghetti into pieces and put them into the pot. Add olive oil and submerge the spaghetti in water.
2. Close the pressure lid and cook on high mode for 5 minutes.
3. Toss the spaghetti using tongs and add the sun-dried tomatoes and pesto. Toss again to coat the spaghetti.
4. Mix the heavy cream and lemon juice. Serve your pesto sauce garnished with cheese, red chili flakes, and basil leaves.

Marinara with Pasta

Preparation time: 5minutes|Cook Time: 25minutes| Servings: 8
Ingredients
Homemade Tomato Sauce:
- 28 oz of tomato puree
- 3 tablespoons of parsley, dried
- 5 garlic cloves (peeled and smashed)
- 2 tablespoons of honey
- 2 tablespoons of essential olive oil
- 2 teaspoons of dried oregano
- 2 teaspoons of kosher salt
- 1/4 teaspoon red pepper flakes, crushed

Pasta:
- 15 oz of tomatoes, diced
- 1/2 cup of dry red wine
- 2 cups of stock
- 1 teaspoon of homemade tomato sauce
- 8 oz of ricotta cheese
- 16 oz of dried pasta
- 1/3 cup of parmesan cheese, freshly grated

Directions
1. Combine all the homemade tomato sauce ingredients with stock, diced tomatoes, and wine.
2. Close the pressure lid and cook on high mode for ten minutes.
3. Quick release the in-built pressure and open the lid. Add the dried pasta and allow it to cover the sauce.
4. Add a dollop of parmesan cheese and close the pressure lid.
5. Cook on high mode for 4 more minutes and natural release the in-built steam.
6. Quick release the rest and open the lid. Stir your marinara and serve.

Meatless Spaghetti

Preparation time: 15minutes|Cook Time: 25minutes| Servings: 4
Ingredients
- A package of pasta, uncooked
- 1 large jar or 3 glasses of pre-made Marinara Sauce
- 1/2 cup of water
- 1/2 package of ricotta cheese
- 1/2 ball of mozzarella cheese, shredded
- 1 package of frozen veggie crumbles

Directions

1. Combine all the ingredients in a Foodi pot (except the cheeses)
2. Close the pressure lid and cook on high mode for 4 minutes. Quick release the accumulated pressure and open the lid.
3. Add the cheeses and stir.

Coconut Mango Arborio Rice Pudding

Preparation time: 5 minutes |Cook Time: 12 minutes| Servings: 2

Ingredients
- 3/4 cup of Arborio Rice
- 1 mango (peeled and cubed)
- A can of light coconut milk
- 1/3 cup of brown sugar
- 1/2 cup of half and half
- 1 1/2 cups of water
- A teaspoon of salt
- 1 teaspoon of vanilla
- 1/4 cup of shredded coconut, pulsed
- 1/4 cup of almonds, pulsed

Directions
1. Combine the rice, coconut milk, water, sugar, and salt in a Foodi.
2. Cook the mixture on low mode for 12 minutes.
3. Quick release the in-built steam and add the vanilla, chopped mango, and the half and half. Stir and transfer into serving bowls.
4. Garnish your pudding with toasted almonds and coconut.

Jumbo Shrimp Pasta

Preparation time: 5minutes| Cook Time: 6minutes| Servings: 6

Ingredients
- 1 lb of dried spaghetti
- A teaspoon of coconut oil
- 3 garlic cloves, minced
- 4 1/4 cups of water
- 1 lb of raw jumbo shrimp (peeled and deveined)
- 3/4 cup of Thai sweet chili sauce
- 3/4 cup of light mayonnaise
- 1/4 cup of lime juice
- 1 tablespoon of sriracha sauce
- 1/2 cup of chopped scallions
- Salt and pepper

Directions
1. Break the spaghetti by half and put them in the Foodi pot.
2. Add the coconut oil, water, garlic, and a teaspoon of salt.
3. Close the pressure lid and cook the mixture on high mode for 5 minutes.
4. Meanwhile, put the mayonnaise in a medium bowl. Add the lime juice, sriracha, and Thai chili sauce. Stir.
5. Open the lid and add the pasta. Stir. Add the scallions and shrimp.
6. Sauté the scallion mixture for two or three minutes and toss. Simmer until the shrimp turns pink.
7. Add salt and pepper. You can also add more sriracha. Enjoy.

Pasta with Meat Sauce

Preparation time: 10minutes| Cook Time: 8minutes| Servings: 4

Ingredients
- 1 onion, chopped
- 2 cloves of garlic, minced
- 24 oz of spaghetti sauce
- 1 lb of ground beef
- 12 oz of rigatoni pasta, uncooked
- 2cups of chicken broth
- 1/2 teaspoon of Italian seasoning
- A teaspoon of basil

Directions
1. Set your Foodi to sauté mode and add the meat, onions, and garlic.
2. Trim the visible fats from the beef and add all the ingredients.
3. Close the pressure lid and cook on high mode for 8 minutes.
4. Quick release the in-built steam and open the lid.
5. Add the pasta and stir well to thicken the sauce.

Pasta with Mediterranean Veggies

Preparation time: 10minutes| Cook Time: 4minutes| Servings: 6

Ingredients
- 1 tablespoon of olive oil
- 2 cloves of garlic, crushed
- 1 red onion, chopped
- 1 eggplant, chopped
- 1 red pepper, chopped
- 1tin (140z) of chopped tomatoes
- 15 oz of pasta
- Vegetable stock
- oz of black olives
- Parmesan, for serving
- Fresh parsley, for serving

Directions
1. Add the olive oil into your Foodi and sauté for a minute.
2. Add the red onion and garlic and cook for two minutes.
3. Add the eggplant and pepper. Cook and stir for 2 minutes.

4. Add the pasta, the chopped tomatoes, and stock. Ensure that the ingredients cover the pasta.
5. Close the pressure lid and cook on high mode for 5 minutes.
6. Quick release the accumulated steam and open the lid.
7. Transfer your pasta into a plate and serve while topped with parsley and parmesan.

Cheese- Rich Pasta

Preparation time: 15 minutes| Cook Time: 30 minutes| servings: 6
Ingredients
- 2 lbs of ground meat
- 1 pound (1 box) of Penne pasta, uncooked
- 3 cups of chicken broth
- 1 large sweet onion, finely chopped
- 2 small cans of sliced mushrooms
- 2 garlic cloves, minced
- 2 cups of mozzarella cheese, shredded
- 2 tablespoons of Italian Seasoning
- 2 tablespoons of essential olive oil
- 1/4 teaspoon of red pepper flakes
- 45 oz (1 jar) of spaghetti sauce
- A cup of red wine
- 1 teaspoon of salt
- 1/2 teaspoon of black pepper

Directions:
1. Sauté the onion and garlic in extra virgin olive oil for two minutes.
2. Brown the meat and add the pasta, mushrooms (inclusive of liquid,) wine, and broth, sauces, and all the seasonings.
3. Close the pressure lid and cook on low mode for 20 minutes.
4. Quick release the in-built pressure and open the lid. Stir and add the mozzarella cheese.
5. Let it stay for 10 minutes before serving.

Med Tuna Noodle

Preparation time: 15 minutes |Cook Time: 15 minutes| Servings: 5
Ingredients
- 8 oz of dry wide egg noodles
- 1 tablespoon of oil
- A can of tuna fish, drained
- 1 can (14 oz) of diced tomatoes
- ½ cup of chopped red onion
- ¼ teaspoon of salt
- 1 jar (7.5 oz) of marinated artichoke hearts
- 1-1/4 glasses of water
- Crumpled feta cheese
- Fresh or dried parsley, chopped
- 1/8 teaspoon of pepper

Directions
1. Sauté the red onion and add the tomatoes, dry noodles, water, salt, and pepper.
2. Close the pressure lid and cook on low mode for 5 minutes. Quick release the in-built steam and add the chopped artichokes. Stir.
3. Add tuna and the artichokes liquid and sauté for 10 minutes. Top your tuna noodles with feta cheese and parsley.

Vegan Miso Risotto

Preparation time: ten minutes| Cook Time: 15 minutes| Servings: 4
Ingredients
- 6 tablespoons of extra-virgin olive oil
- 3 medium cloves garlic, minced (about 1 tablespoon)
- 1 medium shallot, finely minced (about 1/4 cup)
- 2 cups of Nano rice
- 3/4 cup of dry sake
- 2 teaspoons of soy sauce
- 1/4 cup of white miso paste
- 4 cups of vegetable or chicken stock
- 1/2 teaspoon of fresh juice
- Kosher salt
- Fresh chives or scallions, minced for serving

Directions
1. Sauté shallot and garlic in oil until it turns translucent.
2. Add the rice and cook while stirring until it becomes toasted.
3. Add the dry sake and cook for 2 minutes or until it drains. Add the soy sauce and miso paste. Stir.
4. Add the stock and close the pressure lid. Cook the mixture on low mode for 5 minutes and quick release the in-built pressure.
5. Open the lid and add fresh lemon juice. Stir to blend until it becomes creamy.
6. Sauté until it thickens.
7. Season with salt (if desired) and add the chives or scallions. Stir and serve immediately.

APPETIZERS, SNACKS, AND SIDES

Air Fried Rosemary Chips

Preparation time: 40 minutes |Cook time: 30minutes| Servings: 4

Ingredients
- 2 teaspoons of chopped rosemary
- 4 russet potatoes
- 3 teaspoons of oil
- ¼ teaspoon of salt

Directions:
1. Peel the potatoes and slice them into chips. Soak the potato slices in water for 30 minutes. Drain the excess water and pat dry.
2. Preheat the Foodi unit on air crisp at 330°F. Toss some oil and add the chips. Ensure that they mix well with the oil and close the crisping lid.
3. Air-fry the chips for 30 minutes or until golden and crisp.
4. Transfer them into a bowl and add the rosemary and salt. Toss to mix.

Crispy Hot Wings

Preparation time: 5 minutes| Cook Time: 20 minutes| servings:4

Ingredients
- 2 lbs of frozen wings
- 1/2 cup of water
- 2 tablespoons of olive oil
- 2 tablespoons of Frank's Red Hot
- 1 teaspoon of salt

Directions
1. Pour some water into your Foodi. Put the chicken wings in the basket and insert it in the Pot.
2. Close the pressure lid and cook on high mode for 5 minutes.
3. Quick release the in-built steam and open the lid.
4. Pat-dry the wings and add some oil into the basket. Close the crisping lid and air fry at 390°F for 15 minutes. Remember to chuck the wings when crisping using tongs.
5. Combine the hot sauce with salt in a bowl. Transfer it into a bowl and toss the wings to coat. Serve and enjoy!

Slow-Cooked Korean Chicken Wings

Preparation time: 10 minutes| cook time: 10 minutes| Servings: 4

Ingredients
- 2 lb of chicken wings, tips removed
- 1/2 cup of soy sauce
- 1/4 cup of packed brown sugar
- 3 cloves of garlic, minced
- 2 tablespoons of fresh ginger (peeled and chopped)
- 3 green onions, sliced thinly

Directions
1. Sauté the chicken for 5 minutes or until it browns. Turn off the sauté function.
2. Mix the brown sugar with ginger, garlic, soy sauce, and green onions into a bowl.
3. Coat the chicken with the sugar mixture.
4. Close the pressure lid and cook the chicken on low mode for 5 hours.

Pot Stickers Traditional

Preparation time: 20 minutes |Cook Time: 21 minutes| Servings: 4-6

Ingredients
- 1 lb of ground pork, uncooked
- A cup of green cabbage, chopped
- 3/4 cup of shiitake mushrooms, finely chopped
- 2 tablespoons of fresh ginger, minced
- 3 scallions (white and green parts) minced
- 3 cloves garlic (peeled and minced)
- 1 teaspoon of kosher salt
- 1/2 cup and 2 tablespoons of soy sauce
- 36-38 pot sticker or round dumpling wrappers
- 1 3/4 cups of water
- 3 tablespoons of vegetable oil, divided

Directions
1. Combine the pork with mushrooms, cabbage, scallions, garlic, ginger, salt, and 2 tablespoons of soy sauce in a sizable bowl.
2. Put a tablespoon of mixture at the centre of each wrapper and fold.
3. Seal the wrappers by pinching the perimeters together to attain a half-moon shape.
4. Put the sealed wrapper into a plate and cover it with a plastic wrap. Chill.
5. Add a half cup of water into the Foodi and fix the reversible rack.
6. Put a third of the wrappers on the rack and close the pressure lid. Steam the wrappers for 3 minutes and open the lid.
7. Remove the rack using the pot stickers and wipe out any water left.
8. Put a tablespoon of oil in the pot and sauté the steamed stickers on high mode for two minutes or until they turn brown and crisp.
9. Repeat the process for the remaining wrappers.
10. Serve your pot stickers traditional meal with the remaining soy sauce.

Rustic Bell Pepper

Preparation time: 5 minutes| Cook time: 20 minutes| Servings: 4

Ingredients:
- 1/2 cup of extra-virgin essential olive oil
- 1 medium onion, sliced thinly
- 2 garlic cloves, minced
- 6 peppers (yellow, green, red,) seeded and sliced thinly
- 1 can (14.5-oz) of chopped tomatoes
- A tablespoon of balsamic vinegar
- 1 tablespoon of dried oregano
- 1 bunch of basil, torn
- Salt and pepper

Directions:
1. Sauté the onions in oil until they tenderize. Add the garlic and peppers and cook for 5 minutes.
2. Add the chopped tomatoes and stir. Add the oregano, salt, and pepper.
3. Close the pressure lid and cook on high mode for 8 minutes.
4. Quick release the in-built steam and open the lid. Add the vinegar and stir.
5. Take off the peppers using tongs and place them on a platter.
6. Serve your peppers with basil and drizzled with oil.

Pineapple Cilantro Lime Rice

Preparation time: 5 minutes| Cook Time: 50 minutes| Servings: 6

Ingredients
- A cup of pineapple juice
- 1 cup of water
- 1 jalapeno (halved and seeded)
- 2 cloves of garlic, minced
- A cup of brown rice
- 1 teaspoon of salt
- 1 lime zest and juice
- 1 bunch of cilantro (stems off and chopped)

Directions
1. Mix the rice with pineapple juice, garlic, jalapeno, and salt in your Foodi.
2. Add ½ cup of water and close the pressure lid.
3. Cook the rice mixture on high mode for 15 minutes.
4. Let the accumulated steam release naturally for 10 minutes and quick release the rest. Remove the jalapeno and cloves from the pot and add the lime juice, zest, and cilantro.
5. Stir your lime rice and serve hot.

Caponata

Preparation time: 10 minutes| Cook time: 6 minutes| Servings: 8

Ingredients
- 2 medium eggplants, cubed (½ inches)
- 2 garlic cloves, minced
- 1 medium yellow onion, chopped
- 2 red sweet peppers, chopped
- 4 tablespoons of extra-virgin olive oil
- 1/4 cup of red wine vinegar
- 1 tablespoon of capers, rinsed
- 1/2 cup of organic brown sugar
- 15 small pitted green olives, quartered
- A tablespoon of fresh oregano, chopped
- 1 tablespoon of fresh basil, chopped
- Salt and pepper

Directions:
1. Add a cup of water into the Foodi pot. Fix the basket and add the cubed eggplants, garlic, onions, and peppers.
2. Close the pressure lid and cook on high mode for 4 minutes.
3. Quick release the accumulated steam and remove the basket. Drain the pot and return the vegetables into it. Do not put the crisp basket.
4. Add the extra virgin olive oil, sugar, vinegar, capers, olives, basil, and oregano.
5. Add salt and pepper, as desired. Simmer your caponata on sauté mode for two minutes and serve.

Crab Cheese Wontons

Preparation time: 30 minutes |Cook Time: 30 minutes| Servings: 4

Ingredients
- 1 package (12 oz) of imitation crab
- 1/4 cup of mayonnaise
- 2 packages (8 oz each) of cream cheese, softened
- 1/2 teaspoon of kosher salt
- Zest from a lemon
- 1 package (12 oz) of square wonton wrappers

Directions
1. Combine the crab with cream cheese, mayonnaise, lemon zest, and salt in a bowl and mix well.
2. Put a teaspoon of crab mixture at the center of the wonton wrapper.
3. Dip your finger in water and pass it on the internal edges of the wrapper.
4. Fold one corner of the wrapper towards the opposite one.
5. Seal and create a triangle shape by pressing the perimeters. Now make a W-shape by folding the corners diagonally. Do this for the remaining wontons.
6. Place all the filled wontons on a tray and freeze it for 3 hours.
7. Transfer the frozen wontons into a Ziploc bag.

8. Place the basket on the pot and put half of the wrappers on it.
9. Splash them with cooking spray and close the crisping lid. Air-fry the wontons at 390°F for 15 minutes, checking the cooking progress after 10 minutes.

Mediterranean White Bean Dip

Preparation time: 10 minutes| Cook time: 12 minutes |Servings: 2 cups
Ingredients
- 3/4 cup of dried white beans, soaked 8 hours or overnight
- 1/3 cup of extra virgin olive oil
- 2 garlic cloves
- Juice from a lemon
- 1 pinch of red pepper flakes
- 2 teaspoons of dried thyme
- 1 1/2 teaspoons of chili powder
- Salt and freshly ground black pepper
- 3 tablespoons of basil, chopped

Directions:
1. Drain the soaked beans and add them into your Foodi. Cover them with water and close the pressure lid.
2. Cook the beans on high mode for 12 minutes and let the pressure escape naturally.
3. Drain the beans and rinse them. Puree the cooked beans using a blender and add the remaining ingredients (except basil.)
4. Add the basil and stir. Serve your bean dip with tortilla chips or vegetables.

Quinoa Salad

Preparation time: 10 minutes| Cook time: 1 minute| Servings: 6
Ingredients
- A cup of quinoa
- 1 1/2 cups of water
- 1 garlic clove, diced or minced
- 1/2 teaspoon of salt
- 1 large Roma tomato, diced finely
- 1 cucumber (seeded and diced finely)
- A bell pepper, diced finely
- 1/2 cup of scallions, thinly sliced
- 1 bunch of parsley, minced
- A ripe avocado (peeled, pitted, and diced)
- 3 tablespoons of freshly squeezed lime juice
- 2 tablespoons of vegetable broth

Directions:
1. Rinse the quinoa and put them into the Ninja pot. Add water, garlic, and salt.
2. Close the pressure lid and cook the quinoa mixture on high mode for one minute.
3. Let the in-built pressure exit naturally and open the lid. Fluff your quinoa and let it cool.
4. Combine the remaining ingredients in a bowl and add the cooled quinoa. Mix and serve!

Potato with Herbs

Preparation time: 10 minutes| Cook time: 15 minutes| Servings: 4
Ingredients:
- 1 medium onion, diced
- 2 tablespoons of organic olive oil
- 8 medium potatoes, quartered
- 1/2 cup of water
- 1/4 teaspoon of dried basil
- 1/4 teaspoon of dried thyme
- 1/4 teaspoon of dried oregano
- 1/4 teaspoon of dried rosemary
- 1/4 teaspoon of dried sage
- Salt and pepper
- 1/2 lemon

Directions:
1. Preheat your Foodi by sautéing it over medium high heat for three minutes.
2. Add the oil and heat it. Add the potatoes and brown them.
3. Add some water, the herbs, salt, and pepper. Stir and close the pressure lid.
4. Cook the mixture on high mode for 5 minutes.
5. Let the in-built pressure exit naturally and serve while drizzled with lemon juice.

Crispy Kale Chips

Prep: 5 minutes| Cook time: 3 minutes|Servings: 2
Ingredients
- 1 kale head
- 1 tablespoon of vegetable oil
- 1 teaspoon of soya sauce

Directions:
1. Remove the center stem of the kale and tear them up into 1 ½ inch pieces. Wash the pieces and dry.
2. Toss them with the soya sauce and oil.
3. Preheat the unit on air crisp mode at 450°F for a few minutes.
4. Insert the crisping basket into the Foodi and close the air frying lid.
5. Air Crisp the tossed kales at 400°F for 3 minutes.

Jalapeno Hot Popper Dip

Preparation time: 12 minutes| Cook Time: 15 minutes| Servings: 10
Ingredients
- 1 lb of boneless chicken
- 8 oz of cream cheese
- 3 Jalapenos, sliced
- 3/4 cup of sour cream

- 1/2 cup of panko bread crumbs
- 8 oz of cheddar cheese
- 1/2 cup of water

Directions
1. Combine the chicken with jalapenos, cream and water in your Foodi.
2. Close the pressure lid and cook on high mode for 12 minutes.
3. Quick release the in-built pressure and shred the chicken. Add the sour cream and cheddar cheese.
4. Top the shredded chicken mixture with cheese and panko bread crumbs.
5. Close the crisping lid and broil for two minutes.

Buffalo Chicken Dip

Preparation time: 2 minutes| Cook Time: 15 minutes| Servings: 6

Ingredients
- 1lb of chicken white meat
- A cup of hot sauce
- 1 packet of ranch dip
- A stick of butter
- 8 oz of cream cheese
- 16 oz of cheddar cheese

Directions
1. Combine all the ingredients (except the cheddar cheese) in the Foodi and close the pressure lid.
2. Cook the chicken mix on high mode for 15 minutes.
3. Quick release the in-built steam and open the lid. Shred the chicken and add the cheese. Stir and serve with chips.

Asian Barbecue Satay

Preparation time: 15minutes| Cook Time: 15 minutes |Servings: 3

Ingredients
- 4 garlic cloves, chopped
- ¾ pound (12 oz) of boneless and skinless chicken tenders
- ½ cup of pineapple juice
- ½ cup of soy sauce
- ¼ cup of sesame oil
- 4 scallions, chopped
- 2 teaspoons of sesame seeds, toasted
- 1 tablespoon of fresh ginger, grated
- Pinch of black pepper

Directions
1. Skew the chicken tender while trimming extra fat.
2. Combine the remaining ingredients in a bowl. Add the skewered chicken to it.
3. Combine well, cover, and chill for 24 hours.
4. Preheat the unit on air crisp mode at 390°F.
5. Pat-dry the chicken. Add the skewers to the basket and cook for 5 to 7minutes.

Bacon Cheeseburger Dip

Preparation time: 5minutes| Cook Time: 10 minutes| Servings: 4-6

Ingredients
- 4 bacon slices, cut into pieces
- 10 oz of diced tomatoes with green Chile peppers
- 8 oz of cream cheese, cubed
- 8 oz of shredded cheese
- 4 tablespoons of water

Directions
1. Sauté the bacon slices until they turn brown. Transfer the slices onto a paper-lined plate.
2. Brown the beef and drain excess fat.
3. Add the bacon, diced veggies, cream cheese, and water (without stirring) into the Foodi.
4. Cook on high mode for 4 minutes.
5. Quick release the in-built steam and open the lid.
6. Add the cheese and stir. Serve your cheeseburger dip while hot.

Crispy Popcorn Chicken

Preparation time: 5minutes| Cook Time: 10minutes| Servings: 2

Ingredients
- 1 lb of skinless chicken tenders
- ½ cup of corn starch
- 1 cup of coconut milk
- 1 teaspoon of pickle juice
- 3 cups of corn flake cereal, crushed finely
- ½ teaspoon of onion powder
- ½ teaspoon of garlic powder
- ¼ teaspoon of black pepper
- ½ teaspoon of paprika
- ¼ teaspoon of red pepper cayenne (optional)

Directions
1. Cut the chicken into cubes. Put the cornstarch in a plate.
2. Add the pickled juice and coconut milk into a bowl.
3. Add the corn flakes and all the spices in a plastic bag and crush them. Put them in a separate plate.
4. Dip the chicken cubes in the cornstarch and then in the coconut milk. Also, roll the cubes in the flakes.
5. Preheat the Foodi system on air crisp mode at 400°F for 5 minutes.
6. Add the rolled chicken cubes into the basket and fix it in the Foodi.

7. Air-fry the chicken for 10 minutes while tossing and checking the cooking progress.

Peperonata Sauce

Preparation time: 5 minutes| Cook Time: 15 minutes| Servings: 6

Ingredients
- 2 red peppers, sliced thinly
- 1 green pepper, sliced thinly
- 2 yellow pepper, sliced thinly
- 2 medium ripe tomatoes, chopped
- 1 red onion, sliced thinly
- 2 cloves of garlic
- 1 basil or parsley
- Extra virgin organic olive oil
- Salt and pepper

Directions
1. Sauté the onion and add peppers and garlic (wrapped).
2. Cook for 5 minutes without stirring.
3. Add the chopped tomatoes, salt, and pepper. Stir.
4. Close the pressure lid and cook on high mode for 5 minutes. Quick release he accumulated vapor and open the lid.
5. Unwrap the garlic and remove the peppers using tongs.
6. Add a raw clove, chopped basil, and fresh oil. Stir your peperonata and serve.

Nacho Covered Prawns

Preparation time: 30 minutes| Cooking time: 8 minutes| Servings: 3

Ingredients
- 9 ounces of nacho chips
- 1 egg, beaten
- 18 medium-sized prawns

Directions:
1. Remove the prawn's shell and veins. Wash them thoroughly and wipe dry.
2. Grind the chips like breadcrumbs and after that dip each prawn into the egg. Also, coat the prawn using chip crumbs.
3. Preheat the Foodi unit on air crisp mode at 356°F.
4. Add the prawns and cook for 8 minutes. Serve with salsa or sour cream.

Cajun Shrimp

Preparation time: 2minutes| Cook Time: 6minutes| Servings: 2

Ingredients
- 1/2 pound of shrimp, peeled and deveined
- 1/4 teaspoon of red pepper cayenne
- 1/4 teaspoon of smoked paprika
- Pinch of salt
- 1/2 teaspoon of old bay seasoning

Directions
1. Combine all the ingredients in a bowl. Stir the cayenne mixture to coat the shrimp.
2. Close the crisping lid and air crisp at 390°F for 6 minutes.
3. Remember to check the cooking progress and flip the shrimp on the third minute.

Pizza Dip

Preparation time: 15 minutes| Cook Time: 20 minutes| Servings: 4

Ingredients
- 8oz (1 block) of softened cream cheese
- 1/2 cup of pizza sauce
- 1 cup of shredded mozzarella cheese
- 1/2 teaspoon of dried basil
- 2 cups of water

Directions
1. Put the creamy cheese into a Pyrex dish, distributed evenly.
2. Spread the sauce over the cheese using the back of the spoon.
3. Sprinkle the mozzarella cheese and the dried basil.
4. Insert a rack in the Foodi pot and pour some water into it.
5. Place the dish of pizza on the rack and cover with foil.
6. Close the pressure lid and cook on high mode for 20 minutes.
7. Quick release the accumulated steam and open the lid. Let the rack cool for 1-2 minutes before removing it from the pot. Serve your pizza dip cool.

Sweet Potato Tots

Preparation time: 20 minutes| Cook Time: 23 minutes| Servings: 5-6 (28 tots)

Ingredients
- 3 sweet potatoes (about 1 3/4 lb), peeled and cubed
- 4 sprigs of fresh thyme
- 1/4 teaspoon of ground cinnamon or garam Masala
- 1 1/2 cups of water
- 1 1/2 tablespoons of kosher salt, divided
- 1/2 cup of cornstarch, divided
- 2 teaspoons of ground cumin
- 4 cups of panko bread crumbs
- 1 teaspoon of chili powder
- A teaspoon of black pepper, coarsely ground

Directions
1. Put the sweet potatoes, thyme, cinnamon or garam Masala, and a teaspoon of kosher salt into the Foodi.

2. Close the pressure lid and cook on high mode for 8 minutes.
3. Quick release the in-built steam and open the lid. Drain the thyme mixture using a strainer.
4. Rinse and wipe the pot dry and insert the basket into it.
5. Mash the potatoes and two tablespoons of cornstarch in a bowl.
6. Get a separate bowl and add the remaining salt, cornstarch, bread crumbs, chili powder, cumin, and pepper.
7. Form some cylindrical tots from the sweet potato mix.
8. Make them 1-inch long and coat them with the bread crumb mix.
9. Place the tots on a big greased baking sheet and freeze them for 60 minutes.
10. Close the crisping lid and preheat it on air crisp mode at the temperature of 400°F for 5 minutes.
11. Once the time elapses, splash the basket with cooking spray and add tots in a single layer. Sprinkle tots with the cooking spray and air-crisp for 15 minutes.
12. Repeat the process with the remaining tots. Enjoy your potato tots crispy and golden.

Easy Steamed Artichokes

Preparation time: 5 minutes| Cook time: 10 minutes| Servings: 4
Ingredients:
- 2 medium artichokes, washed and damaged leaves removed
- 1 lemon, halved
- 1 tablespoon of freshly squeezed lemon juice
- 1 bay leaf
- A garlic clove
- 1 teaspoon of Dijon mustard
- 2 tablespoons of mayonnaise (vegan)
- 1/2 teaspoon of lemon zest
- 1/4 teaspoon of ground black pepper

Directions:
1. Cut off the top edges of the washed artichokes (remove the damaged leaves first).
2. Trim off the spines and then wipe the lemon edge (on the cut) to prevent oxidation.
3. Add a cup of water, garlic, and bay leaf to the Foodi pot.
4. Insert the basket and put artichokes in it. Drizzle with lemon juice.
5. Close the pressure lid and cook on high mode for 15 minutes. Let the in-built vapor exit naturally and open the lid.
6. Combine the mustard with lemon zest, mayonnaise, and black pepper in a small bowl. Enjoy your artichokes warm.

Southwest Asian Falafel

Preparation time: 15 minutes| Cook Time: 44 minutes| Servings: 4
Ingredients
- 2 cans (15 oz each) of chickpeas, drained and rinsed
- 1 small onion, peeled and chopped
- 1/4 cup of bread crumbs
- 2 tablespoons of lemon juice
- 1/4 cup of flat-leaf Italian parsley, chopped
- 2 teaspoons of ground cumin
- 2 cloves of garlic, peeled and smashed
- A teaspoon of kosher salt
- 1/2 teaspoon of ground black pepper
- 1 teaspoon of ground coriander
- 5 tablespoons of extra virgin organic olive oil, divided
- A large egg

Directions:
1. Line the tray with paper towels. Spread the chickpeas on it to dry.
2. Put the bread crumbs, onion, fresh lemon juice, parsley, coriander, black pepper, salt, and cumin into and minced.
3. Add a whisked egg, chickpeas, and 3 tablespoons of oil and pulse until they are well mixed.
4. Transfer the egg mixture into a bowl and make 16 patties from it.
5. Cover the patties for 45 minutes and then brush them with oil.
6. Insert a basket in the Foodi pot and preheat it on air crisp mode for 5 minutes.
7. Add 8 patties into the basket and crisp over 375°F for 22 minutes. Remember to flip the patties halfway.
8. Remove the air crisped patties and cook the remaining ones. Enjoy while warm!

Rosemary Beets

Preparation time: 20 minutes| Cook Time: 20 minutes| Servings: 8
Ingredients
- 5 large fresh beets (about 3-1/2 lb), scrubbed and top-trimmed to 1"
- 1 medium red onion, chopped
- 1 tablespoon of extra virgin olive oil
- 2 cloves of garlic, minced
- 1 medium orange, peeled and chopped
- 1/4 cup of white balsamic vinegar
- 1/3 cup of honey
- A teaspoon of dried and crushed rosemary or 1 tablespoon of fresh and minced rosemary
- 3/4 teaspoon of dried thyme or 2 teaspoons of fresh thyme, minced
- 1/2 teaspoon of Chinese five-spice powder

- 3/4 teaspoon of salt
- 1/2 teaspoon of pepper, coarsely ground
- A cup of crumbled feta cheese

Directions
1. Fix the reversible rack in the Foodi. Add 1 cup of water. Place the scrubbed and trimmed beets on the rack.
2. Close the pressure lid and cook on high mode for 20 minutes. Let the accumulated vapor exit naturally and open the lid.
3. Remove and cool the beets. Take off the rack and discard juices. Clean the removable pot for more cooking.
4. Peel the beets and cut them into wedges. Keep the wedges warm.
5. Preheat your Foodi by sautéing it on medium high heat for three minutes.
6. Add the oil and heat it. Add the onion and stir. Let it cook for 5 minutes.
7. Add the minced garlic and cook for one minute.
8. Add the orange, vinegar, honey, thyme, rosemary, Chinese five-spice, salt, pepper, and the beets.
9. Let the ingredients heat on sauté mode. Serve warm or cold while sprinkled with cheese.

Easy pickled Green Chilies

Preparation time: 10 minutes| Cook Time: 11 minutes| Servings: 1½ cups
Ingredients
- 1 lb of green chilies or jalapeno, sliced
- 1½ cups of apple cider vinegar
- 1½ teaspoons of sugar
- 1 teaspoon of pickling or canning salt
- ¼ teaspoon of garlic powder

Directions
1. Combine all the ingredients into the Foodi pot.
2. Close the pressure lid and cook on high mode for a minute. Let the pressure exit naturally and open the lid.
3. Ladle your green chilies into jars and combine it with vinegar. You can also add more fluids if necessary.

Beet, Endives and Spinach Salad

Preparation time: 5 minutes| Cook time: 25 minutes| Servings: 5
Ingredients
- 1 cup of water
- 4 medium-sized beets (cleaned and tops removed)
- 1/2 cup of candied walnuts
- 2 medium heads of Belgian endive (rinsed and sliced)
- 4 cups of fresh spinach, chopped

Dressing:
- 1 large garlic oil, chopped
- 1 teaspoon of dried thyme, crushed
- 2 tablespoons of white balsamic vinegar
- A tablespoon of lemon juice
- 1 tablespoons of essential olive oil
- 1/2 teaspoon of salt
- Pinch black pepper

Directions:
1. Add some water into the Foodi and insert the basket.
2. Put the cleaned beets into the basket and close the pressure lid. Cook on high mode for 20 minutes.
3. Meanwhile, prepare the dressing by combining all the ingredients in a small jar.
4. Quick release the in-built vapor and open the lid.
5. Pierce the beets with a fork to check whether it's cooked. If not, close the lid and cook for 10 more minutes.
6. Transfer the cooked beets on a cutting board and slice it. Put the beets into a platter.
7. Add the walnuts, endives, and spinach. Top your beets meal with the dressing.

Hoisin Meatballs

Preparation time: 20 minutes| Cook Time: 20 minutes| Servings: 12
Ingredients
- A cup of beef broth or dry red wine
- 3 tablespoons of hoisin sauce
- 1 large egg, lightly beaten
- 2 tablespoons of soy sauce
- 4 green onions, chopped
- 1/4 cup of onion, finely chopped
- 2 garlic cloves, minced
- 1/4 cup of minced fresh cilantro
- 1/2 teaspoon of pepper
- 1/2 teaspoon of salt
- A pound of ground beef
- 1 pound of ground pork
- Sesame seeds

Directions
1. Combine the broth or wine with soy sauce and hoisin sauce in the Foodi.
2. Let the mixture boil on sauté mode and allow it to simmer to reduce the fluid.
3. Mix the remaining ingredients (except the beef, pork, and sesame seeds) in a bowl.
4. Add the beef and pork. Mix well and shape meatballs from it.

5. Close the pressure lid and cook on high mode for 10 minutes.
6. Quick release the in-built pressure and sprinkle with sesame seeds. Cool and freeze for later use.

Cheddar Bacon Ale Dip

Preparation time: 15 minutes| Cook Time: 10 minutes| Servings: 4-1/2 cups
Ingredients
- 1/4 cup of sour cream
- 18 oz of cream cheese, softened
- 2 tablespoons of Dijon mustard
- 1 teaspoon of garlic powder
- 1 pound of bacon strips, cooked and crumbled
- 1 cup of beer
- 2 cups of cheddar cheese, shredded
- 1/4 cup of heavy cream
- 1 green onion, sliced thinly
- Soft pretzel bites

Directions
1. Combine the sour cream with cream cheese, garlic powder, and mustard in the Foodi.
2. Add the beer and bacon (reserve 2 tablespoons.)
3. Close the pressure lid and cook on high mode for 5 minutes.
4. Quick release the in-built pressure and open the lid.
5. Reset the Foodi to sauté mode and add the cream mixture.
6. Let it cook and thicken for 2 minutes.
7. Transfer it into a bowl and sprinkle with the reserved bacon and onions.

Bok Choy and Mushrooms Salad

Preparation time: 15 minutes| Cook Time: 12 minutes| Servings: 4
Ingredients
- 2 pounds of bok Choy, washed and chopped
- 2 cups of sliced fresh mushrooms
- 1 1/2 cups of water
- 1 onion, sliced
- A teaspoon of crushed red pepper flakes
- 2 garlic cloves, crushed
- Salt
- Pepper
- 3 tablespoons of vegetable broth

Directions:
1. Pour some water into the Foodi and fix the rack. Add bok Choy and mushrooms into it.
2. Close the pressure lid and cook on high mode for 5 minutes.
3. Remove the rack, drain the pot and wipe it dry.
4. Sauté the onions, red pepper, garlic, salt, and pepper in oil.
5. Cook and stir for 5 minutes. Add the vegetable broth, bok Choy, and mushrooms. Stir.
6. Continue cooking while adding more seasonings. Serve with noodles or rice.

Black Bean Dip

Preparation time: 15 minutes| Cook Time: 30 minutes| Servings: 8
Ingredients
- 1.5 cups of dried black beans
- 1 medium onion, diced
- 4 cloves of garlic, peeled and minced
- 2 medium jalapeños (chopped)
- 14.5 oz of diced tomatoes, or crushed
- 1 + 3/4 cups of canola broth
- 1 1/2 tablespoons of avocado oil
- Juice extracted from a lime
- 1 teaspoon of smoked paprika
- 2 teaspoon of ground cumin
- 1/2 teaspoon of chili powder
- 3/4 teaspoon of sea salt
- 1/2 teaspoon of ground coriander

Directions
1. Rinse the beans and put them into the Foodi. Add the vegetables, tomatoes, garlic, oil, broth, spices, and lime juice. Mix thoroughly.
2. Close the pressure lid and cook on high mode for 30 minutes.
3. Let the accumulated pressure exit naturally for 10 minutes and quick release the rest.
4. Puree the ingredients using an immersion blender. Add the desired toppings and enjoy.

Chickpeas Meal

Preparation time: 10 minutes| Cook Time: 25 minutes| Servings: 6
Ingredients
- 1 lb of dried chickpeas
- A teaspoon of kosher salt

Directions
1. Put the chickpeas into the removable pot.
2. Add around 5 glasses of water and season with salt.
3. Close the pressure lid and cook the chickpeas on high mode for 2 minutes.
4. Once the cooking time elapses, let the in-built pressure exit naturally for 20 minutes and quick release the rest.
5. Open the lid carefully and drain the chickpeas. Taste them. If not tender, cook them on high mode for ten more minutes.
6. Quick release the in-built steam and serve immediately or refrigerate for 5 days.

Broiled Grapefruit

Preparation time: 5 minutes| Cook Time: 6-8 minutes| Servings: 2

Ingredients
- 3 tablespoons of brown sugar
- 1/4 teaspoon of ground ginger
- 2 teaspoons of honey
- 1/8 teaspoon of ground cinnamon
- 1 chilled grapefruit

Directions
1. Combine the honey with brown sugar, ginger, and cinnamon in a bowl.
2. Close the crisping lid and preheat the unit for 5 minutes.
3. Half the grapefruit and loosen the edge (from the flesh of the grapefruit through the white pith) using a paring knife.
4. Spread the sugar mix evenly over the halves.
5. Line the reversible rack with foil and set the grape fruits on it.
6. Insert the rack in the preheated multi-cooker and close the crisping lid.
7. Broil for 8 minutes having checked its doneness on the sixth minute.
8. Cool for two minutes before serving.

Texas Cheese Fries in Melted Cheese

Preparation time: 5 minutes| Cook Time: 25 minutes| Servings: 2

Ingredients
- 1 package (2 lb bag) of seasoned frozen French fries
- 4 slices of bacon
- 1 cup of mozzarella cheese, shredded
- A cup of cheddar cheese, shredded
- *For dipping*: Ranch dressing

Directions
1. Set the unit to sauté mode and preheat it for 5 minutes.
2. Cook the bacon until crispy. Remove and switch off the sauté function.
3. Insert a rack or basket in Foodi pot and add the French fries onto it.
4. Close crisping lid and set the Foodi to air-fry mode.
5. Cook at the temperature of 375°F for 20 minutes.
6. Sprinkle the cheeses at the last 2 minutes and continue cooking.
7. Remove the melted cheese from the pot and sprinkle with the crumbled bacon and ranch dressing.

Broccoli, Cherries, and Raisins

Preparation time: 5 minutes| Cook Time: 2 minutes| Servings: 4

Ingredients
- A head of broccoli, cut into pieces
- 1 tablespoon of fresh lemon juice
- 1 cup of water
- 1/4 cup of raisins
- 1/4 cup of cherries, dried
- 2 garlic cloves, minced
- 1 medium onion, finely chopped
- 1 teaspoon of extra virgin olive oil
- 2 tablespoons of red vinegar
- 1/8 teaspoon of cayenne pepper

Directions
1. Combine water with fresh lemon juice and broccoli in the Foodi.
2. Close the pressure lid and cook on high mode for 2 minutes.
3. Quick release the accumulated vapor and open the lid.
4. Mix the raisins with cherries, garlic, onion, extra-virgin olive oil, vinegar, and cayenne in a bowl.
5. Add the broccoli and toss.

Mashed Potatoes

Preparation time: 5minutes| Cook Time: 15 minutes| Servings: 4

Ingredients
- 3 lbs of russet potatoes (peeled and quartered)
- 2 cup of water
- 2 cups of butter
- Kosher salt
- 1/2 cup of sour cream
- 1/2 cup of milk
- Freshly ground black pepper

Directions
1. Put water, potatoes, and salt in the Foodi.
2. Close the pressure lid and cook on high mode for 12 minutes.
3. Quick release the in-built pressure and open the lid.
4. Drain the excess liquid and transfer the potatoes into a large bowl.
5. Mash the potato mixture using a masher until it smoothens.
6. Meanwhile, melt butter in a microwave and add the milk. Warm the milk and pour it over the mash. Stir until the mixture turns creamy.
7. Add the sour cream and stir. Season it with salt and pepper.
8. Transfer the potatoes into serving bowls and top them with butter. If desired, season with additional pepper.

Creamy Parmesan Mashed Cauliflower

Preparation time: 10 minutes| Cook Time: 25 minutes| Servings: 4

Ingredients

- 1 head cauliflower (leaves and stems removed)
- 4 cloves of garlic
- 1 cup of stock
- 6 sprigs of fresh thyme
- 1/2 cup of plain Greek yogurt
- 1/2 cup of cheese, grated freshly
- 1/2 teaspoon of black pepper
- 1/2 teaspoon of salt

Directions
1. Put the stock, cloves, and thyme into a Foodi. Fix the reversible rack and place the cauliflower on it.
2. Close the pressure lid and cook the mixture on low mode for 15 minutes.
3. Quick release the in-built pressure and open the lid carefully.
4. Let the cauliflower cools and remove it from the Foodi.
5. Add the cheese, yoghurt, salt, and pepper. Mash well. Add more seasonings if necessary.

Spanish Tortilla

Preparation time: 15 minutes| Cook Time: 13 minutes| Servings: 6-8

Ingredients
- 1 1/2 lbs of Yukon Gold potatoes (peeled and sliced thinly into ¼" rounds)
- An onion (peeled and sliced into 1/4-inch thickness)
- 1/2 cup of water
- 1 1/2 teaspoons of kosher salt, divided
- 1/4 cup of extra virgin essential olive oil
- 8 large eggs
- 1/2 teaspoon of ground black pepper

Directions
1. Pour some water into the Foodi pot and add potatoes, onions, oil, and a half teaspoon of salt.
2. Close the pressure lid and cook on high mode for a minute.
3. Reset the Foodi to sauté mode and brown for 5 minutes or until the cooking liquid drains. Do not stir.
4. Meanwhile, mix the eggs, the remaining salt, and pepper in a large bowl.Whisk well.
5. Add the egg mixture into the Foodi pot and turn off the sauté function.
6. Bake the potatoes at a temperature of 400°F for 7 minutes or until the eggs set.
7. Transfer your tortilla onto a big plate and slice it into wedges.

Air Fried Bacon Wrapped Asparagus

Preparation time: 5 minutes |Cook Time: 10 minutes| Servings: 10

Ingredients

1 bunch of fresh asparagus
Olive oil spray
10 slices of raw bacon, halved

Directions
1. Wrap each bacon piece around 2 asparagus stalks and spray it with olive oil and salt.
2. Insert the reversible rack or basket and close the Crisping lid.
3. Air-crisp the asparagus over a temperature of 390°F for 10 minutes.

Hummus

Preparation time: 10 minutes |Cook Time: 35 minutes| Servings: 2

Ingredients
- 1 cup of dried chickpeas
- 1/2 teaspoon of salt
- 3 cups of water
- A cube of vegetable stock

For the dip:
- 2 tablespoons of organic olive oil
- 1/4 cup + 2 tablespoons of fresh lemon juice
- 3 tablespoons of tahini
- 2 garlic cloves, chopped
- 1 teaspoon of cumin powder
- Pinch of salt
- 2/3 cup of cooking liquid

Directions
1. Put the chickpeas into the Foodi pot and cover them with water.
2. Add the stock cubes and close the pressure lid.
3. Cook the chickpeas on high mode for 35 minutes. Let the in-built pressure release naturally for 10 minutes and quick release the rest.
4. Pass the cooked chickpeas via a strainer but reserve the cooking liquid.
5. Put the cooked chickpeas, extra virgin olive oil, fresh lemon juice, tahini, cumin, garlic, and salt into a blender.
6. Add a half cup of the cooking liquid and pulse.
7. Scrape the mixture from the sides after each process.
8. Add the remaining liquid and pulse again while adding a tablespoon of cooking liquid or water to soften, as desired.
9. Serve your hummus while drizzled with olive oil and sprinkled with paprika and cumin.

Puff Pastry Banana Rolls

Preparation time: 10 minutes | Cook Time: 10 minutes| Servings: 3

Ingredients
- 2 puffs of pastry sheets

- 3 medium-sized bananas, peeled

Directions
1. Cut the pastry sheets into thin strips. Twine two strips to make a cord.
2. Make as many cords as required.
3. Wind the bananas with the cords and heat the Foodi on 356°F.
4. Cook the wrapped bananas for ten minutes or until golden.

Crispy Chicken Wings

Preparation time: 10 minutes | Cook Time: 30 minutes| Servings: 12

Ingredients
- 12 chicken wings
- 1/2 cup of chicken broth
- All-seasoned salt
- 1/4 cup of melted butter

Directions
1. Pour the broth into the Foodi.
2. Put the chicken in the Crisp basket and fix it in the pot.
3. Close the pressure lid and cook the wings on high mode for 8 minutes.
4. Quick release the accumulated steam and wipe the chicken using paper towels.
5. Pour the melted butter over the wings and sprinkle with all the seasoning.
6. Close the crisping lid and air-fry for 20 minutes. Remember to check the cooking progress on the 10th minute using tongs.
7. Cook your crispy chicken wings to the desired crispiness and enjoy.

Air Fried Blooming Onion

Preparation time: 120 minutes | Cook Time: 20 minutes| Servings: 1

Ingredients
- 1 large onion
- 2 tablespoons of milk
- 2 eggs
- A cup of panko bread crumbs
- 1 teaspoon of garlic powder
- A teaspoon of paprika
- Olive oil

Directions
1. Begin by peeling the onion and subdividing it into 8 slices.
2. Dip the onion in cold water (facedown) for two hours.
3. Combine the bread crumbs with seasonings in a bowl and coat the onion using the egg/ crumb mix.
4. Tip over to drip off excess coatings. Sprinkle the panko over the onion and put it in a basket. Splash the panko with cooking spray and close the crisping lid.
5. Air-crisp your blooming onion for over 390°F for 10 minutes.

Bow Tie Pasta Chips

Cute snacks!
Preparation time: 10 minutes| Cook Time: 2minutes| Servings: 2

Ingredients
- 2 cups of dry whole wheat grains bow tie pasta
- 1 tablespoon of nutritional yeast
- 1 tablespoon of extra virgin olive oil
- 1/2 teaspoon of salt
- 1 1/2 teaspoon of Italian Seasoning Blend

Directions
1. Cook the pasta for half of the time indicated in its package.
2. Drain it and drizzle with organic olive oil, the Italian seasoning, and salt.
3. Insert the basket in the Foodi pot and put the half-cooked pasta in it.
4. Close the crisping lid and air crisp over 390°F for 5 minute while shaking regularly.
5. Hint: the longer it cools, the crispier it gets.

Asian Sticky Wings

Preparation time: 5 minutes| Cook Time: 40 minutes| Servings: 2

Ingredients
- 2 cups of water
- 1 lb of chicken wings
- A teaspoon of sea salt, divided
- 1/4 cup of honey
- 1/2 cup of rice vinegar
- 2 teaspoons of store bought red chili pepper
- 1 teaspoon of ginger fresh, grated
- A small orange zest and juice

Directions
1. Pour water into the Foodi pot and insert the rack.
2. Put the chicken wings on the rack and close the pressure lid.
3. Cook the chicken on high mode for 2 minutes and quick release the accumulated vapor.
4. Combine vinegar with juice, zest, freshly grated ginger, red pepper paste, honey, and a half teaspoon of salt in a bowl.
5. Remove your wings from the rack and pat dry using paper towels.
6. Add the sauce to the Foodi and return the rack.

7. Place the dried wings on the rack and air crisp at 390° F for 30 minutes, flipping in ten minutes intervals.
8. Coat the wings with all the sauce and serve hot.

Brussels sprouts and Walnuts

Preparation time: 5 minutes| Cook time: 4 minutes| Servings: 6

Ingredients
- 1 lb of Brussels sprouts
- 1/2 cup of walnuts (toasted and coarsely chopped)
- 2 teaspoons of fresh lemon juice
- Extra virgin olive oil
- Salt and black pepper

Directions:
1. Begin by washing the Brussels sprouts. Take out the outer leaves and trim the stems.
2. Half the sprouts and put them in a bowl.
3. Add a cup of water into the Foodi pot and insert the rack basket. Add the Brussels sprouts into it and close the pressure lid.
4. Cook the sprouts on high mode for 4 minutes and quick release the in-built pressure.
5. Transfer the vegetables into a serving dish and toss with fresh lemon juice, essential olive oil, walnuts, salt, and pepper. Enjoy.

Fried Ravioli

Preparation time: 5 minutes |Cook Time: 13 minutes |Serving: 4

Ingredients
- Pre-packaged ravioli, frozen
- A cup of bread crumbs
- 1 tablespoon of Italian seasoning
- 1 tablespoon of garlic powder
- ½ cup of mozzarella cheese
- 2 eggs, whisked
- Cooking Spray

Directions
1. Combine the bread crumbs with the Italian seasoning, garlic, and the mozzarella.
2. Whisk eggs in another bowl.
3. Dip the ravioli into the egg mixture and then into the breadcrumb mixture.
4. Preheat the Foodi on air fry mode over a temperature of 350°F for two minutes.
5. Put the breaded ravioli in the basket and splash it with the cooking spray.
6. Cook 15 minutes having flipped on the eighth minute.

DESSERTS

Vanilla Tapioca Pudding

Preparation time: 5 minutes| Cook time: 15minutes| Servings: 4

Ingredients
- 1 1/4 cups of water
- 1/3 cup of small tapioca pearls (rinsed and drained)
- 4 tablespoons of your preferred sweetener
- 1 1/4 cups of unsweetened almond milk
- 1/2 teaspoon of vanilla flavor
- A teaspoon of corn starch

Directions:
1. Combine the rinsed tapioca pearls with water in your Ninja pot.
2. Close the pressure lid and cook on high mode for 8 minutes.
3. Let the accumulated steam exit naturally for 10 minutes and quick release the rest.
4. Add the sweetener, almond milk, and corn starch in the Foodi.
5. Sauté the mixture until it begins to boil. Add the vanilla extract and stir.
6. Cool the pudding and stir occasionally to thicken it.
7. Transfer your vanilla tapioca pudding to a dish and refrigerate while covered for 3 hours.

Strawberry Jam

Preparation time: 10 minutes| Cook time: 10minutes| Servings: 5

Ingredients
- 1 cup of raw honey
- 1 pound of organic strawberries, diced

Directions:
1. Melt the honey on sauté mode and add the strawberries. Boil until they turn pink.
2. Close the pressure lid and cook on high mode for 3 minutes.
3. Let the pressure exit naturally and open the lid. Mash the cooked strawberries and boil the cooking fluid on sauté mode.
4. Pour your strawberry jam into a jar ready for use.

Cinnamon Maple Apples

Preparation time: 5 minutes| Cook time: 2 minutes| Servings: 5

Ingredients
- 3 gala apples (peeled, cored, and sliced)
- 2 tablespoons of water
- A teaspoon of maple syrup
- 1 teaspoon of cinnamon

Directions:
1. Put all the ingredients into your Foodi pot and stir well.
2. Close the pressure lid and cook the apple mixture on high mode for 2 minutes.
3. Quick release the in-built steam and open the lid. Serve your cinnamon maple apple cool.

Citrus Canola Cake

Preparation time: 10 minutes| Cook Time: 40 minutes| Servings: 8

Ingredients
- 4 eggs
- 1 cup of canola oil
- A cup of sugar
- 1 orange, juice and zest
- 1 lemon, juice and zest
- A tablespoon of baking powder
- 1 cup of all-purpose flour
- 1/4 teaspoon of kosher salt
- Powdered sugar, for garnishing

Directions
1. Combine the eggs with canola oil, sugar, juices, and zests in a food processor. Pulse well.
2. Mix the flour with baking powder and salt in a mixing bowl.
3. Add the salted baking into the mixer and pulse.
4. Grease an 8- inch baking pan with oil and add butter.
5. Place the buttered pan on the rack.
6. Close the crisping lid and bake over 325°F for 3minutes.
7. Pour the puree in the pan and close the crisping lid again. Bake the puree over the same temperature for 40 minutes.
8. Remove the pan from the Foodi and allow the cake to cool for around 15 minutes. Garnish your citrus canola cake with powdered sugar.

Dump Cake

Preparation time: 5 minutes| Cooking time: 25 minutes |Servings: 6

Ingredients
- 3 tablespoons of butter, melted
- 2 cups of cake mix
- 1 can of pie filling

Directions:
1. Combine the cake mix with the melted butter in a bowl. Stir and add the filling.
2. Transfer the mixture into a baking pan and cover it with a foil.
3. Insert the reversible rack and place the pan containing batter into it.
4. Close the Crisping lid and preheat the Foodi on bake mode over 325°F for two minutes.

5. Once preheated, cook the dump cake for 25 minutes. Cool it and serve in slices.

Vanilla Cake

Preparation time: 10 minutes| Cook time: 50 minutes| Servings: 6
Ingredients
- 1 ½ cups of pie filling
- 1 ½ glasses of cake mix
- ½ tube of melted vanilla frosting
- 2 eggs

Directions:
1. Grease a baking pan with the cooking spray.
2. Combine the cake mix with eggs in a bowl and fold the filling in it.
3. Transfer the mixture to pan and cover with foil.
4. Fix the reversible rack and place the pan containing the cake mix on it.
5. Close the Crisping lid and preheat the Foodi on bake mode over 325°F for two minutes.
6. After that, bake your vanilla cake over the same temperature for 50 minutes.

Dried Fruits in Wine Sauce

Preparation time: 10 minutes| Cook time: 10 minutes |Servings: 6
Ingredients
- 1 garlic clove, minced
- 1 medium onion, diced
- 2 tablespoons of extra virgin olive oil
- 1 cup of dried peaches, cut into small pieces
- A cup of dried apricots, cut into small pieces
- 1 cup of dried figs
- 1 1/2 cups of red wine
- 1/2 cup of water
- 3/4 cup of packed brown sugar
- 2 lemon slices
- 1 cinnamon stick

Directions
1. Sauté the onion and garlic in olive oil for three minutes.
2. Add the remaining ingredients and boil them while stirring constantly to dissolve the sugar.
3. Close the pressure lid and cook on high mode for 5 minutes. Quick release the accumulated vapor and serve your wine sauce warm.

Banana/ Rum Mix

Preparation time: 5 minutes| Cooking time: 5 minutes| Servings: 4
Ingredients
- 1/2 cup of butter
- A cup of dark brown sugar
- 1 teaspoon of ground cinnamon
- 4 small bananas
- 1/2 cup of rum
- Vanilla ice cream, for serving

Directions
1. Peel the bananas and half them lengthwise. Half them again and set aside.
2. Preheat your Foodi on sauté mode and add the butter, brown sugar, and cinnamon.
3. Stir to dissolve the brown sugar and butter.
4. Add the bananas and ladle the sauce over them. Cook the mixture until it bubbles.
5. Add the rum and cook for 2 minutes.
6. Serve your bananas with vanilla ice cream.

Peach Cobbler

Preparation time: 15 minutes| Cooking time: 10 minutes| Servings: 6
Ingredients
- 1 box (15.25-oz) of white cake mix, divided
- 6 peaches (peeled and sliced)
- ¼ cup of softened butter

Directions:
1. Put half of the dessert mix in a large bowl. Add the butter and mix well.
2. Arrange the peaches on a multi-purpose pan and sprinkle them with the cake butter mix.
3. Cover the mixture with foil and place it on a reversible rack.
4. Insert the pan in the rack and close the crisping lid.
5. Bake your peach cobbler over 550°F for thirty minutes.

Upside-Down Cheesecake

Preparation time: 30 minutes| Cook Time: 35| Servings: 4
Ingredients
- 2 packages (8 oz each) of creamy cheese
- 2 large eggs
- 2/3 cup of sugar
- 1 teaspoon of vanilla extract
- 1 cup of water
- 2 tablespoons of melted butter
- 1/2 package (8 oz) of sandwich cookies, of preference
- Chocolate, caramel, or strawberry syrup

Directions
1. Combine the sugar with cream cheese in a mixing bowl. Add the vanilla and eggs. Stir.
2. Pour the sugar mixture into a 7- inch greased pan and cover with a foil.
3. Pour water and fix the steam rack in the Foodi.
4. Cook the mixture on low mode for 35 minutes. Let the pressure exit naturally for 15 minutes and remove the foil.

5. Set it aside for thirty minutes and refrigerate for at least two hours.
6. Pulse the cookies and melted butter and cover the cooled cheesecake with it.
7. Drizzle the cake with the strawberry syrup and refrigerate for 30 minutes.

Blueberry Pancake Muffins

Preparation time: 15 minutes| Cook Time: 25 minutes| Servings: 6
Ingredients
- A cup of all-purpose flour
- 1 1/2 teaspoons of baking powder
- 1/4 teaspoon of baking soda
- 2 teaspoons of sugar
- 1/4 teaspoon of salt
- 3/4 cup of buttermilk
- 1 tablespoon of canola oil
- 1 egg
- 3 tablespoons of canned blueberries, drained
- 1 1/2 cups of hot water
- Cooking spray

Directions
1. Combine the flour with the baking powder, baking soda, salt, and sugar in bowl.
2. Mix the buttermilk with oil and eggs in another bowl.
3. Combine the buttermilk mixture with the flour mixture. Add the blueberries and stir.
4. Treat a 6-cup muffin pan with cooking spray and spoon the batter into the muffin cups. Pour water into the pot and insert the rack. Place the pan containing butter on the rack and close the crisping lid.
5. Bake the batter over 350 °F for 25 minutes.

Pear Cranberry Honey Sauce

Preparation time: 10 minutes| Cooking time: 10 minutes |Servings: 10
Ingredients
- 3 pears (peeled, cored, and diced)
- A (12-ounce) package cranberries, frozen
- 3/4 cup of water
- 1/2 cup of white sugar
- A cup of maple syrup
- 1 clove
- 1/2 teaspoon of ground nutmeg
- A pinch of cinnamon

Directions
1. Mix water with sugar, maple syrup, and clove in a Foodi pot. Stir to dissolve the sugar.
2. Add nutmeg and cinnamon. Stir and add pears and cranberries.
3. Close the pressure lid and cook the cranberry mixture on low mode for 7 minutes.
4. Quick release the accumulated steam and open the lid.

Mango Cheesecake

Preparation time: 8 minutes| Cooking time: 30 minutes| Servings: 2
Ingredients
- 1 can (14-oz) of sweetened condensed milk
- 1/4 cup of mango puree
- 1 cup of Greek yogurt

Directions:
1. Grease a pan with nonstick cooking spray.
2. Mix the remaining ingredients in a bowl and transfer them to a coated pan. Cover the pan with aluminum foil and put it in a rack.
3. Add water to the Foodi pot and fix the rack containing a yogurt mix.
4. Close the pressure lid and cook on high mode for 30 minutes.
5. Release the in-built pressure naturally for 20 minutes and quick release the rest.
6. Cool the cheesecake on a wire rack for 5 hours.
7. Top it with the mango puree and garnish with cardamom powder or nuts.

Mexican Pot du Crème

Preparation time: 10 minutes| Cooking time: 10 minutes| Servings: 6
Ingredients
- 1 1/2 cups of heavy cream
- 1/2 teaspoon of ground cinnamon
- 2 tablespoons of coffee-flavored liqueur
- 1/4 teaspoon of chili powder
- 1/4 cup of sugar
- 5 egg yolks
- A pinch of kosher salt
- 2 bars of bittersweet chocolate, melted (4 oz each)
- 1 cup of water

Directions
1. Preheat the Foodi unit on sauté mode and add the milk, heavy cream, cinnamon, liqueur, and chili powder.
2. Whisk the egg yolks, sugar, and salt in a large bowl and add the warm cream mix, whisking gently.
3. Whisk the melted chocolate and share it between six ramekins. Wrap each ramekin with a foil.
4. Add water to the pot and fix the rack in it.
5. Place the ramekins on the rack and stack the rest on top. Close the pressure lid and cook on high mode for 8 minutes.
6. Let the in-built steam exit naturally for 10 minutes and quick release the rest.

7. Remove the ramekins using tongs, remove the foil, chill, and serve the crème with whipped cream, if desired.

Pressure Cooked Apples

Preparation time: 5 minutes| Cooking time: 10 minutes |Servings: 4
Ingredients
- 4 apples, cored
- 1 1/2 cup of water
- 1/2 cup of sugar
- 1/2 cup of dates, roughly chopped
- 1/4 cup of walnuts or raisins, roughly chopped
- 2 tablespoons of Goji berries
- 1 teaspoon of cinnamon powder

Directions:
1. Cut off the bottom and top of cored apples. Place them in the Foodi and add water, sugar, nuts, dates, Goji berries, and cinnamon.
2. Close the pressure lid and cook on high mode for 10 minutes.
3. Let the accumulated steam release naturally and open the lid.
4. Serve your cooked apples with the cooking liquid.

Baked Apples

Preparation time: 5 minutes| Cook Time: 45 minutes |Servings: 4
Ingredients
- 2 apples (halved, core removed, but skin intact)
- 4 teaspoons of light brown sugar
- Juice from a lemon
- 1/4 cup (1/2 stick) of butter, cut in 16 pieces
- 8 teaspoons of granulated sugar

Directions
1. Pierce the apple halves 6 times.
2. Put the crisper plate in the basket and fix it in the Foodi.
3. Preheat the unit on air fry mode on 325°F for 3 minutes.
4. Cover both the basket and the plate with a foil and squeeze apple pieces around the foil (cut side up.)
5. Sprinkle with brown sugar and lemon juice, top with butter.
6. Air-fry the apples over the same temperature for 45 minutes.
7. Half way, remove the basket and sprinkle the apples with sugar. Cook until softened and serve with your preferred toppings.

Dulce de Leche Cake

Preparation time: 10 minutes| Cooking time: 11 minutes |Servings: 3
Ingredients
- 1 2/3 servings of Dulce de Leche
- A cup of water
- 4 tablespoons of all-purpose flour, divided
- 2 egg yolks
- 1 large egg

Directions:
1. Grease 3 ramekins with cooking spray.
2. Whisk the eggs until fluffy and thick.
3. Add the Dulce de Leche and stir again.
4. Add the flour and whisk again. Transfer everything into the ramekins.
5. Close the crisping lid and preheat the Foodi unit on 375°F.
6. Place ramekins on the reversible rack and fix it in the pot.
7. Close crisping lid and bake your cake over 375°F for 11 minutes. Check its doneness and leave it to cool.

Peach Dump Cake

Preparation time: 5 minutes |Cooking time: 25 minutes |Servings: 6
Ingredients
- 2 cans (15-oz) of peaches with juice
- 1 teaspoon of ground cinnamon
- 1/4 cup of butter, cut into pieces
- 1/2 box of vanilla cake mix
- A cup of water

Directions
1. Pour the halved peaches into a greased baking pan. Add the cinnamon and stir.
2. Squeeze the cake mix in the peaches and swirl. Set the butter slices over the cake mix.
3. Pour some water into the Foodi and insert the rack into it.
4. Place the greased pan on the rack and cover it with foil.
5. Close the pressure lid and cook on high mode for 25 minutes. Quick release the accumulated vapor and open the lid.
6. Close the crisping lid and broil your dump cake for 5 minutes. Cool and serve.

Easy Applesauce

Preparation time: 10 minutes| Cooking time: 4 minutes| Servings: 4
Ingredients
- 3 pounds of apples
- 1/4 cup of sugar
- 1/2 cups of apple juice
- Pinch of salt
- 1/2 teaspoon of ground cinnamon
- 1/2 teaspoon of ground cardamom

- 1 tablespoon of freshly-squeezed lemon juice

Directions:
1. Peel the apples, remove the cores, and slice them.
2. Combine all the ingredients and close the pressure lid.
3. Cook the apple mixture on high mode for 4 minutes.
4. Quick release the in-built steam and open the lid.
5. Puree the mixture using an immersion blender.

Baked Spice Cookies

Preparation time: 10 minutes |Cooking time: 15 minutes |Servings: 18

Ingredients
- 2 ½ cups of almond flour
- ½ cup of sugar
- 4 tablespoons of butter, softened
- 2 tablespoons of water
- A large egg
- 1 teaspoon of ground cinnamon
- 2 teaspoons of ground ginger
- 1 teaspoon of baking soda
- ¼ teaspoon of salt
- ½ teaspoon of ground nutmeg

Directions:
1. Mix the butter with sugar, egg, and water in a blender. Puree well.
2. Combine the flour with cinnamon, ginger, baking soda, salt, and nutmeg in a bowl.
3. Add the puree to the bowl content.
4. Roll some balls from the mixture and place them on a lined baking pan.
5. Close the crisping lid and bake the balls over 350°F for fifteen minutes or until the cookies' tops turns slightly brown.

Chocolaty Rice Pudding

Preparation time: 5minutes|Cook time: 14minutes| Servings: 5

Ingredients
- A cup of rice, uncooked
- 1/2 cup of sugar
- 2 tablespoons of butter
- 2 tablespoons of cocoa powder, unsweetened
- 1 teaspoon of vanilla flavor
- 2 cups of milk
- ½ cup of evaporated milk
- A cup of water
- 1 egg

Directions
1. Melt butter on sauté mode.
2. Add the rice, milk, and water. Stir and add vanilla, cocoa, and sugar.
3. Stir thoroughly and leave it clump-free.
4. Close the pressure lid and cook the butter mixture on high mode for 14 minutes.
5. Quick release the in-built steam and open the lid.
6. Mix the evaporated milk and egg in a small bowl.
7. Add a half cup of the hot rice pudding and mix. Add another ½ cup of the rice pudding and stir. Stir and transfer the mixture into the Foodi pot.
8. Sauté it for 2 minutes or until it thicken.

Cranberry Oat Bars

Preparation time: 10 minutes| Cooking time: 30 minutes| Servings: 8

Ingredients
- 1 cup of all-purpose flour
- 1 cup of rolled oats, quick-cooking
- 1/4 teaspoon of baking soda
- 1/3 cup of brown sugar
- 1/2 cup (1 stick) of butter, room temperature
- 1 cup of whole cranberry sauce

Directions
1. Combine the flour with oats, baking soda, and brown sugar in a bowl.
2. Add butter and blend using a pastry cutter until it forms coarse crumbs.
3. Close the crisping lid and preheat the Foodi unit on bake mode over 325 °F for 5 minutes.
4. Press the mixture over a greased 8 inch pan (Set aside 1 cup). Spread the cranberry sauce over the crumb mix.
5. Close crisping lid and bake on same temperature for 30 minutes. Remove, cool, and cut into bars.

Candied Lemon Peels

Preparation time: 20 minutes| Cooking time: 20 minutes| Servings: 30

Ingredients
- 6 organic lemons, top and bottoms cut off and peeled
- 3 cups of sugar, divided
- 6 cups of water, divided

Directions:
1. Add the lemon peels to the Foodi. Add 4 cups of water and close the pressure lid.
2. Cook the lemons on high mode for 3 minutes.
3. Let the pressure exit naturally for ten minutes and quick release the rest.
4. Drain water and rinse the lemon peels with cold water.

5. Rinse the pot and add the rinsed lemon peels, 2 1/2 cups of sugar and the remaining water.
6. Set your Foodi to sauté mode and cook-stir your lemon for 5 minutes to melt the sugar. Close the pressure lid and cook on high mode for ten minutes.
7. Let the pressure exit naturally and open the lid.
8. Transfer the peels on a parchment paper and let it cool for twenty minutes.
9. Spread the remaining sugar over a wide plate and toss the cool lemon peels with it. Shake off excess sugar. Put the sugary peels on a sheet pan and chill for 6 hours.
10. You can put it into glass jars and refrigerate for 2 months.
11. Enjoy with coffee or use as a garnish for cakes.

Pumpkin Pie Pudding

Preparation time: 10 minutes| Cook Time: 30 minutes | servings 6
Ingredients
- 2 eggs
- 1/2 cup of heavy cream
- 3/4 cup of sweetener
- 1 teaspoon of pumpkin pie spice
- 15 oz of canned pumpkin puree
- 1 teaspoon of vanilla extract

Directions
1. Whisk the eggs with the remaining ingredients and pour the pumpkin mixture into a greased pan.
2. Add water to the Foodi pot and insert the rack. Place the greased pan on the rack and cover it with a foil.
3. Secure the pressure lid and cook on high mode for 20 minutes. Let the in-built steam exit naturally for 10 minutes and quick release the rest.
4. Open the lid and drain all the water from the pudding.
5. Refrigerate your pie pudding for at least 7 hours and serve with the whipped cream.

Hot Peach and Blackberry Cobbler

Preparation time: ten minutes| Cook Time: 20 minutes |Servings: 6
Ingredients
- 4 cups of sliced peaches, frozen
- 2 cups of frozen blackberries
- Zest from a lemon
- Juice from 2 lemons (1/3 cup juice)
- 2/3 cup of sugar
- A teaspoon of ground cinnamon
- 5 tablespoons of cornstarch
- 2 cups of water

For the Topping:
- 1 1/2 cups of flour
- 1 tablespoon of ground cinnamon
- A cup of light brown sugar, packed
- 1/4 teaspoon of kosher sea salt
- 1 1/2 teaspoons of vanilla extract
- 2/3 cup of unsalted butter, melted

Directions
1. Mix the blackberries with the sliced peaches in a baking pan.
2. Combine the lemon zest with the fresh lemon juice, cornstarch, sugar, and a teaspoon of cinnamon in a bowl. Pour the mixture over the pan content and stir. Set aside for 10 minutes.
3. Place the pan on the rack and pour some water in the pot.
4. Fix the rack in the Foodi and close the pressure lid. Cook the lemon mixture on high mode for 7 minutes.
5. Meanwhile, combine the flour with the brown sugar, a tablespoon of cinnamon, and salt in a bowl. Stir well. Add the butter and vanilla and stir.
6. Allow the in-built pressure to exit naturally for 10 minutes and quick release the rest. Open the lid and add the fruit mixture.
7. Let it rest for 15 minutes as it thickens. Spread the toppings over the fruit mix and close the crisping rid.
8. Air-crisp the cobbler at 350°F for 10 minutes. Cool and serve with frozen vanilla.

Apple Dumplings

Preparation time: 10 minutes| Cooking time: 10 minutes| Servings: 8
Ingredients
- 8 oz (1 can) of crescent rolls
- 1 large Granny Smith apple
- 4 tablespoons of butter
- 1/2 cup of brown sugar
- A teaspoon of ground cinnamon
- 1/2 teaspoon of vanilla extract
- A pinch of ground nutmeg
- 3/4 cup of apple cider juice

Direction
1. Core the apples, peel, and cut it into 8 wedges.
2. Preheat the Foodi unit and open the rolls.
3. Roll the dough flat and the apple wedges in crescent rolls.
4. Melt butter in a pot and add the sugar, cinnamon, vanilla, and nutmeg. Stir.
5. Put the dumplings in the Foodi and drizzle with the apple cider.
6. Close the pressure lid and cook on high mode for 10 minutes.

7. Let the accumulated steam exit naturally. Allow your apple dumplings to cool and serve, while drizzled with cider syrup and sugar.

Egg Leche Flan

Preparation time: 10 minutes| Cooking time: 15 minutes| Servings: 4

Ingredients
- ½ cup of white sugar
- 2 tablespoons of water
- 4 large eggs
- A can (12 oz) of evaporated milk
- 1 can (14 oz) of sweetened condensed milk
- 1 teaspoon of lemon zest
- 1 1/2 glasses of water

Directions
1. Combine sugar with water in a bowl. Stir.
2. Microwave the mixture for four minutes and avoid burning it. Remove and transfer the mixture to a ramekin or pan.
3. Combine the eggs with evaporated milk, condensed milk, and lemon zest in a bowl. Transfer the mixture into a ramekin or pan
4. Add water to the Foodi pot and insert the rack in it. Place the ramekins on the rack and close the pressure lid. Cook the mixture on high mode for ten minutes.
5. Let the accumulated steam exit naturally for ten minutes and quick release the rest.
6. Open the lid and remove the rack. Drain excess fluids on the flan using a paper towel and chill for 12 hours.

Easy Pumpkin Puree

Preparation time: 15 minutes| Cooking time: 15 minutes| Servings: 10

Ingredients
- 3 1/2 to 4 lbs of pie pumpkin
- 1 cup of water

Directions
1. Remove the pumpkin stem. Fix the rack on your Foodi and put a cup of pumpkin in it.
2. Close the pressure lid and cook the pumpkin on high mode for 12 minutes.
3. Let the accumulated steam exit naturally and open the lid.
4. Transfer the cooked pies of a cutting board and slice into two.
5. Take your seeds and peel the skin off. Blend the slices to a puree and refrigerate.

APPENDIX : RECIPES INDEX

30-MINUTES MOROCCAN CHICKEN 66

A

African Lamb Stew 104
Air Fried Bacon Wrapped Asparagus 137
Air Fried Beef Satay 71
Air Fried Blooming Onion 138
Air Fried Breakfast Sausage 28
Air fried chicken wings 17
Air fried plate nachos 17
Air Fried Rosemary Chips 128
Air fried sausage casserole 18
Air Fried Turkey Breast 68
Air fryer Lamb Chops 73
Air Fryer Pork Taquitos 90
Air fryer tacos 17
Air-fried seasoned asparagus 17
Almond and Berries Cut Oats 26
Almond Eggs 29
Apple Dumplings 145
Apples Pork Chops 83
Asian Barbecue Satay 131
Asian Chicken Delight 52
Asian Sticky Wings 138
Asian Style Chickpeas 39
Asparagus and Mushroom Risotto 122

B

Baby Carrots 34
Bacon and Corn Bake 27
Bacon Cheeseburger Dip 131
Bacon Cheeseburger Soup 108
Bacon Potato Soup 111
Bacon Pulled Pork 86
Bacon Veggies Combo 24
Baked Apples 143
Baked Mushrooms 40
Baked Omelet 27
Baked Spice Cookies 144
Balsamic Beef Pot Roast 77
Balsamic Roast Beef 72
Banana Breakfast Mix 29
Banana/ Rum Mix 141
Barbeque Pulled Chicken 68
Barley and Mushroom Soup 100
BBQ Pork Chops 86
Bean Pasta 118
Beans and Tomatoes Mix 38
Beans Chicken Chili 111
Beef and Egg Noodles 75
Beef and Old-School Calico Beans 78
Beef and Wheat Berry Soup 102
Beef Bourguignon 70
Beef Brisket 72
Beef Gyros 77

Beef Short Ribs and Vegetables 78
Beef Stock Recipe 47
Beef Stroganoff with Egg Noodles 70
Beef Taco Soup 106
Beet, Endives and Spinach Salad 134
Belize Chicken Stew 103
Black Bean Dip 135
Black Bean Soup 43
Black Beans and Potato 119
Blueberries Breakfast Mix 22
Blueberry Pancake Muffins 142
Bok Choy and Mushrooms Salad 135
Bow Tie Pasta Chips 138
Braised Pork Belly with Potato and Eggs 86
Brazilian Fish Stew (Moqueca) 93
Breakfast Burritos 27
Breakfast Casserole 24
Breakfast Quinoa 23
Breakfast Roll Casserole 31
Broccoli Mash 41
Broccoli, Cherries, and Raisins 136
Broiled Grapefruit 136
Brown Rice Breakfast Risotto 31
Bruschetta Chicken 65
Brussels sprouts 34
Brussels sprouts 39
Brussels sprouts and Walnuts 139
Buffalo Chicken Dip 131
Buffalo Chicken Meatballs 60
Buffalo Wing Potatoes 116
Butter and Ham Sandwich 24
Butternut Squash and Apple Soup 102
Butternut Squash Soup with Chicken 54
Buttery Broccoli 35
Buttery Brussels sprouts 39
Buttery Mushrooms 36

C

Cabbage Risotto 121
Cabbage Roll Soup 112
Cajun Shrimp 132
Calamari with Tomato Stew 98
Candied Lemon Peels 144
Caponata 129
Carbonnade 75
Carnitas 83
Carrot Fries 42
Carrot Ginger and Turmeric Soup 106
Carrot Puree 40
Catfish with French Sauce 95
Cauliflower and Pineapple Salad 36
Cauliflower Mix 33
Cauliflower Risotto 41
Cauliflower Soup 109

Cereal-Crusted Tenders 61
Cheddar Bacon Ale Dip 135
Cheddar Chicken Breast 52
Cheese- Rich Pasta 127
Cheese steak Casserole 75
Cheesy Meat Oatmeal 27
Cheesy White Wine Risotto 122
Cherries Oat 22
Chicken and Brown Rice 69
Chicken and Chimichurri 44
Chicken and Dumplings 64
Chicken and Kale Stew 103
Chicken and Mushrooms Mix 50
Chicken and Rice Casserole 65
Chicken and Rice with Yogurt Sauce 56
Chicken and Tomatoes 45
Chicken and Vegetable Noodle Soup 107
Chicken Casserole 53
Chicken Curry 57
Chicken Drumsticks 49
Chicken Enchilada Dish 62
Chicken Lemon Sauce Pasta 60
Chicken Noodle Soup Recipe 47
Chicken Pie Casserole 63
Chicken Pot Pie Recipe 53
Chicken Puttanesca 62
Chicken Stock Recipe 43
Chicken Strips 48
Chicken Taco Soup 101
Chicken Thigh Soup 99
Chicken Thighs 66
Chicken with Cashew Cream and Naan 68
Chicken Zoodle Soup 108
Chickpea Tagine 117
Chickpeas Meal 135
Chicory and Carrots Salad 114
Chili Queso Chicken Soup 109
Chimichurri Chili Chicken 56
Chinese BBQ Pork with Ginger Almond Sweet Potatoes 90
Chinese Hot and Sour Soup 103
Chinese Pork Soup 105
Chinese Pork with Ginger Coconut Potatoes 87
Chipotle Pulled Pork 82
Chocolaty Rice Pudding 144
Cinnamon Maple Apples 140
Citrus Canola Cake 140
Coconut Mango Arborio Rice Pudding 126
Coconut Scramble 25
Colombian Style Chicken Soup Recipe 54
Corned Beef and Cabbage 75
Corned Beef Hash 28
Country Grouper 95
Country Style Ribs 80

Crab Cheese Wontons 129
Crack Chicken 64
Cranberry Oat Bars 144
Cream Cheese and Bread 30
Cream of Sweet Potato Soup Recipe 53
Creamy Artichokes 41
Creamy Asparagus Soup 45
Creamy Cauliflower 38
Creamy Crab 92
Creamy Mushrooms 42
Creamy Parmesan Mashed Cauliflower 136
Creamy Shrimp Scampi 93
Creamy Spaghetti in Pesto Sauce 125
Creamy Tomato Feta Soup 109
Crispy Breaded Air Fried Chicken 67
Crispy Chicken Thighs with Carrots and Rice Pilaf 50
Crispy Chicken Wings 138
Crispy Hot Wings 128
Crispy Kale Chips 130
Crispy Popcorn Chicken 131
Crispy Pork Carnitas 81
Crunchy Cut Oats 24
Crust-less Quiche 25
Cumin Chicken Wings 44
Cumin Green Beans 42
Curried Peppers Stuffed With Lentil 115

D

Deli Salmon Veggies Cakes 31
Delicious Frozen Chicken Dinner 51
Dinner of Beef Short Ribs 77
Directions 87
Double Bean and Ham Soup 99
Dried Fruits in Wine Sauce 141
Dulce de Leche Cake 143
Dump Cake 140

E

Easy Applesauce 143
Easy Gnocchi 34
Easy pickled Green Chilies 134
Easy Pumpkin Puree 146
Easy Steamed Artichokes 133
Egg and Cheese Scramble 22
Egg Leche Flan 146
Egg, Sausage, and Cheese Cake 30
Ethiopian Spinach Lentil Soup 110

F

Fall-Apart Pot Roast 70
Feta and Bacon Omelet 25
Fish Steaks with Olive Sauce and Tomato 98
French Fries and Cheese 25
French Onion Soup 104
French Onion Soup Recipe 54
Fried Ravioli 139

G

Garlic Mushrooms 38
Garlic Shrimp with Risotto Primavera 94
Garlicky Broccoli 34
Garlicky Chicken Adobo 57
Garlicky Shrimp Scampi 92
Gold Potatoes and Bacon 28
Great Chicken Wings 44
Green Beans Salad 37
Ground Beef Cabbage Soup 100

H

Ham and Greens 84
Hash Brown Casserole 22
Hawaiian Pork Roast 89
Hazelnut Cauliflower Rice 36
Hearty Ratatouille 119
Herbed Sweet Potatoes 35
Herbed Whole Roasted Chicken 43
Herb-Roasted Chicken 56
Hoisin Meatballs 134
Homemade Hot Sauce 108
Homemade Marinara Sauce 111
Hot and Spicy Pork Shoulder 88
Hot Peach and Blackberry Cobbler 145
Hot Prawns with Cocktail Sauce 94
Hummus 137
Hungarian Chicken Paprikash 61
Hungarian Paprika Turkey 65

I

Indian Butter Chicken 55
Indian Chicken Vindaloo 60
Indian Fish Curry 91
Italian Chicken Masala 55
Italian Chicken, Lentil, and Bacon Stew 106

J

Jalapeno Hot Popper Dip 130
Jamaican Jerk Pork Roast 80
Juicy Kalua Pork 84
Jumbo Shrimp Pasta 126

K

Kale - Egg Frittata 22
Kale Chicken Soup 99
Kalua Pork with Green Cabbage 83
Keto Chicken Pot Pie 61
Keto Chunky Chili 74
Keto Clam Chowder 94
Keto Coq Au Vin 58
Keto Curried Beef 76
Keto Indian Kheema 71
Keto No- Beans Chili 104
Keto Pulled Pork 80
Keto Steak Rolls and Asparagus 76
Kimchi Beef Stew 101
Kimchi Fried Rice 125

L

Leek, Potato, and Pea Soup 100
Lemon Dill Chicken and Potatoes 57
Lemon Rotisserie Chicken 65
Lemony Broccoli 118
Lemony Carrots 42
Lentil Vegetable Risotto 123
Low Town Shrimp Boil 97
Low-Carb Mexican Pulled Pork 85

M

Mac 'N' Cheese 121
Mango Cheesecake 142
Maple Carrots 36
Maple Giant Pancake 28
Marinara with Pasta 125
Mashed Potatoes 136
Matzo Ball Soup 111
Meatless Spaghetti 125
Med Tuna Noodle 127
Mediterranean White Bean Dip 130
Mexican Beans 37
Mexican Pork Soup 107
Mexican Pot du Crème 142
Mexican Rice 123
Mexican- styled Pork Pozole 88
Millet and Pinto Bean Chili 116
Millet, Beans, and Quinoa 116
Minestrone Soup 102
Mississippi Pot Roast 72
Moroccan Frozen Chicken 66
Mushroom Omelet 26
Mushroom Pork 89
Mushroom Rice Pilaf 113
Mushroom Stroganoff 124
Mussels and Chorizo 91

N

Nacho Covered Prawns 132
Ninja Foodi yoghurt 19
North African Lentil and Spinach Soup 99

O

Oatmeal with Carrot 29
Olive and Lemon Ligurian Chicken 49
Onion Tofu Scramble 23
Orange Chicken 64
Orange Roughy with Black Olive Sauce 95
Oregano Potatoes 40
Oxtails Stew 101

P

Paella 92
Paprika Beets 41
Pasta with Arugula Pesto 123
Pasta with Meat Sauce 126
Pasta with Mediterranean Veggies 126
Peach Cobbler 141

Peach Dump Cake 143
Pear Cranberry Honey Sauce 142
Peperonata Sauce 132
Pepper Jack Pork Chops 85
Peppercinis Pot Roast 77
Peppered Chicken and Potatoes 69
Pesto Chicken Breasts 50
Pineapple and Cauliflower Rice 124
Pineapple Cilantro Lime Rice 129
Piripiri Chicken 59
Pizza Dip 132
Polenta Breakfast 24
Pork and Fennel Sausage Risotto 87
Pork and Pinto Bean Nachos 81
Pork Chops with Potato Purée and Gravy 81
Pork Loin with Vegetables 87
Pork Loin, Stuffing, and Gravy 84
Pork Roast Bacon with Potato Bourbon Mash 84
Pork Tenderloin with Gravy 89
Portuguese Style Chicken 58
Pot Roast 74
Pot Roast Soup 112
Pot Stickers Traditional 128
Potato Leek Soup 102
Potato Mash 37
Potato Salad 33
Potato with Herbs 130
Potato, Carrot, and Leek Soup Recipe 47
Potatoes and Tomatoes 38
Pressure Cooked Apples 143
Pressure-cooked lasagna soup 18
Pressure-cooked pork chops with cabbage 18
Pressure-Cooked Summer Squash 117
Pressure-cooked-chicken Masala 18
Puerto Rican Pork Roast 86
Puff Pastry Banana Rolls 137
Pulled Pork with Crispy Biscuits 83
Pumpkin Pie Pudding 145

Q

Quinoa Salad 130

R

Ragù Bolognese 71
Red Cabbage 37
Red Snapper with miso 97
Rice Pilaf with Veggies 122
Rich Spaghetti Dish 123
Risotto with Lima Beans 118
Roasted Potatoes 40
Roasted Red Pepper Chicken 67
Roasted Tomato Salad 37
Ropa Vieja 73
Rosemary Beets 133
Rosemary Turkey 45

Rustic Bell Pepper 128

S

Saffron Rice 122
Salmon with Orange Ginger Sauce 95
Salsa Chicken 62
Scrambled Eggs 24
Seared Shrimp and Rice with Fruity Salsa 93
Shredded Beef Sloppy Joes 78
Shredded Chicken Breast 59
Shrimp and Cheesy Butter Grits 96
Shrimp Chicken Jambalaya 91
Shrimp with Tomatoes and Feta 96
Sicilian Steamed Leeks 118
Silky Creamy Chicken Mulligatawny Soup 110
Simple Corned Beef Hash 29
Simple Pulled Pork 81
Slow- Cooked Pulled Pork Apple Sliders 85
Slow-Cooked Korean Chicken Wings 128
Smoky Lentils and Rice 115
Smoky White Beans and Ham 82
Smothered Pork Chops 82
Sourdough Bread 26
Southwest Asian Falafel 133
Spaghetti Squash Chicken Alfredo 62
Spaghetti Squash with Tomatoes 113
Spanish Tortilla 137
Spiced Squash 38
Spicy Chicken 49
Spicy Chili Verde 55
Spicy Cranberry Sauce 110
Spicy Farfalle Pasta 124
Spicy Pasta Sauce 110
Spicy Thai Chicken Wings 58
Spicy Tomato Eggs 30
Spicy Turkey Chili 51
Spinach Chana Dal 115
Spinach Quiche 26
Squash Mash 36
Steak, Potatoes and Asparagus 73
Steamed White Rice 121
Sticky St. Louis Ribs 78
Stir-Fried Pork and Noodles 89
Strawberry Jam 140
Stuffed Acorn Squash with Pecans 119
Stuffed Chicken Recipe 46
Sumac Eggplant 35
Sunrise Millet Pudding 23
Sweet and Sour Pork 88
Sweet Chipotle Chicken Wings 51
Sweet Potato and Black-Eyed Peas 113
Sweet Potato and Mayo 39
Sweet Potato Mash 40
Sweet Potato Tots 132

T

Sweet Potatoes with Thai Peanut Butter Sauce 114
Sweet Tomato Chutney 112

Tasty Chicken Ramen 67
Tasty Chicken Soup 54
Teriyaki Chicken with Rice and Broccoli 59
Texas Cheese Fries in Melted Cheese 136
Tex-Mex Meatloaf 76
Thai Shrimp Soup 96
Thyme Red Potatoes 35
Tofu with Mixed Veggies 30
Tomato Basil Soup 104
Tomato Soup Recipe 48
Tortellini Soup 109
Tuna Bowls 29
Turkey Breast 45
Turkey Burrito 32
Turkey Gluten Free Gravy 52
Turkey Meatballs in Tomato Sauce 48
Turkey Meatballs with Pasta 63
Turmeric Cauliflower 33
Turmeric Chicken 50
Turmeric Nutty Chicken 67

U

Un-Stuffed Beef and Cabbage 72
Upside-Down Cheesecake 141

V

Vanilla Cake 141
Vanilla Tapioca Pudding 140
Vegan Bread 117
Vegan Miso Risotto 127
Vegan Pasta Puttanesca 124
Vegetable Biryani 114
Vegetable Mélange 119
Vegetable Soup 105
Vegetable Stock 107
Vegetable Stock Recipe 43
Vegetarian Chili Mac 121
Veggie Side Salad 35
Very Tender Pork Roast 90

W

Walnut Bowls 23
Warm Potato Salad 34
White Chicken Chili 100
Wild Rice Soup 108
Wild Salmon Tagine 97

Y

Yummy Eggplant 39

Z

Zucchini Fries 34
Zucchini Pasta Sauce 107
Zucchini Spaghetti 33
Zucchini Tomato Medley 115
Zuppa Toscana Soup 105

www.ingramcontent.com/pod-product-compliance
Lightning Source LLC
Chambersburg PA
CBHW081414080526
44589CB00016B/2533